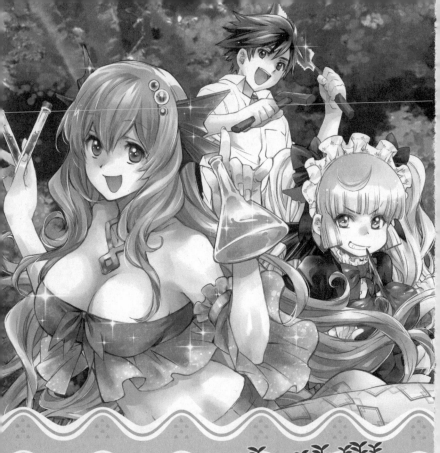

LET'S BUY THE LAND 2 and CULTIVATE IT IN A DIFFERENT WORLD

story by
ROKUJYUUYON OKAZAWA

art by
JUN SASAMEYUKI

character design by
YUICHI MURAKAMI

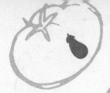

Characters

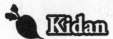

Kidan

His real name is Itonami Norio. Before, he was your normal, everyday paper pusher, but then he got caught up in a hero summoning to another world. Though he was deemed skill-less and told he was unnecessary, he actually possesses a gift called the Supreme Wielder, bestowed unto him by the gods. This powerful skill allows him to become a master of *any* tool he holds in his hands.

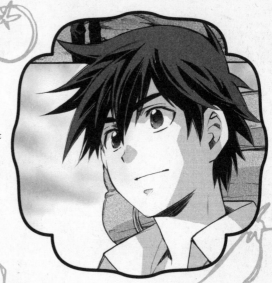

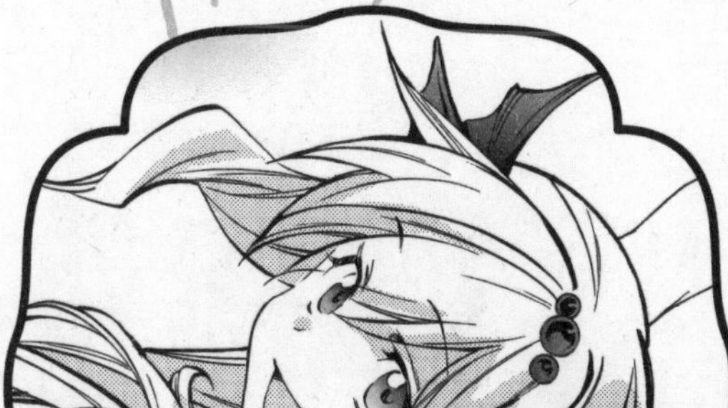

Plattie

Hails from the Merfolk Kingdom. She's a prideful mermaid who looks down on land-dwellers and their treatment of the seas. But since she was fished up by Kidan, she became determined to be his wife. She's also famous for making magical potions and contributes greatly to Kidan's efforts in developing the land.

Story

Though summoned to a different world, Kidan, deemed useless and skill-less, acquired a plot of undeveloped land. He began cultivating the land, his second chance at a relaxing life in another world. His supposedly slow and easy-going life changed drastically when he fished up a mermaid, Plattie, who demanded to become his wife. When he befriended the Undead King and a young dragoness, it seemed like his peaceful life was about to be upended!

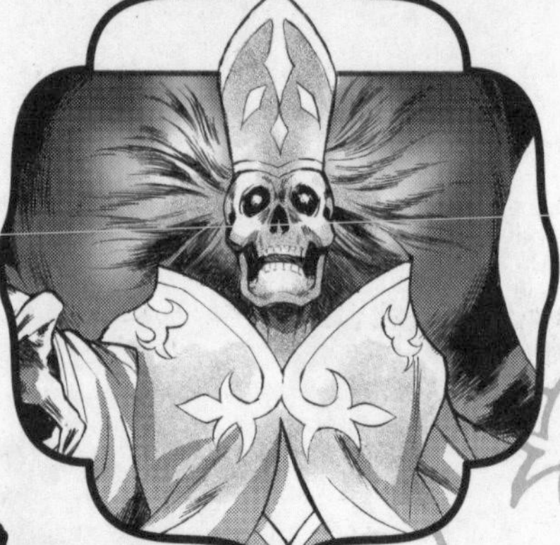

Sensei

The Ruler of the Undead, the Unliving King. Kidan's neighbor who reigns over the dungeon nearby. He calls Kidan the "Chosen One" because he was chosen by the Unliving King's holy sword. The two have become good friends.

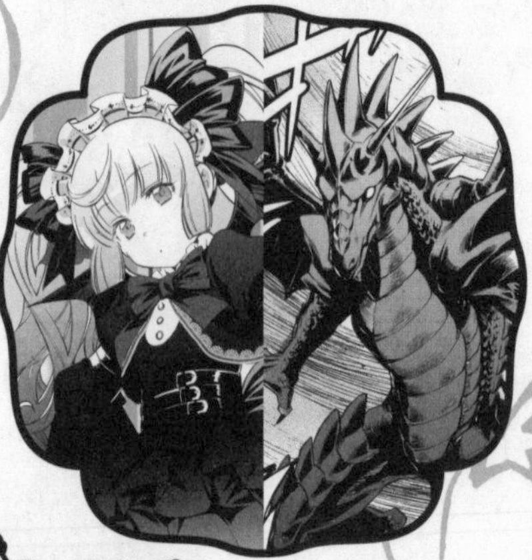

Veel

The Grinzell Dragon. Currently under training to become the heir to the Geyser Dragon. She came to ambush Kidan and Plattie after the couple laid waste to her dungeon, but she became enraptured with Kidan's cooking. She turns into a cutie-patootie when in human form.

Contents

CHAPTER
7
005

CHAPTER
8
025

CHAPTER
9
049

CHAPTER
10
073

CHAPTER
11
097

CHAPTER
12
121

SPECIAL
CHAPTER
145

EXTRA STORY
Astareth and the
Witch's Strike
151

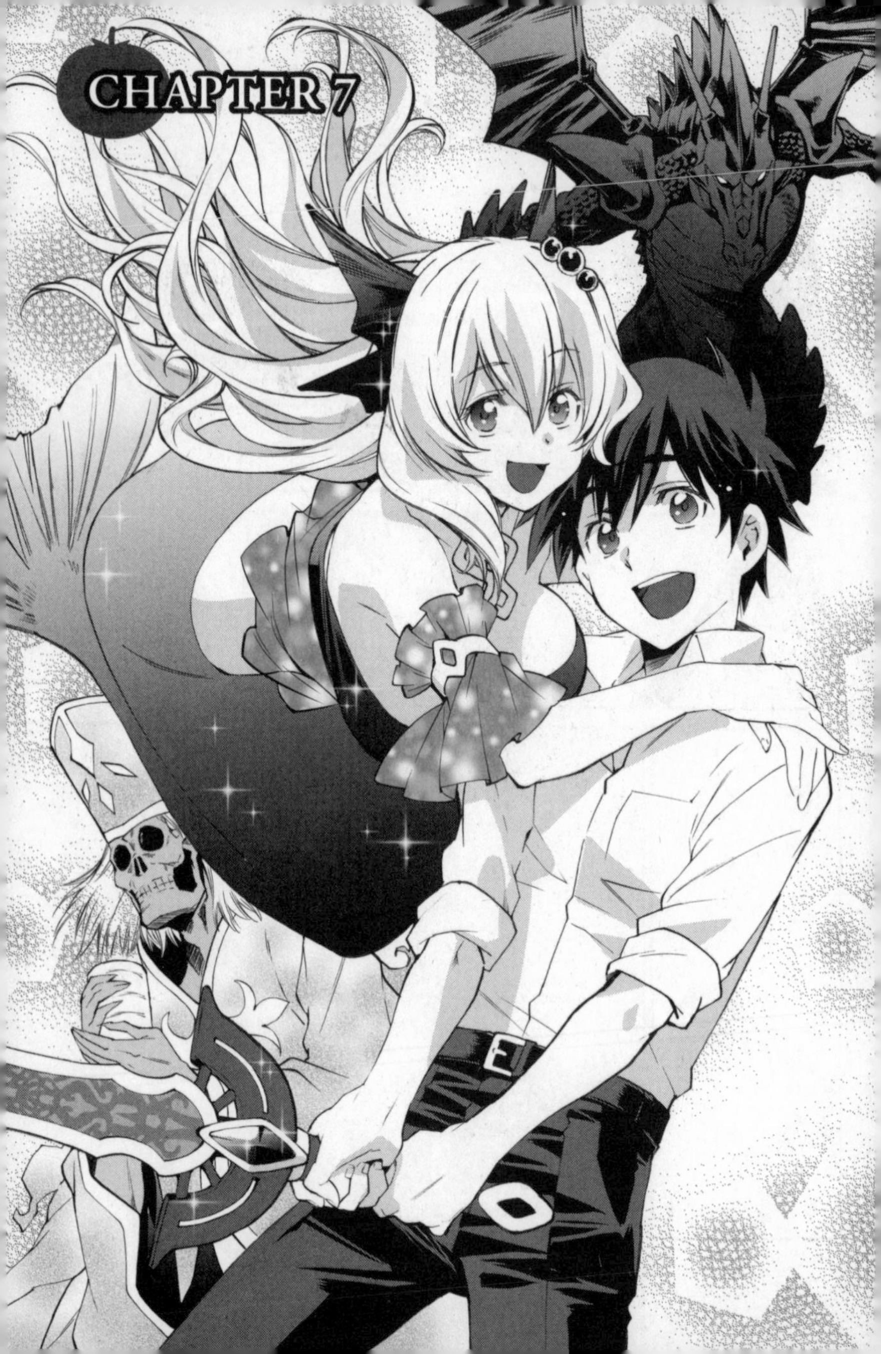
CHAPTER 7

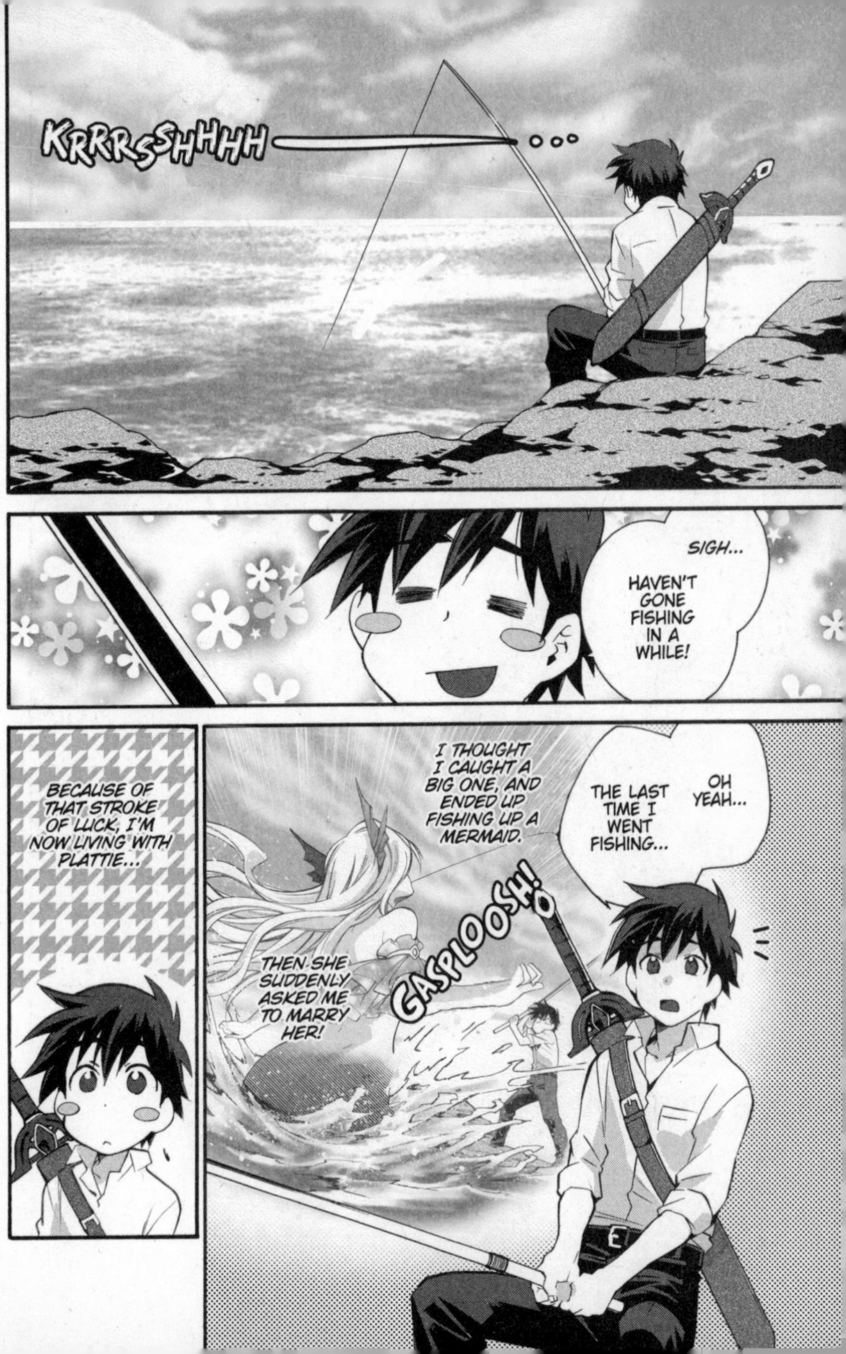
KRRRSSHHHH
...
SIGH...
HAVEN'T GONE FISHING IN A WHILE!
OH YEAH...
THE LAST TIME I WENT FISHING...
I THOUGHT I CAUGHT A BIG ONE, AND ENDED UP FISHING UP A MERMAID.
GASPLOOSH!
THEN SHE SUDDENLY ASKED ME TO MARRY HER!
BECAUSE OF THAT STROKE OF LUCK, I'M NOW LIVING WITH PLATTIE...

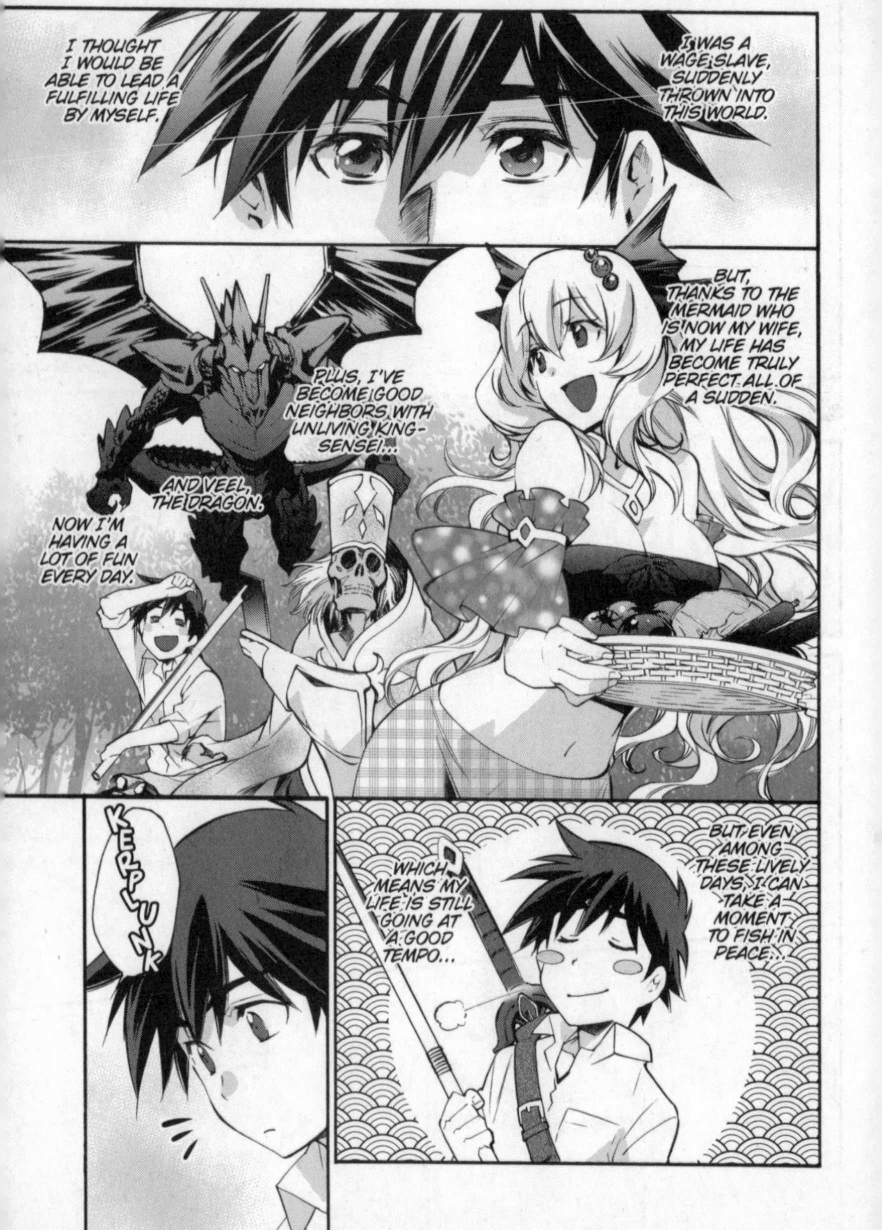
I WAS A WAGE SLAVE, SUDDENLY THROWN INTO THIS WORLD.
I THOUGHT I WOULD BE ABLE TO LEAD A FULFILLING LIFE BY MYSELF.
BUT, THANKS TO THE MERMAID WHO IS NOW MY WIFE, MY LIFE HAS BECOME TRULY PERFECT ALL OF A SUDDEN.
PLUS, I'VE BECOME GOOD NEIGHBORS WITH UNLIVING KING-SENSEI...
AND VEEL, THE DRAGON.
NOW I'M HAVING A LOT OF FUN EVERY DAY.
BUT EVEN AMONG THESE LIVELY DAYS, I CAN TAKE A MOMENT TO FISH IN PEACE...
WHICH MEANS MY LIFE IS STILL GOING AT A GOOD TEMPO...
KERPLUNK

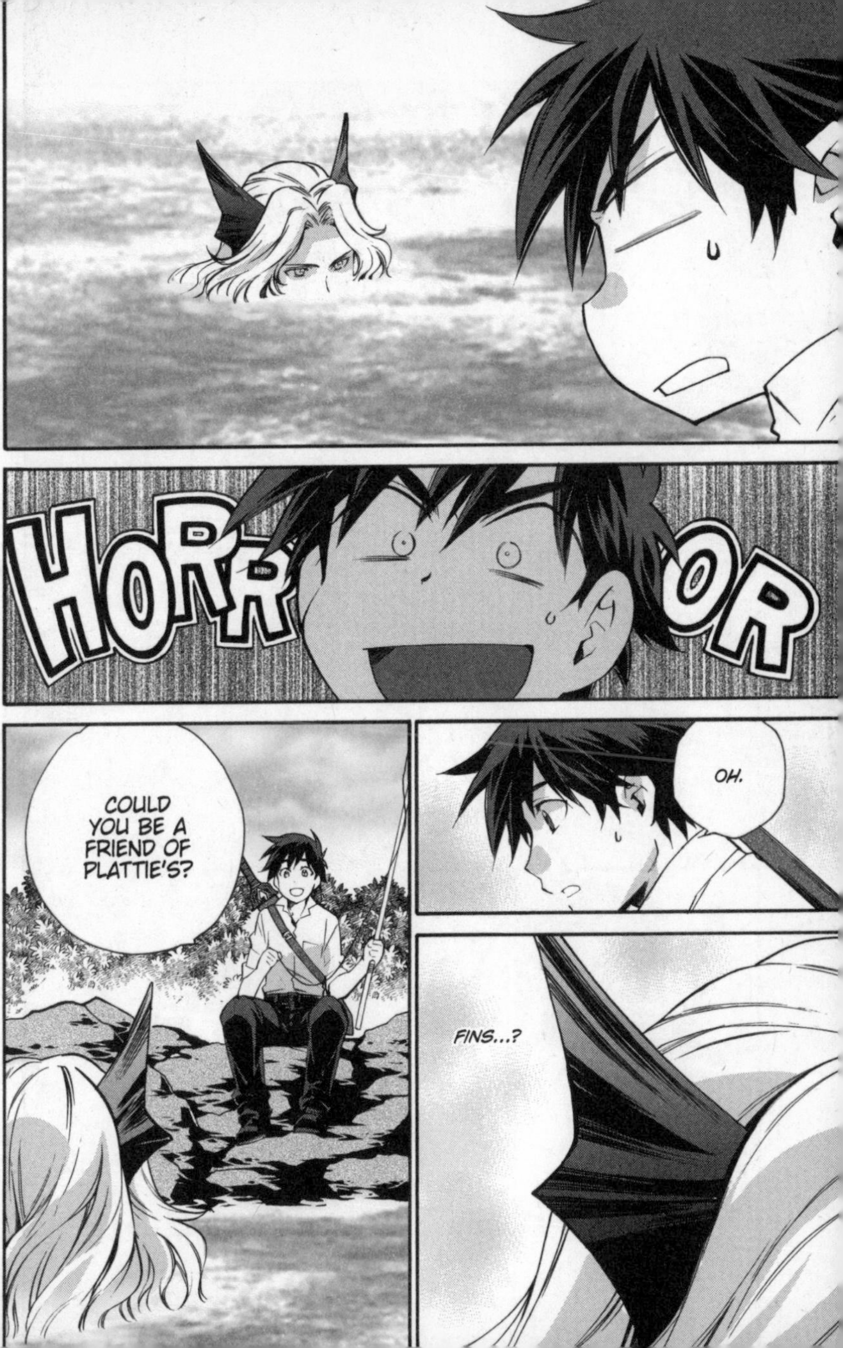
HORROR
OH.
FINS...?
COULD YOU BE A FRIEND OF PLATTIE'S?

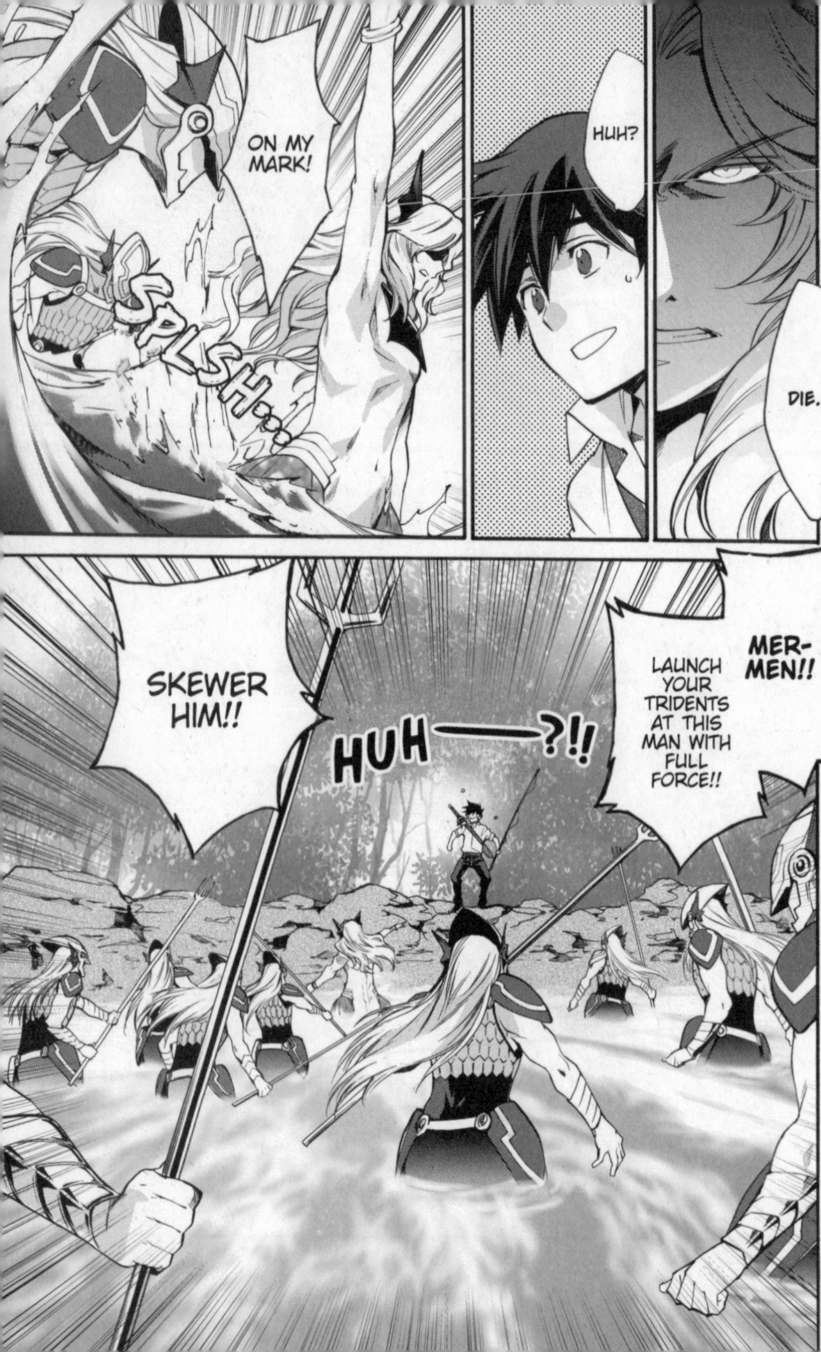
DIE...
HUH?
ON MY MARK!
SPLSH...
MER-MEN!!
LAUNCH YOUR TRIDENTS AT THIS MAN WITH FULL FORCE!!
HUH——?!!
SKEWER HIM!!

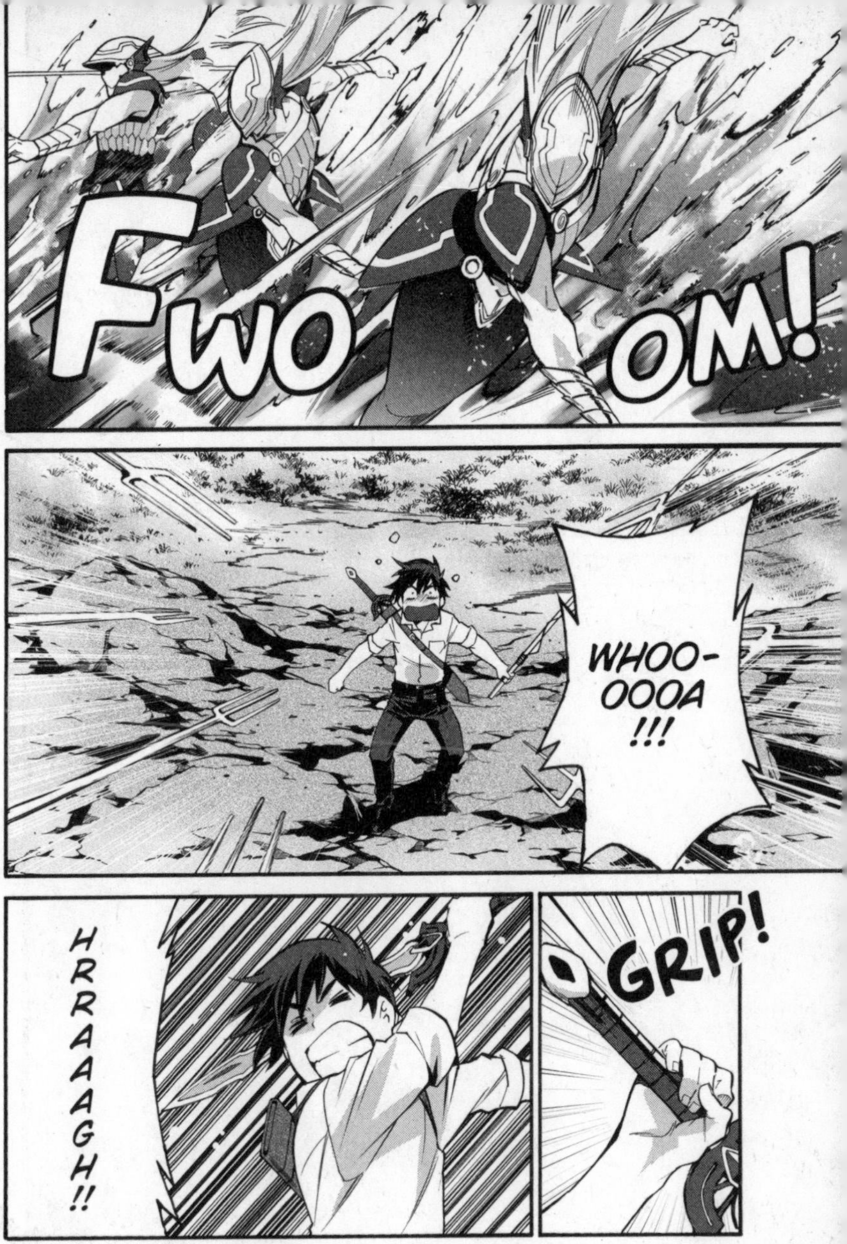
FWOOM!
WHOO-OOOA!!!
GRIP!
HRRAAAAGH!!

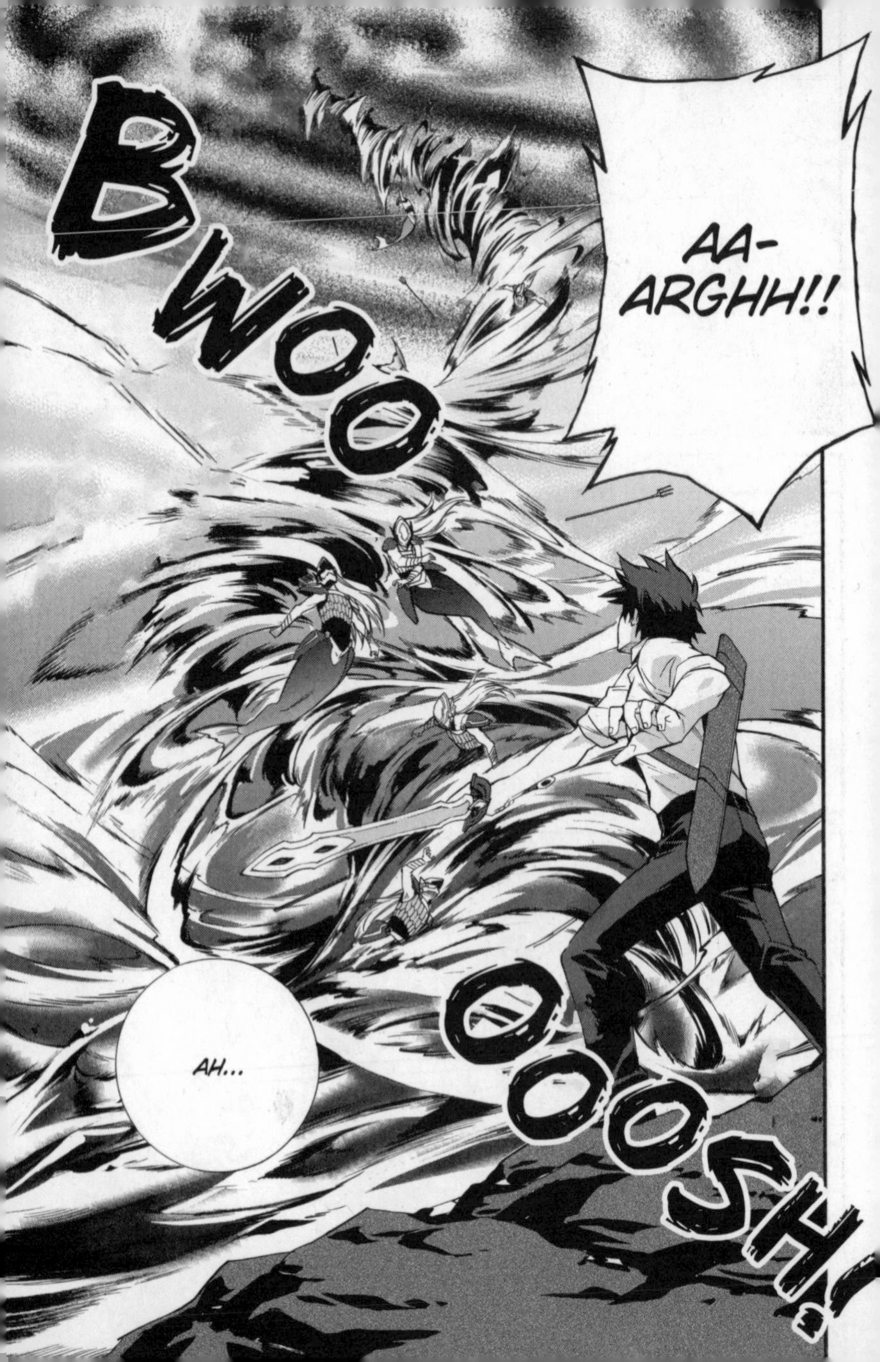
AA-
ARGHH!!
BWOOOOOOSH!
AH...

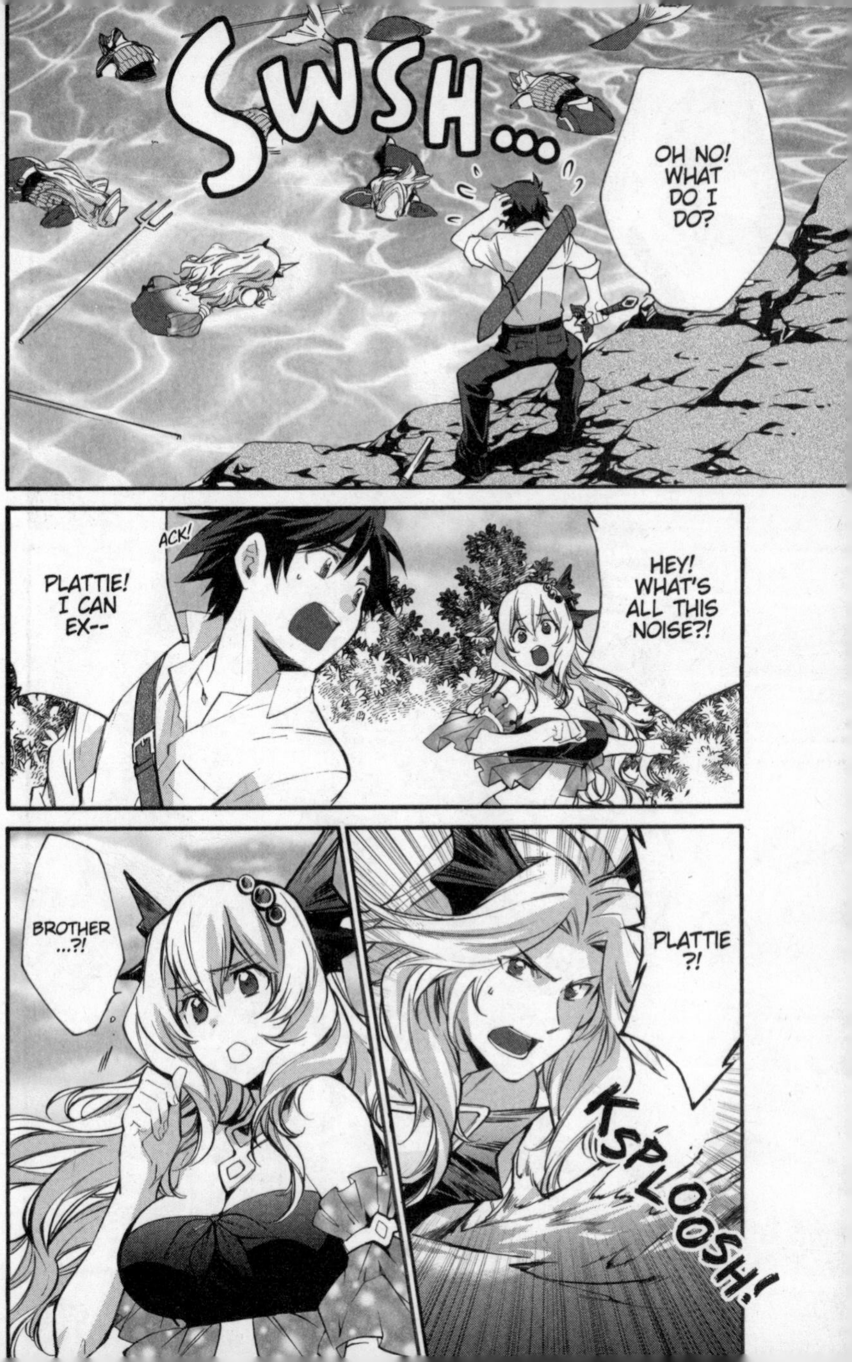
SWSH...
OH NO! WHAT DO I DO?
HEY! WHAT'S ALL THIS NOISE?!
ACK!
PLATTIE! I CAN EX--
PLATTIE ?!
TSPLOOSH!
BROTHER ...?!

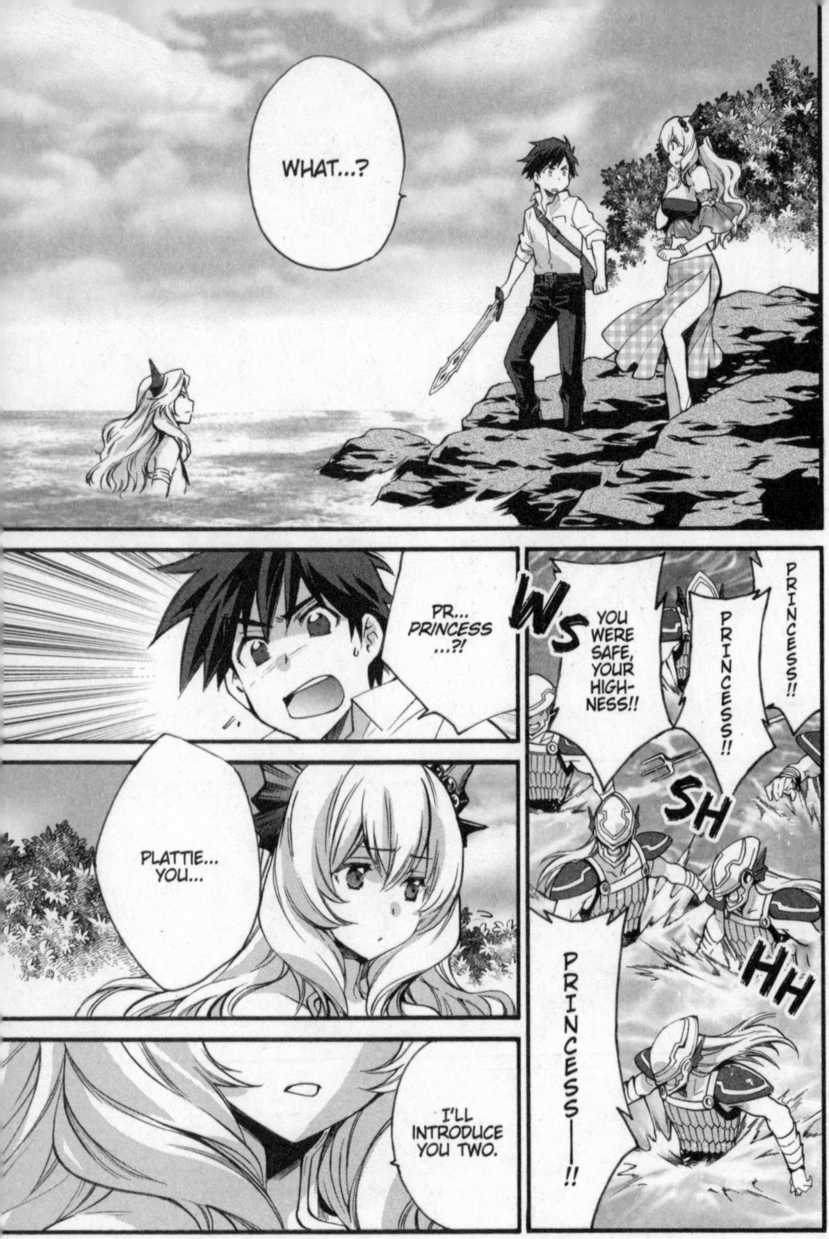
WHAT...?
PRINCESS!!
PRINCESS!!
YOU WERE SAFE, YOUR HIGHNESS!!
WS
SH
HH
PRINCESS—!!
PR... PRINCESS ...?!
PLATTIE... YOU...
I'LL INTRODUCE YOU TWO.

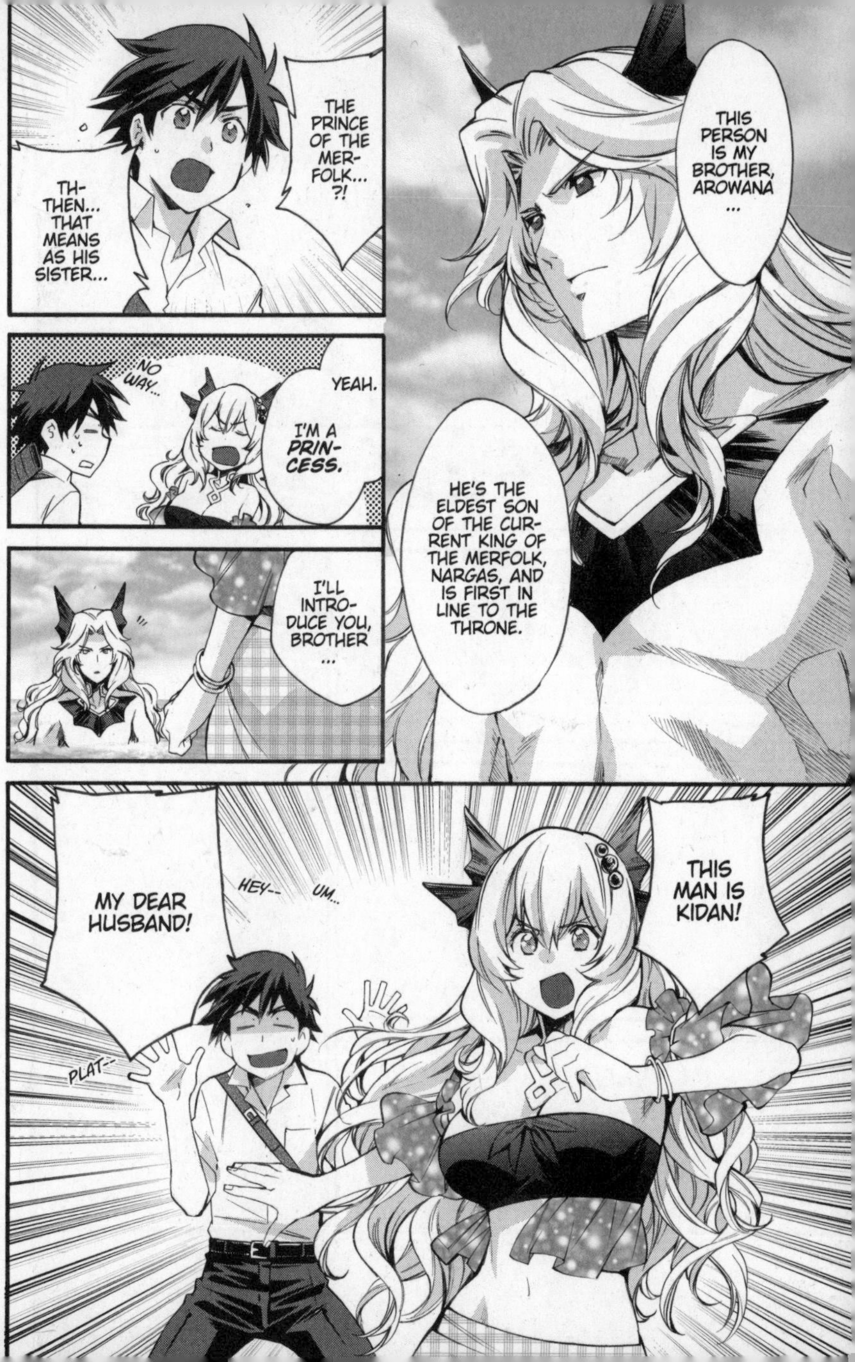
THIS PERSON IS MY BROTHER, AROWANA ...
HE'S THE ELDEST SON OF THE CUR-RENT KING OF THE MERFOLK, NARGAS, AND IS FIRST IN LINE TO THE THRONE.
THE PRINCE OF THE MER-FOLK...?!
TH-THEN... THAT MEANS AS HIS SISTER...
YEAH.
I'M A PRIN-CESS.
NO WAY...
I'LL INTRO-DUCE YOU, BROTHER ...
THIS MAN IS KIDAN!
UM...
HEY--
MY DEAR HUSBAND!
PLAT--

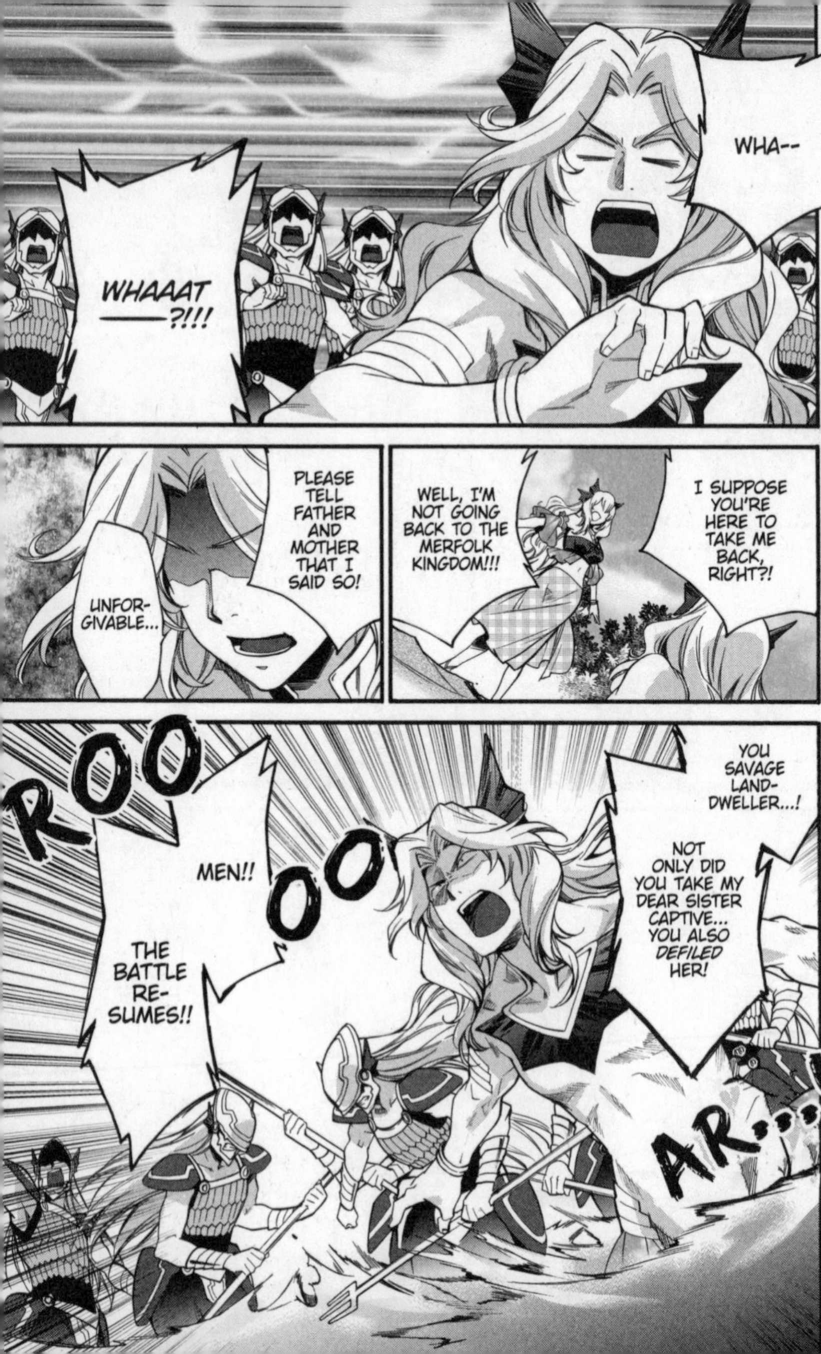

WHA--
WHAAAT ——?!!!
I SUPPOSE YOU'RE HERE TO TAKE ME BACK, RIGHT?!
WELL, I'M NOT GOING BACK TO THE MERFOLK KINGDOM!!!
PLEASE TELL FATHER AND MOTHER THAT I SAID SO!
UNFORGIVABLE...
YOU SAVAGE LAND-DWELLER...!
NOT ONLY DID YOU TAKE MY DEAR SISTER CAPTIVE... YOU ALSO DEFILED HER!
MEN!!
THE BATTLE RESUMES!!
ROOOOAR...!

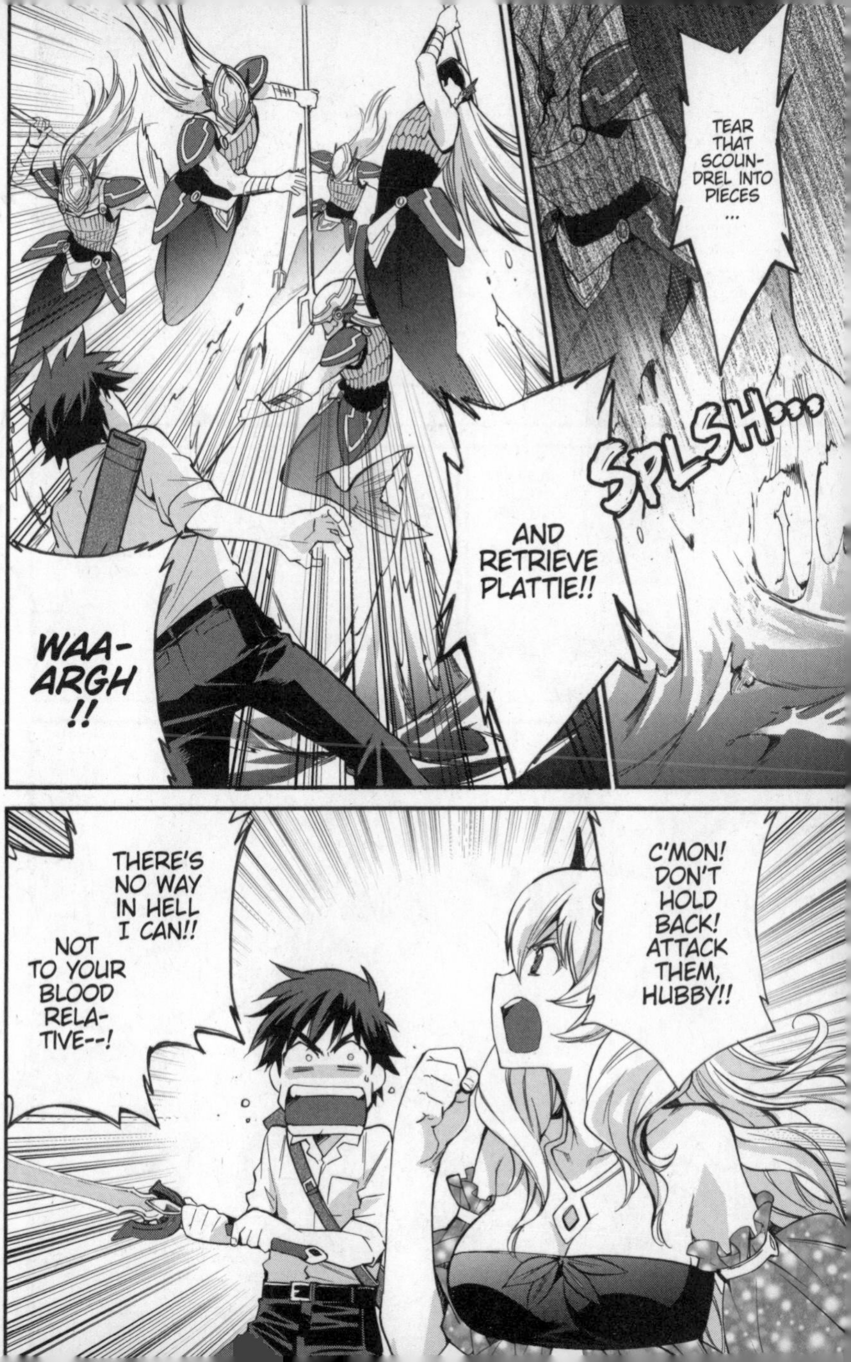
TEAR THAT SCOUN-DREL INTO PIECES ...
SPLSH...
AND RETRIEVE PLATTIE!!
WAA-ARGH!!
C'MON! DON'T HOLD BACK! ATTACK THEM, HUBBY!!
THERE'S NO WAY IN HELL I CAN!!
NOT TO YOUR BLOOD RELA-TIVE--!

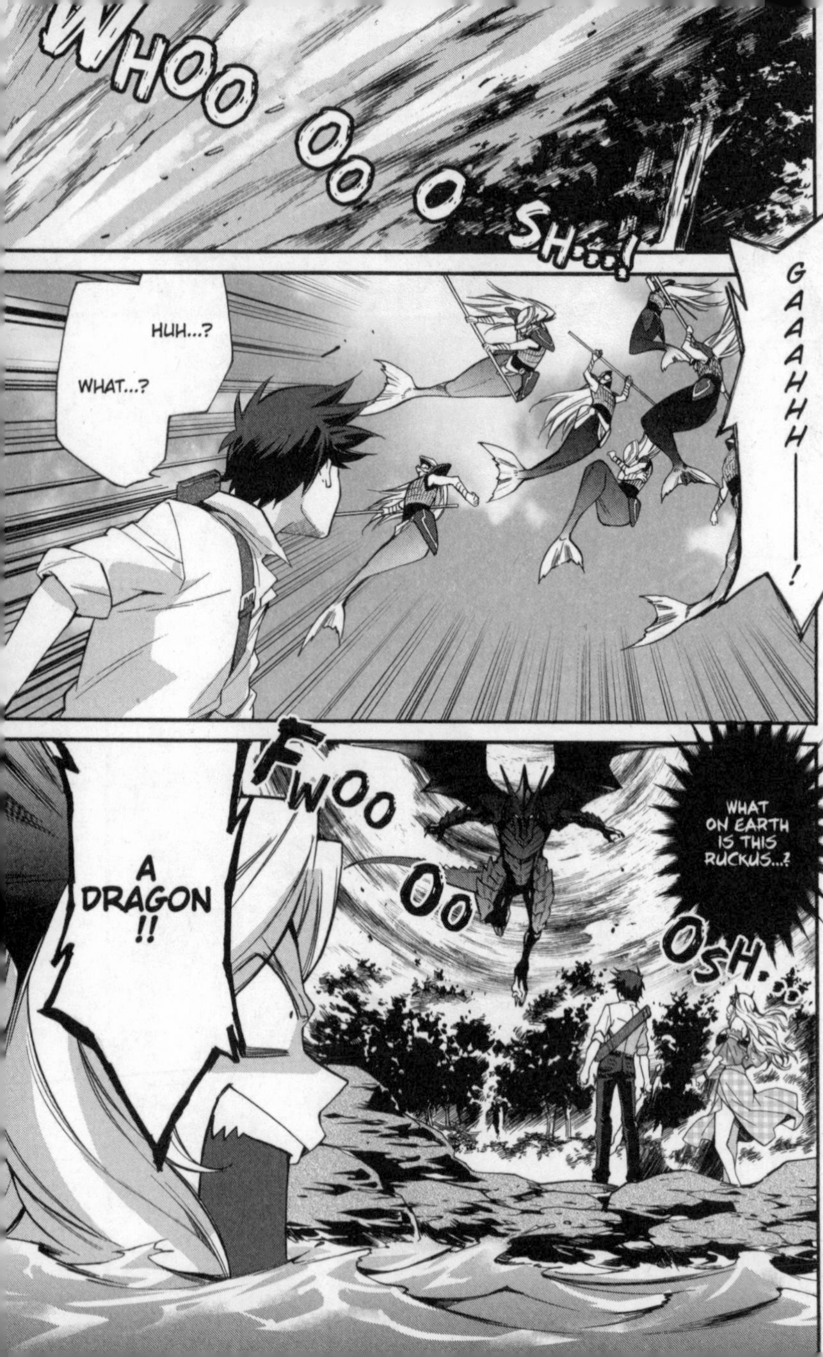
WHOOOOOO SH...!
GAAAHHH—!
HUH...?
WHAT...?
WHAT ON EARTH IS THIS RUCKUS...?
FWOOOOOSH...
A DRAGON!!

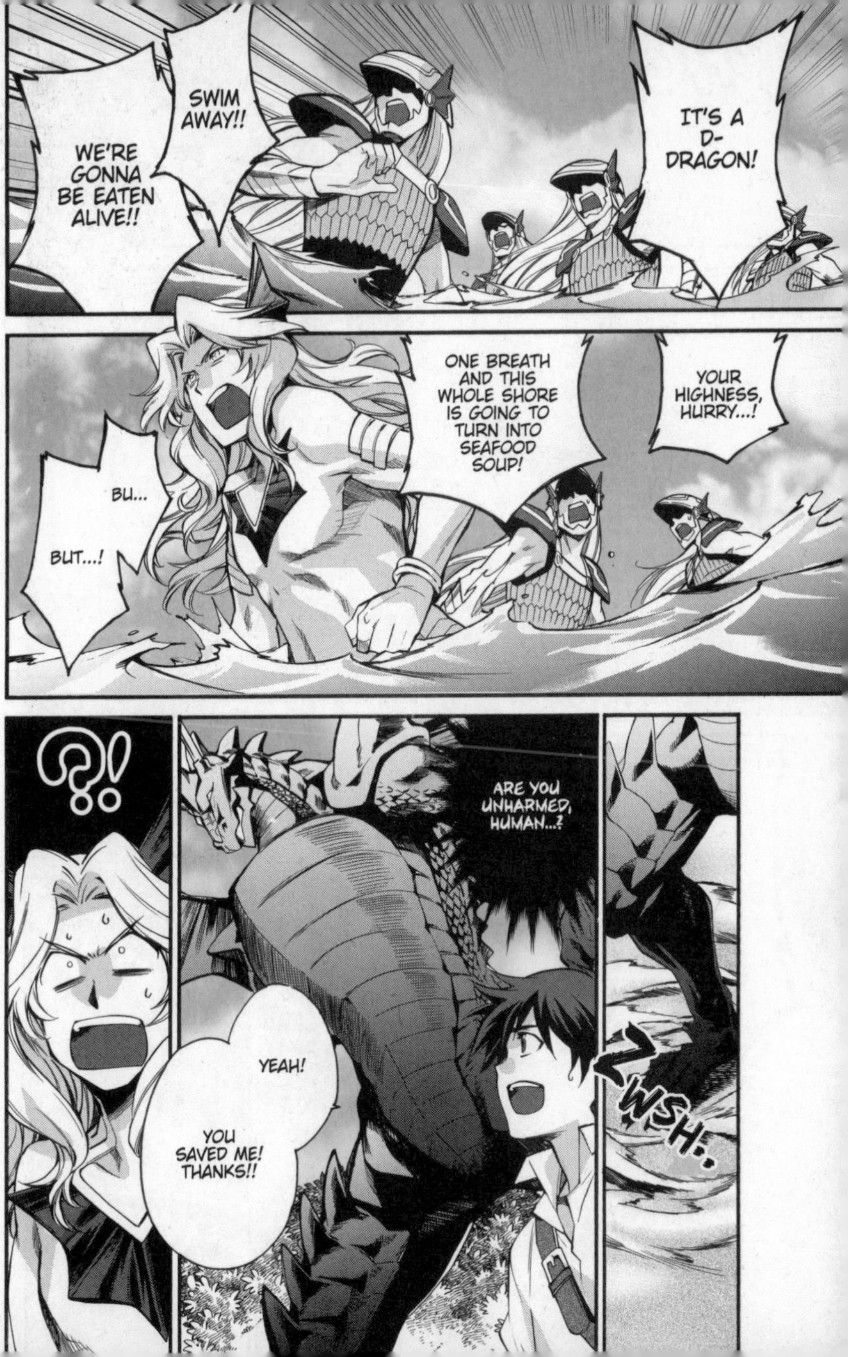
IT'S A D-DRAGON!
SWIM AWAY!!
WE'RE GONNA BE EATEN ALIVE!!
YOUR HIGHNESS, HURRY...!
ONE BREATH AND THIS WHOLE SHORE IS GOING TO TURN INTO SEAFOOD SOUP!
BU...
BUT...!
ZWSH..
ARE YOU UNHARMED, HUMAN...?
YEAH!
YOU SAVED ME! THANKS!!
?!

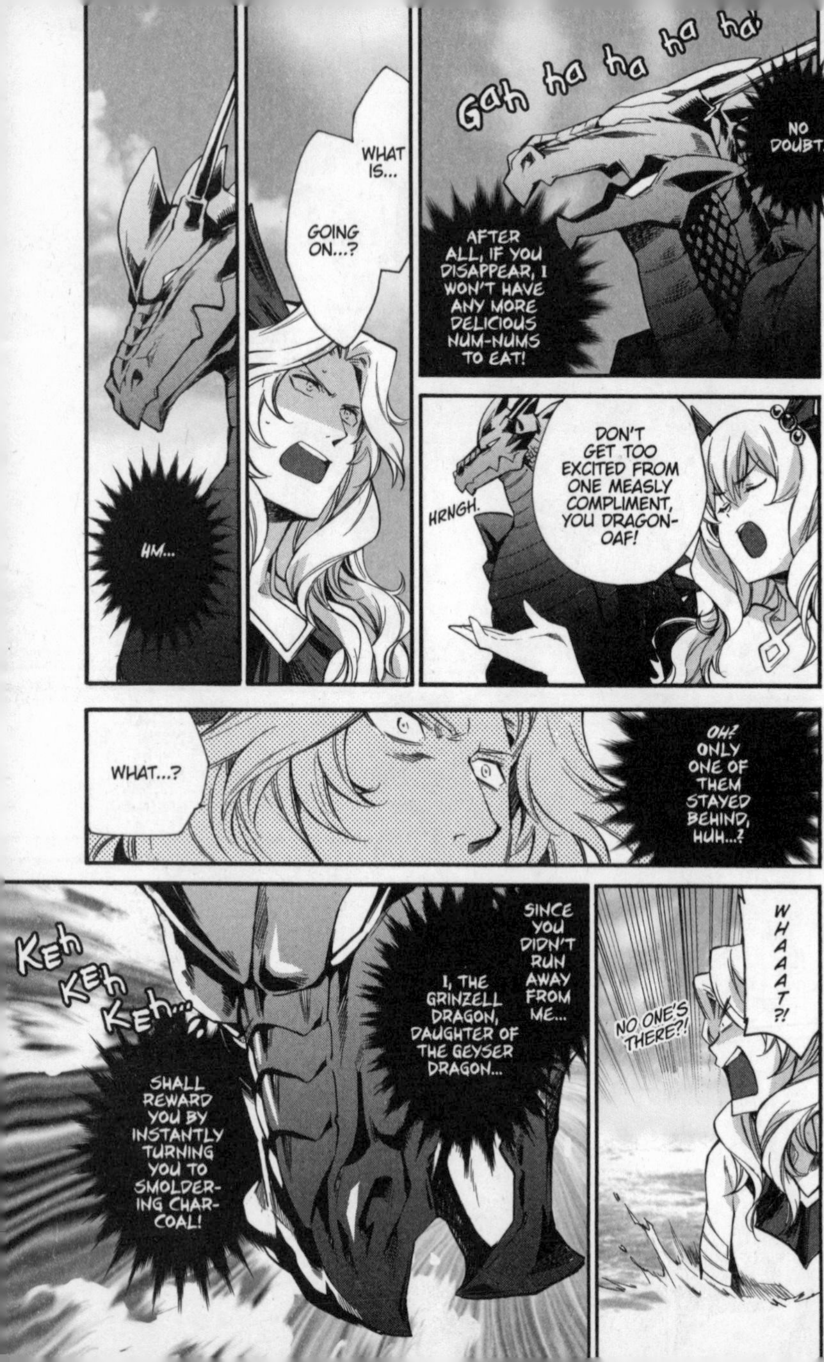
Gah ha ha ha ha
NO DOUBT.
AFTER ALL, IF YOU DISAPPEAR, I WON'T HAVE ANY MORE DELICIOUS NUM-NUMS TO EAT!
DON'T GET TOO EXCITED FROM ONE MEASLY COMPLIMENT, YOU DRAGON-OAF!
HRNGH.
WHAT IS...
GOING ON...?
HM...
OH? ONLY ONE OF THEM STAYED BEHIND, HUH...?
WHAT...?
WHAAAAT?!
NO ONE'S THERE?!
SINCE YOU DIDN'T RUN AWAY FROM ME...
I, THE GRINZELL DRAGON, DAUGHTER OF THE GEYSER DRAGON...
SHALL REWARD YOU BY INSTANTLY TURNING YOU TO SMOLDER-ING CHAR-COAL!
KEh KEh KEh...

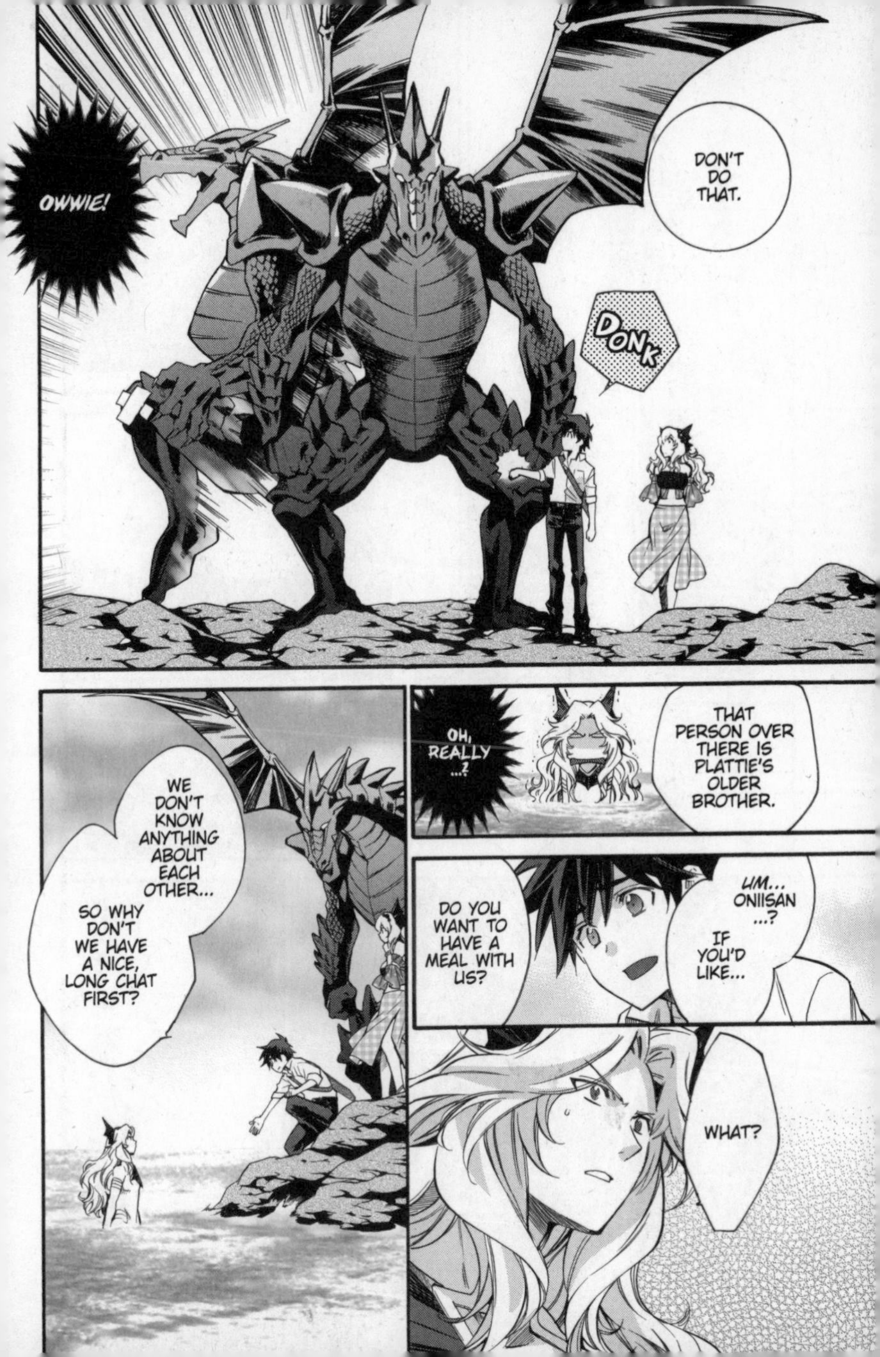
DON'T DO THAT.
DONK
OWWIE!
THAT PERSON OVER THERE IS PLATTIE'S OLDER BROTHER.
OH, REALLY ...?
UM... ONIISAN ...?
IF YOU'D LIKE...
DO YOU WANT TO HAVE A MEAL WITH US?
WHAT?
WE DON'T KNOW ANYTHING ABOUT EACH OTHER...
SO WHY DON'T WE HAVE A NICE, LONG CHAT FIRST?

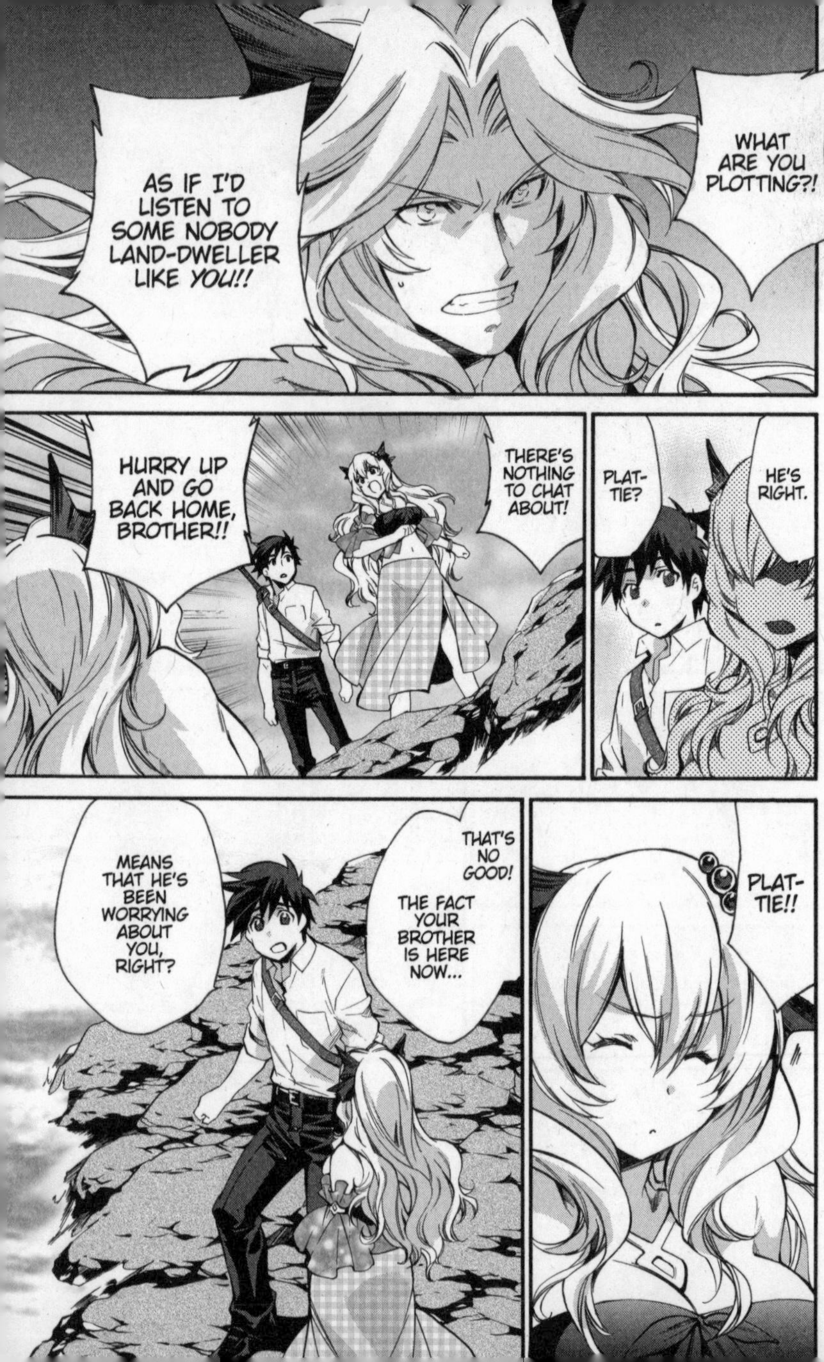
WHAT ARE YOU PLOTTING?!
AS IF I'D LISTEN TO SOME NOBODY LAND-DWELLER LIKE *YOU*!!
HE'S RIGHT.
PLAT-TIE?
THERE'S NOTHING TO CHAT ABOUT!
HURRY UP AND GO BACK HOME, BROTHER!!
PLAT-TIE!!
THAT'S NO GOOD!
THE FACT YOUR BROTHER IS HERE NOW...
MEANS THAT HE'S BEEN WORRYING ABOUT YOU, RIGHT?

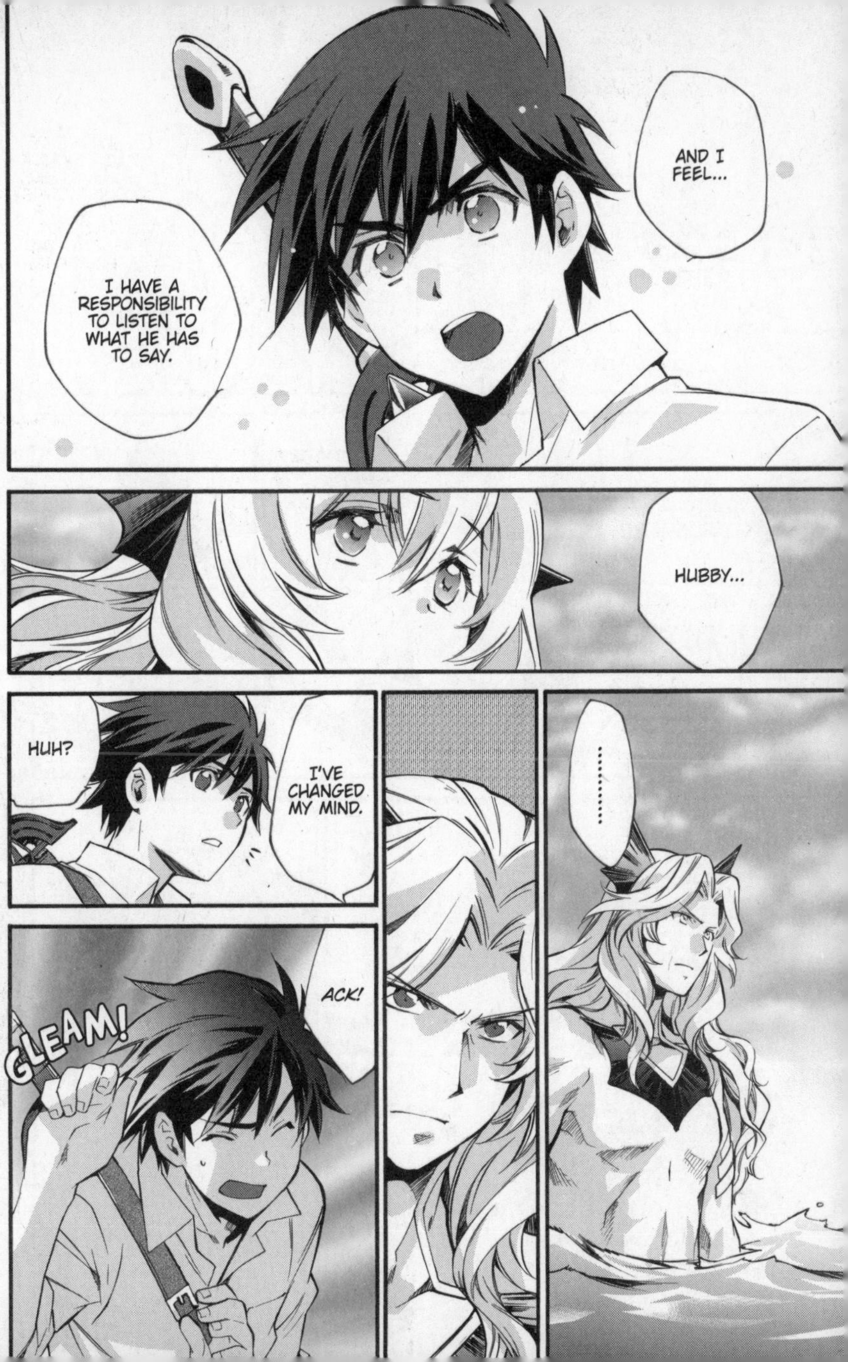
AND I FEEL...
I HAVE A RESPONSIBILITY TO LISTEN TO WHAT HE HAS TO SAY.
HUBBY...
......
I'VE CHANGED MY MIND.
HUH?
ACK!
GLEAM!

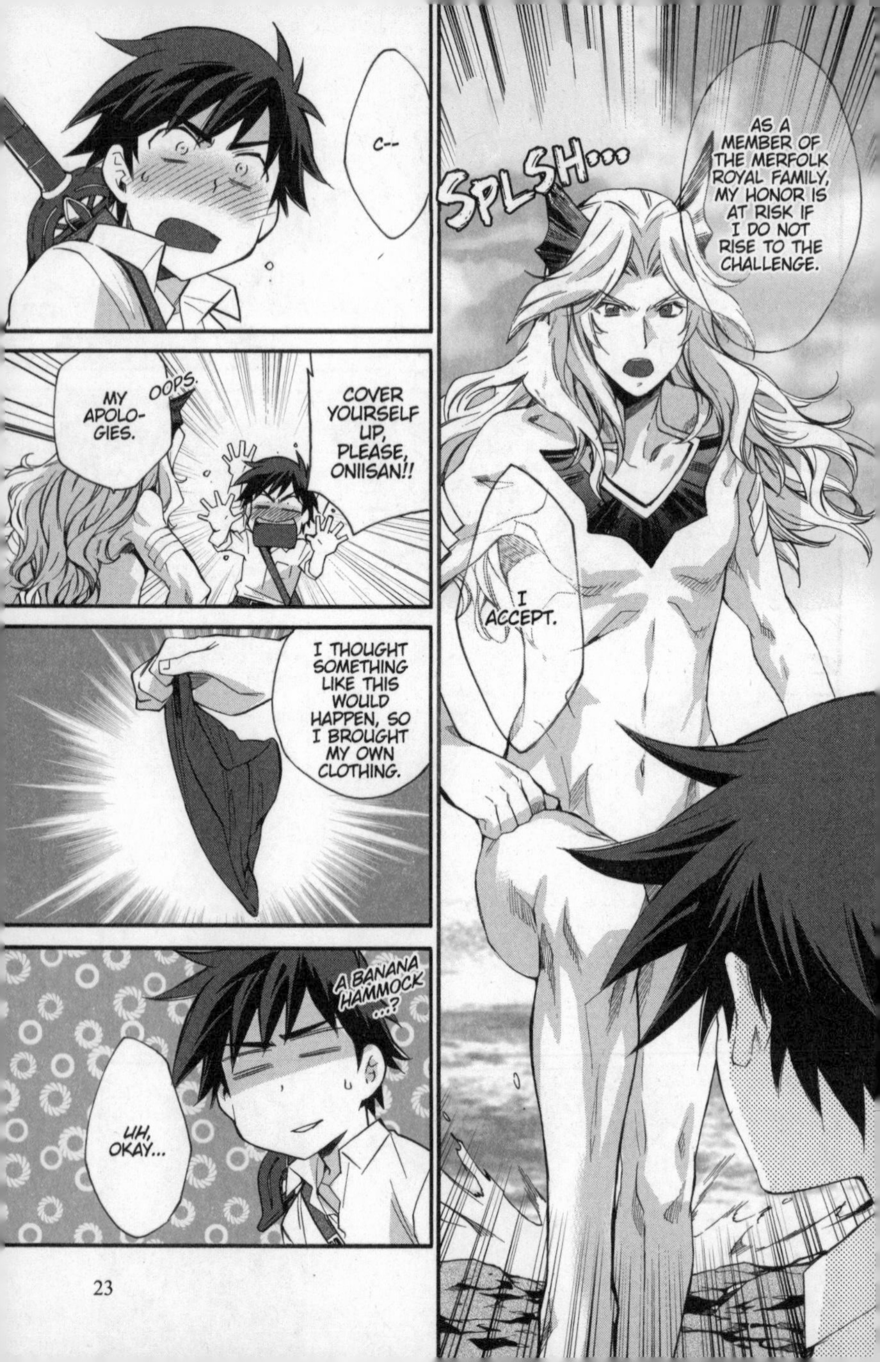
AS A MEMBER OF THE MERFOLK ROYAL FAMILY, MY HONOR IS AT RISK IF I DO NOT RISE TO THE CHALLENGE.
SPLSH...
I ACCEPT.
C--
COVER YOURSELF UP, PLEASE, ONIISAN!!
OOPS.
MY APOLOGIES.
I THOUGHT SOMETHING LIKE THIS WOULD HAPPEN, SO I BROUGHT MY OWN CLOTHING.
A BANANA HAMMOCK ...?
UH, OKAY...

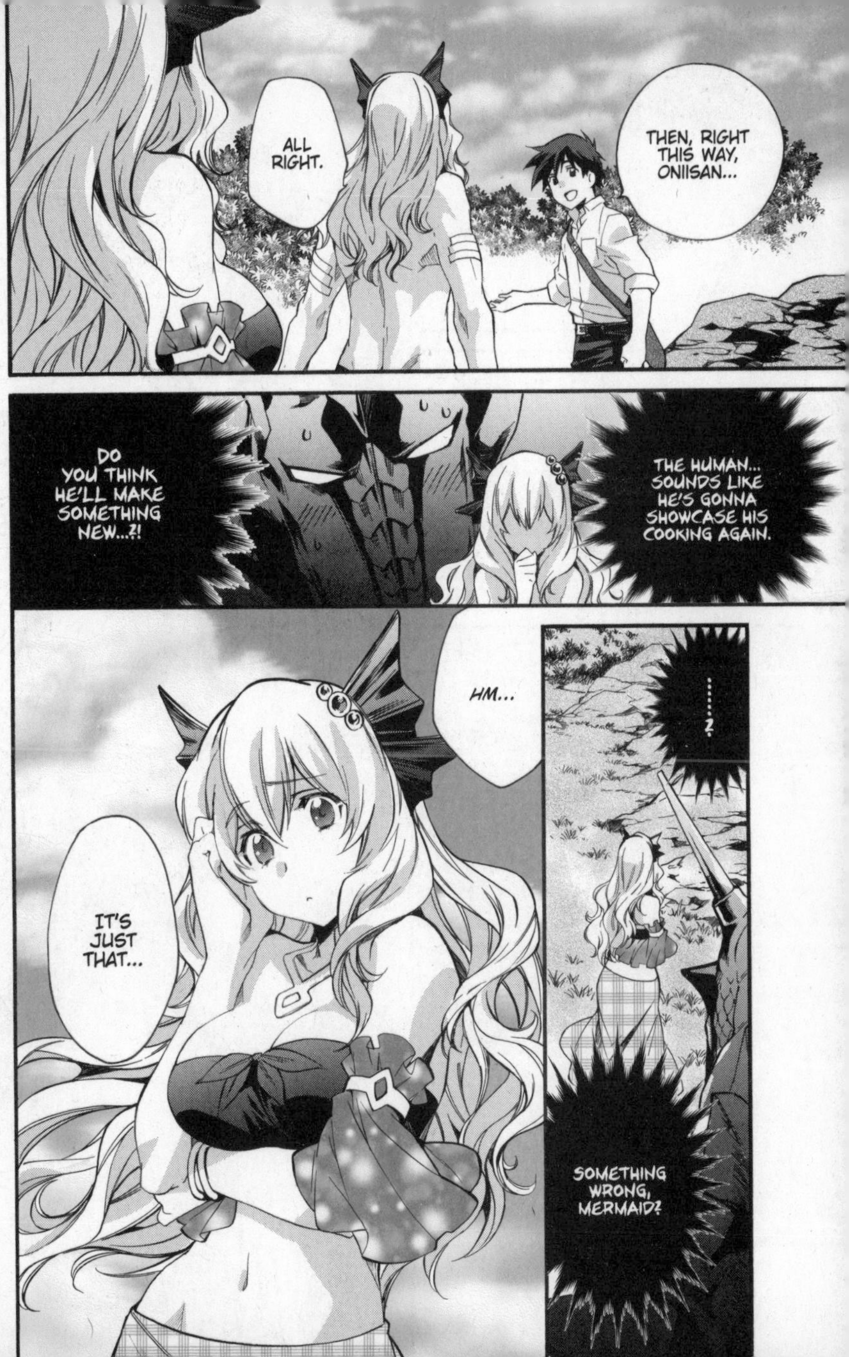
THEN, RIGHT THIS WAY, ONIISAN...
ALL RIGHT.
THE HUMAN... SOUNDS LIKE HE'S GONNA SHOWCASE HIS COOKING AGAIN.
DO YOU THINK HE'LL MAKE SOMETHING NEW...?!
......?
SOMETHING WRONG, MERMAID?
HM...
IT'S JUST THAT...

CHAPTER 8

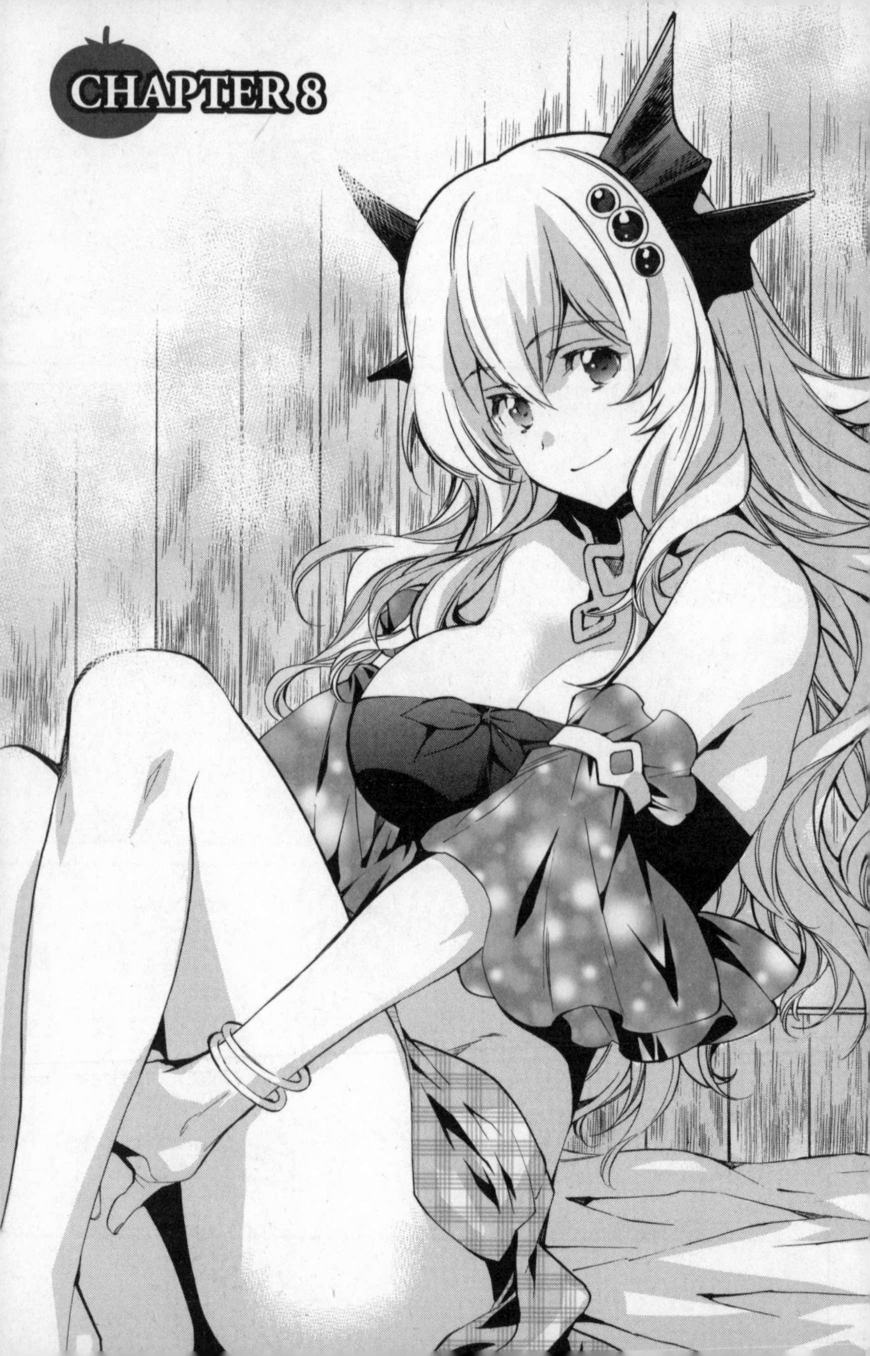

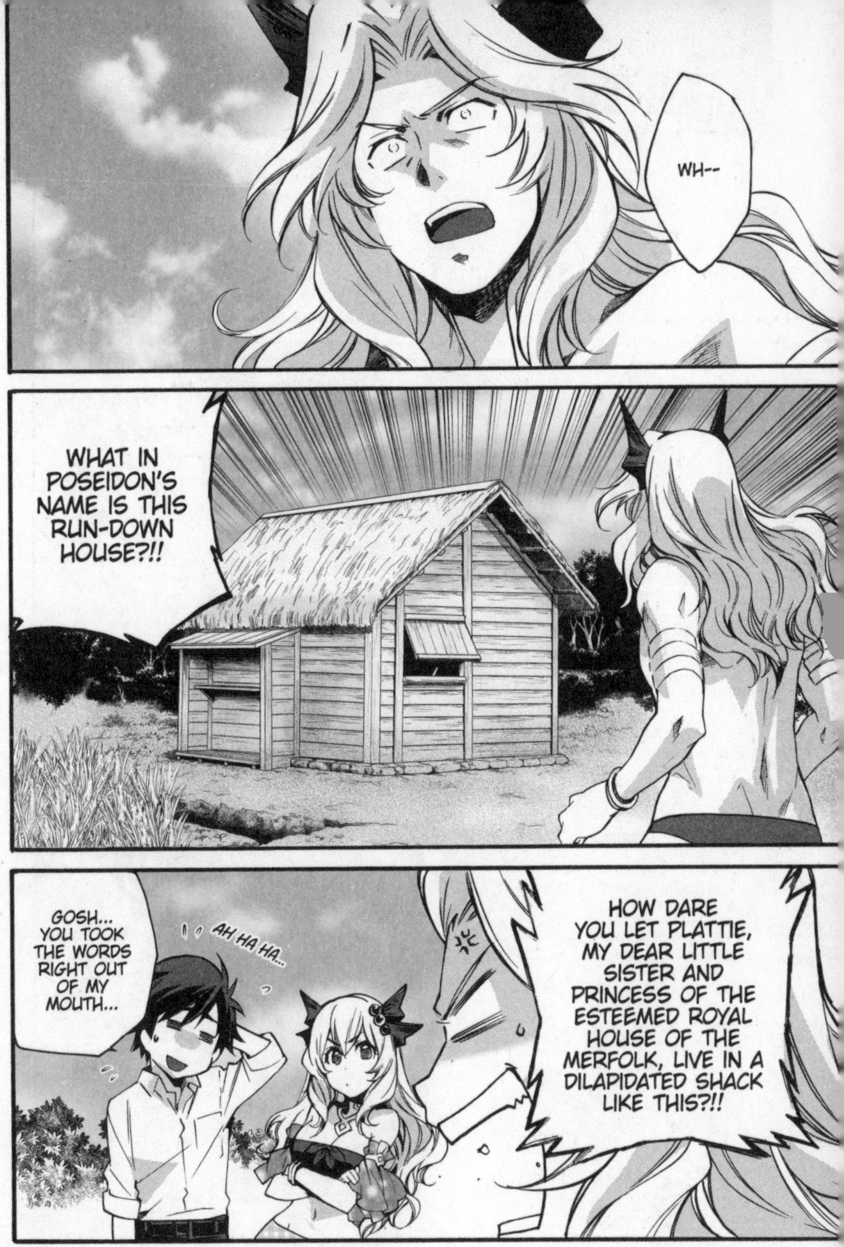
WH--
WHAT IN POSEIDON'S NAME IS THIS RUN-DOWN HOUSE?!!
HOW DARE YOU LET PLATTIE, MY DEAR LITTLE SISTER AND PRINCESS OF THE ESTEEMED ROYAL HOUSE OF THE MERFOLK, LIVE IN A DILAPIDATED SHACK LIKE THIS?!!
AH HA HA...
GOSH... YOU TOOK THE WORDS RIGHT OUT OF MY MOUTH...

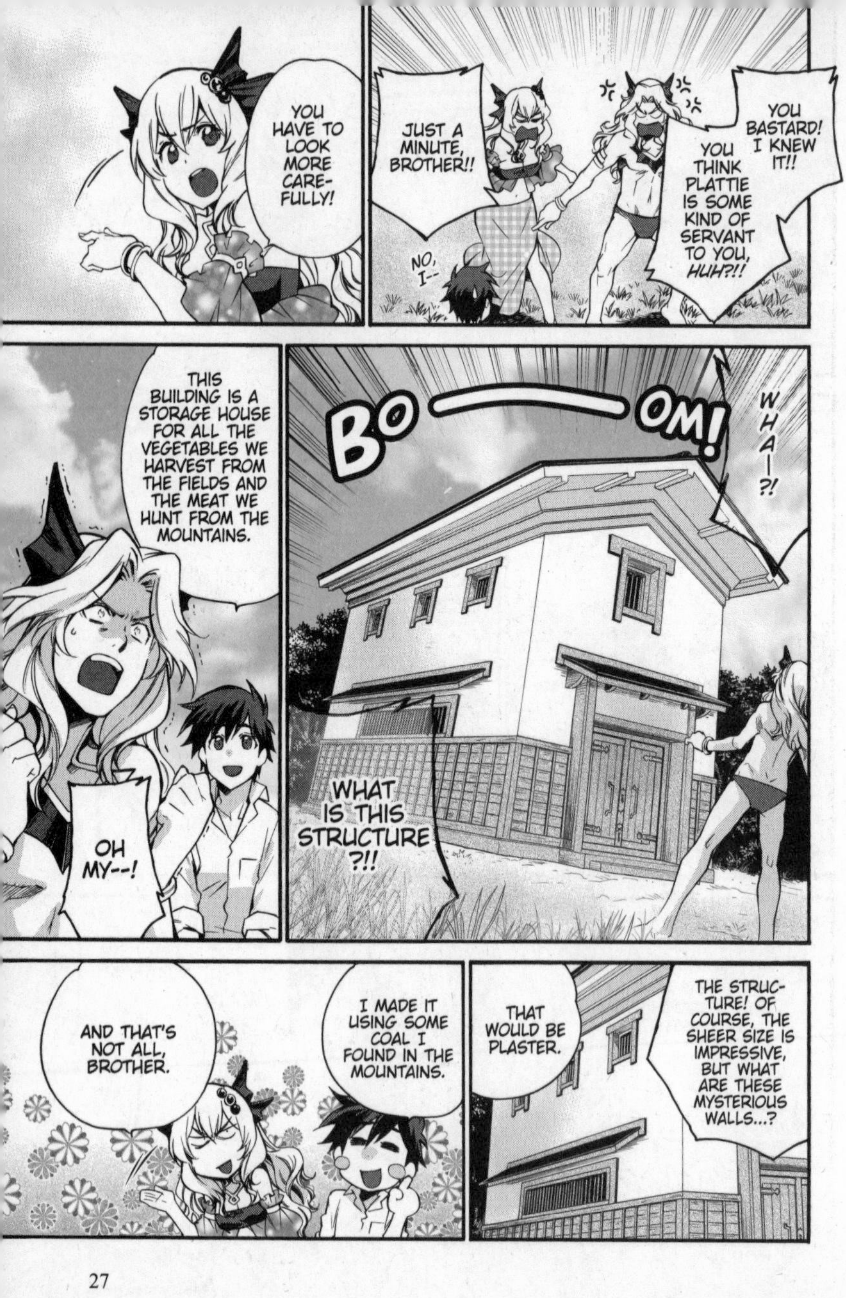
YOU BASTARD! I KNEW IT!!
YOU THINK PLATTIE IS SOME KIND OF SERVANT TO YOU, HUH?!!
JUST A MINUTE, BROTHER!!
NO, I--
YOU HAVE TO LOOK MORE CARE-FULLY!
WHA--?!
BO——OM!
WHAT IS THIS STRUCTURE?!!
THIS BUILDING IS A STORAGE HOUSE FOR ALL THE VEGETABLES WE HARVEST FROM THE FIELDS AND THE MEAT WE HUNT FROM THE MOUNTAINS.
OH MY--!
THE STRUC-TURE! OF COURSE, THE SHEER SIZE IS IMPRESSIVE, BUT WHAT ARE THESE MYSTERIOUS WALLS...?
THAT WOULD BE PLASTER.
I MADE IT USING SOME COAL I FOUND IN THE MOUNTAINS.
AND THAT'S NOT ALL, BROTHER.

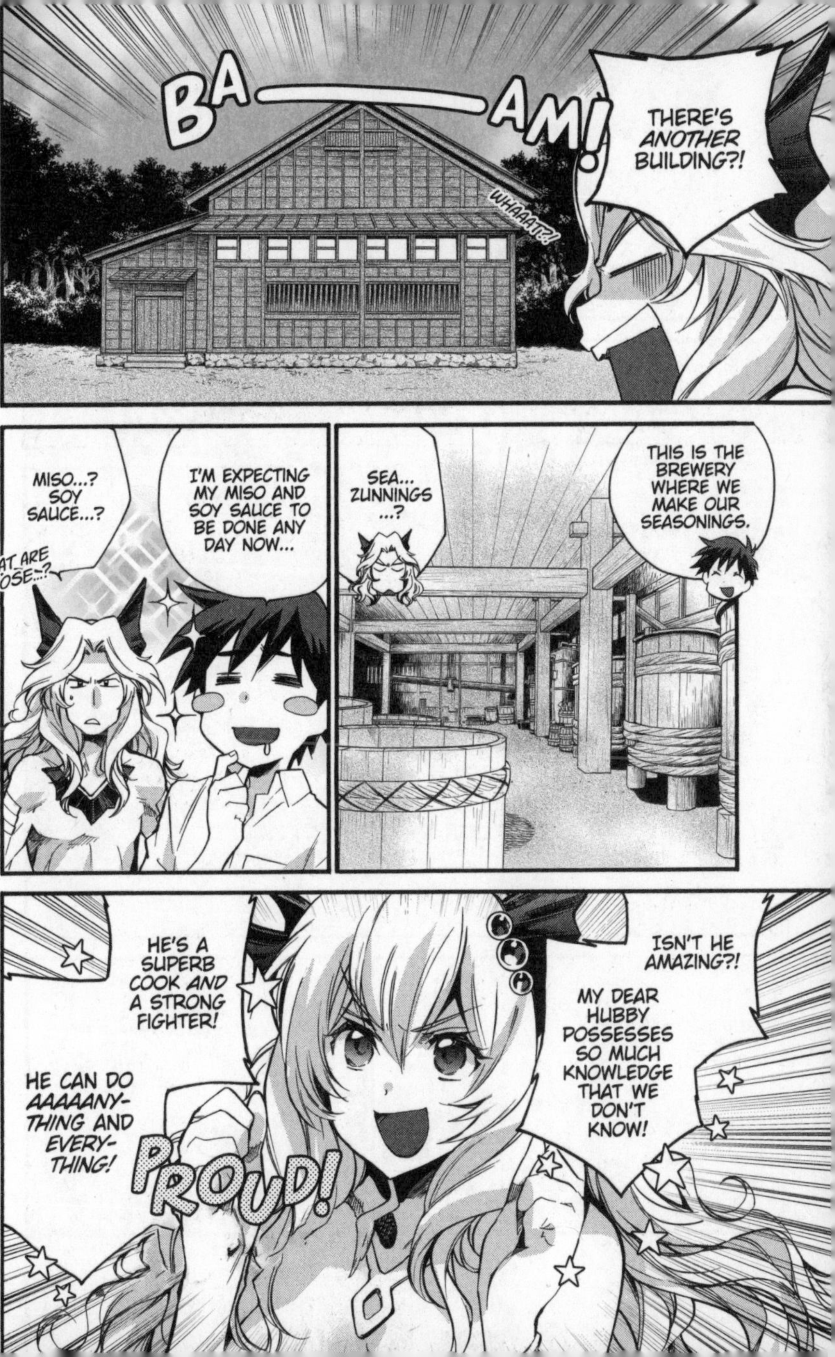
THERE'S ANOTHER BUILDING?!
BA——AM!
WHAAAAT?!
THIS IS THE BREWERY WHERE WE MAKE OUR SEASONINGS.
SEA... ZUNNINGS ...?
I'M EXPECTING MY MISO AND SOY SAUCE TO BE DONE ANY DAY NOW...
MISO...? SOY SAUCE...?
WHAT ARE THOSE...?
ISN'T HE AMAZING?!
MY DEAR HUBBY POSSESSES SO MUCH KNOWLEDGE THAT WE DON'T KNOW!
HE'S A SUPERB COOK AND A STRONG FIGHTER!
HE CAN DO AAAAANY-THING AND EVERY-THING!
PROUD!

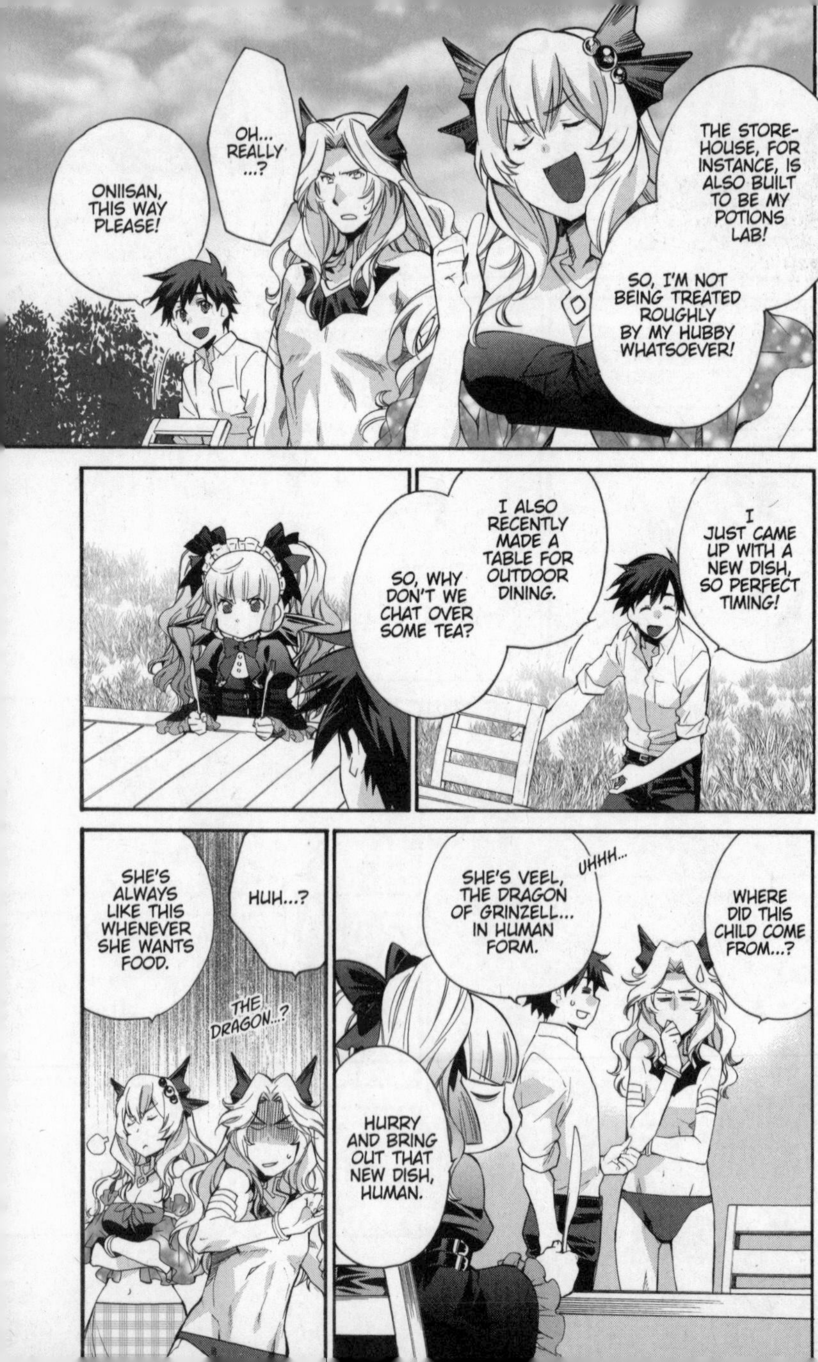
THE STORE-HOUSE, FOR INSTANCE, IS ALSO BUILT TO BE MY POTIONS LAB!
SO, I'M NOT BEING TREATED ROUGHLY BY MY HUBBY WHATSOEVER!
OH... REALLY ...?
ONIISAN, THIS WAY PLEASE!
I JUST CAME UP WITH A NEW DISH, SO PERFECT TIMING!
I ALSO RECENTLY MADE A TABLE FOR OUTDOOR DINING.
SO, WHY DON'T WE CHAT OVER SOME TEA?
WHERE DID THIS CHILD COME FROM...?
UHHH...
SHE'S VEEL, THE DRAGON OF GRINZELL... IN HUMAN FORM.
HURRY AND BRING OUT THAT NEW DISH, HUMAN.
HUH...?
SHE'S ALWAYS LIKE THIS WHENEVER SHE WANTS FOOD.
THE DRAGON...?

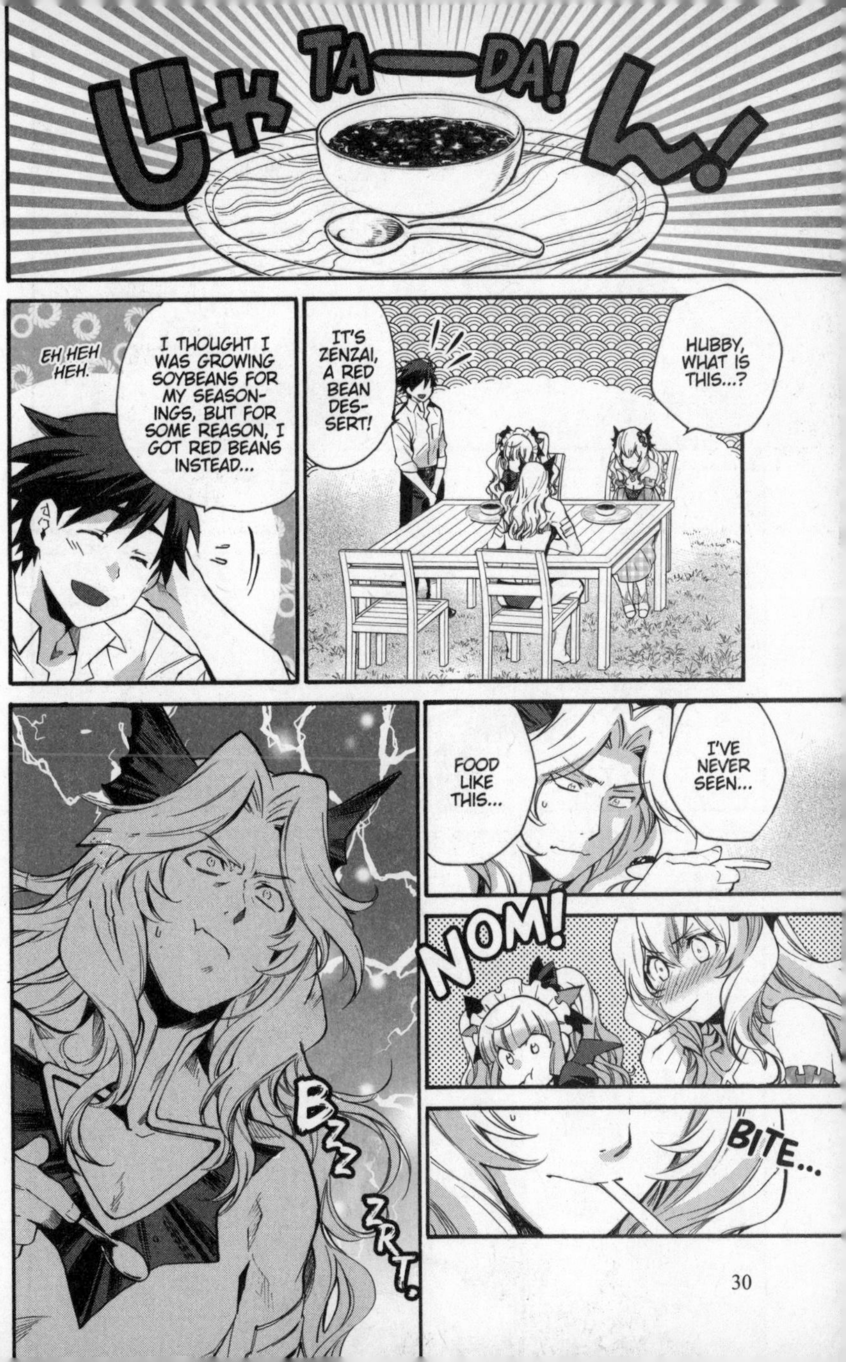
じゃ
TA—DA!
ん!
HUBBY, WHAT IS THIS...?
IT'S ZENZAI, A RED BEAN DES-SERT!
I THOUGHT I WAS GROWING SOYBEANS FOR MY SEASON-INGS, BUT FOR SOME REASON, I GOT RED BEANS INSTEAD...
EH HEH HEH.
I'VE NEVER SEEN...
FOOD LIKE THIS...
NOM!
BITE...
BZZ
ZRT.

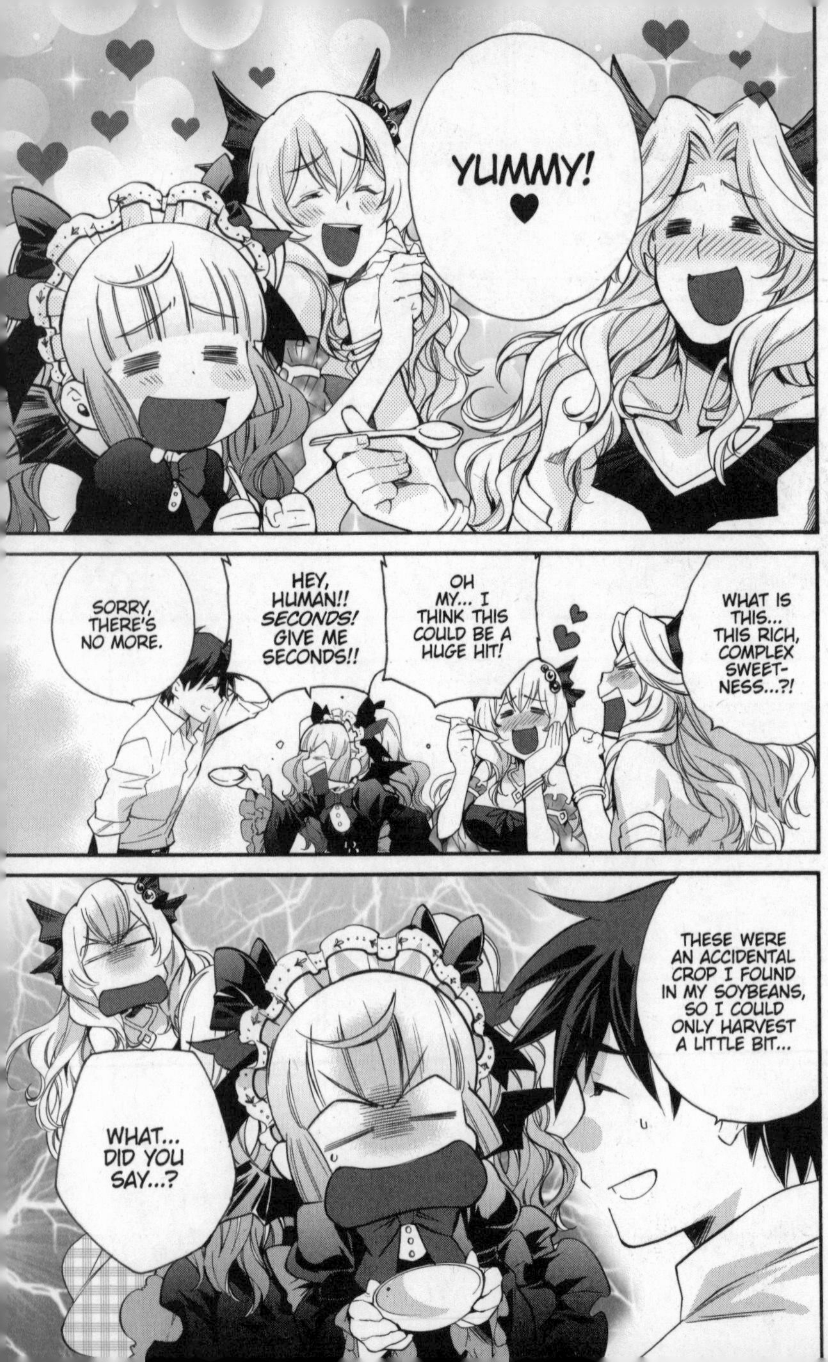
YUMMY! ♥
WHAT IS THIS... THIS RICH, COMPLEX SWEETNESS...?!
OH MY... I THINK THIS COULD BE A HUGE HIT!
HEY, HUMAN!! *SECONDS!* GIVE ME SECONDS!!
SORRY, THERE'S NO MORE.
THESE WERE AN ACCIDENTAL CROP I FOUND IN MY SOYBEANS, SO I COULD ONLY HARVEST A LITTLE BIT...
WHAT... DID YOU SAY...?

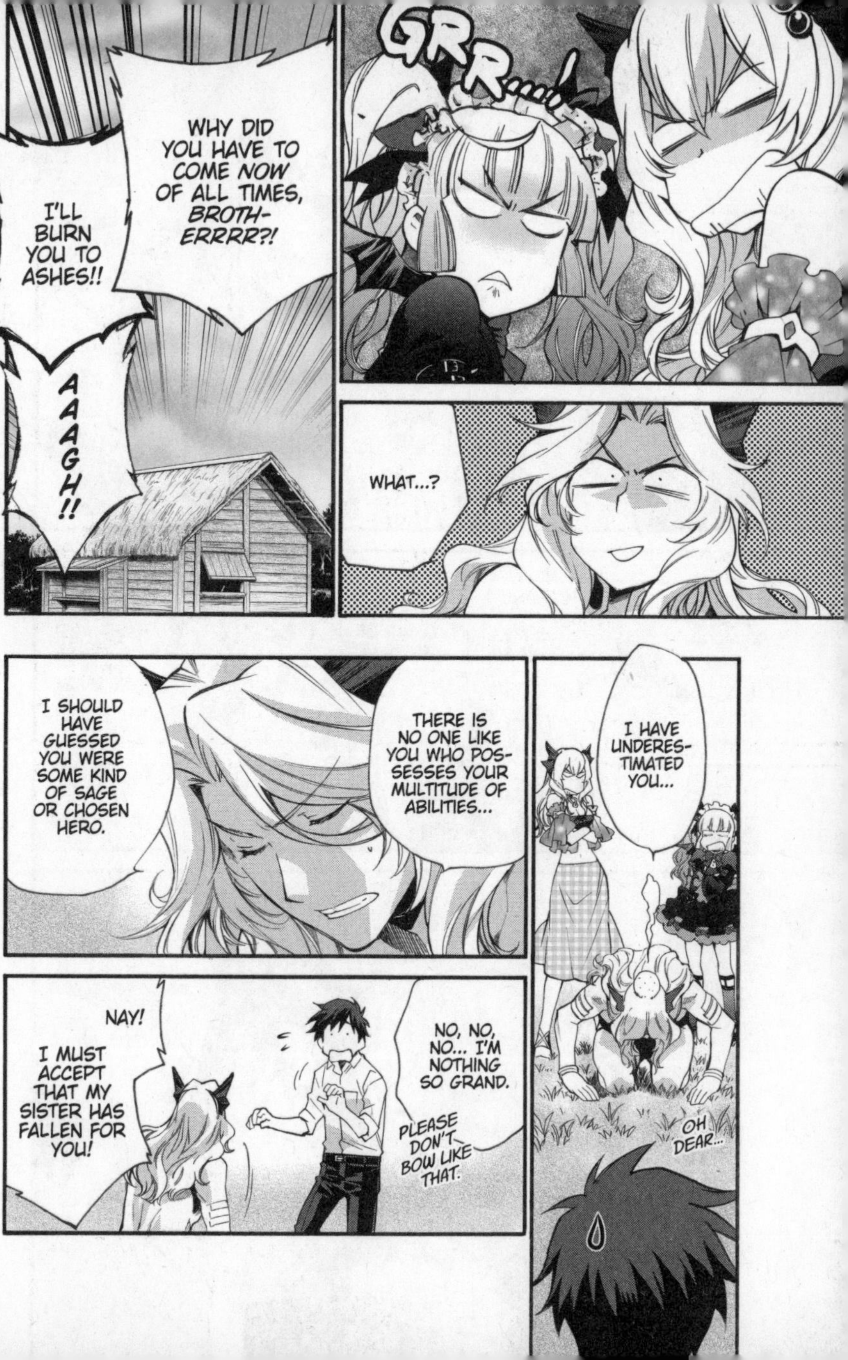
GRR...!
WHAT...?
WHY DID YOU HAVE TO COME NOW OF ALL TIMES, BROTH-ERRRR?!
I'LL BURN YOU TO ASHES!!
AAAAGH!!
I HAVE UNDERES-TIMATED YOU...
OH DEAR...
THERE IS NO ONE LIKE YOU WHO POS-SESSES YOUR MULTITUDE OF ABILITIES...
I SHOULD HAVE GUESSED YOU WERE SOME KIND OF SAGE OR CHOSEN HERO.
NO, NO, NO... I'M NOTHING SO GRAND.
PLEASE DON'T BOW LIKE THAT.
NAY!
I MUST ACCEPT THAT MY SISTER HAS FALLEN FOR YOU!

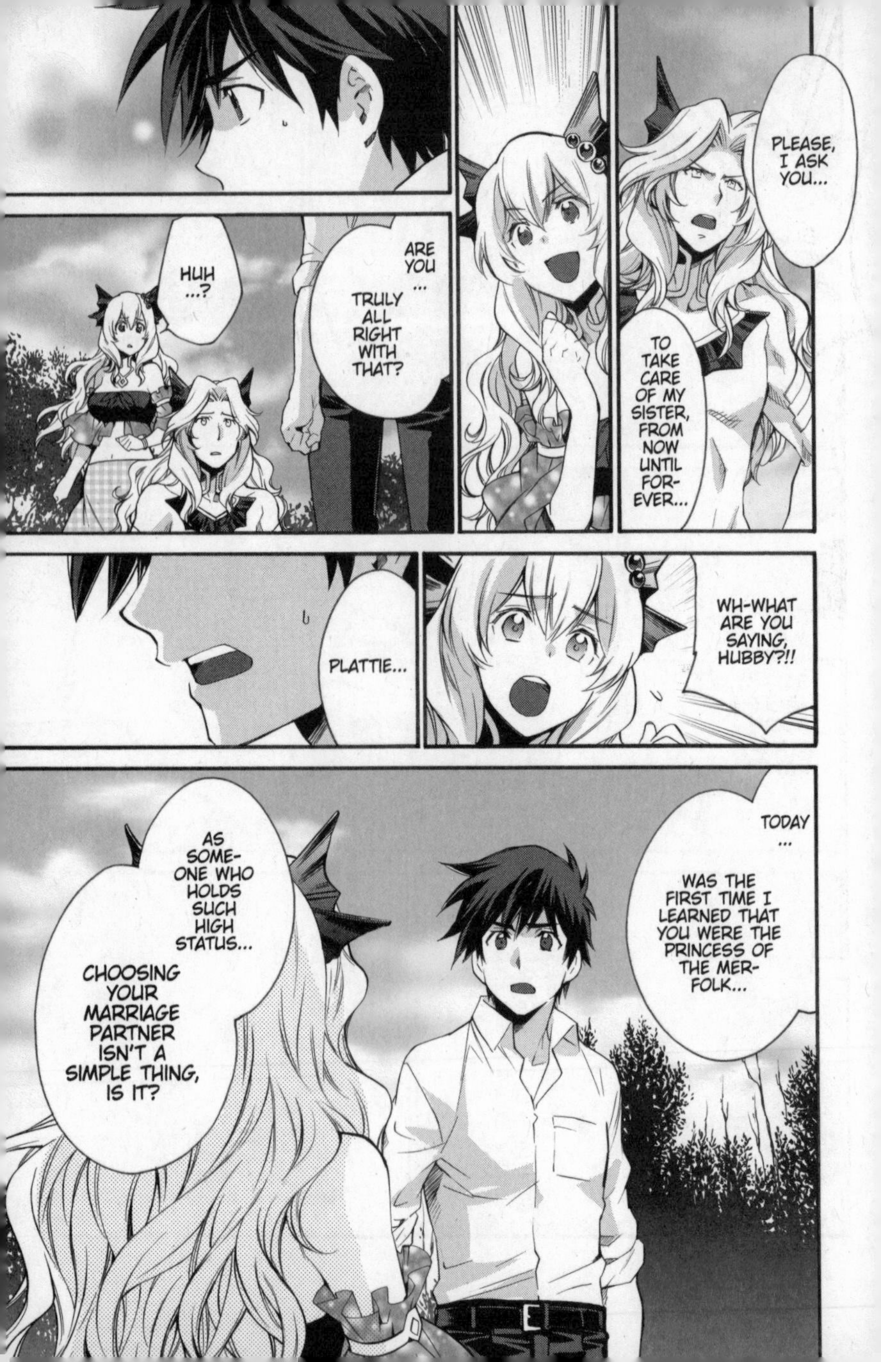
PLEASE, I ASK YOU...
TO TAKE CARE OF MY SISTER, FROM NOW UNTIL FOR-EVER...
ARE YOU ... TRULY ALL RIGHT WITH THAT?
HUH ...?
WH-WHAT ARE YOU SAYING, HUBBY?!!
PLATTIE...
TODAY ...
WAS THE FIRST TIME I LEARNED THAT YOU WERE THE PRINCESS OF THE MER-FOLK...
AS SOME-ONE WHO HOLDS SUCH HIGH STATUS...
CHOOSING YOUR MARRIAGE PARTNER ISN'T A SIMPLE THING, IS IT?

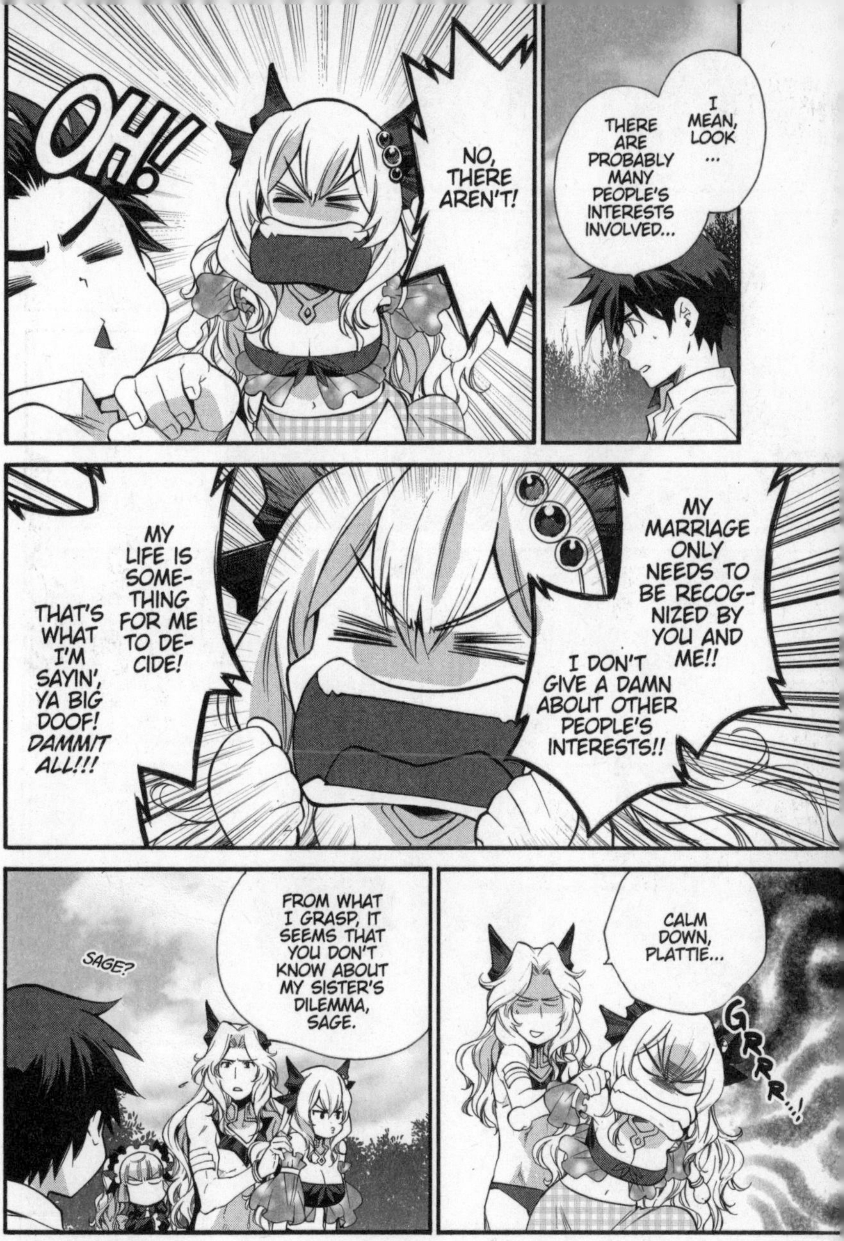
I MEAN, LOOK ...
THERE ARE PROBABLY MANY PEOPLE'S INTERESTS INVOLVED...
NO, THERE AREN'T!
OH!!
MY MARRIAGE ONLY NEEDS TO BE RECOG-NIZED BY YOU AND ME!!
I DON'T GIVE A DAMN ABOUT OTHER PEOPLE'S INTERESTS!!
MY LIFE IS SOME-THING FOR ME TO DE-CIDE!
THAT'S WHAT I'M SAYIN', YA BIG DOOF! DAMMIT ALL!!!
CALM DOWN, PLATTIE...
GRRRR...!
FROM WHAT I GRASP, IT SEEMS THAT YOU DON'T KNOW ABOUT MY SISTER'S DILEMMA, SAGE.
SAGE?

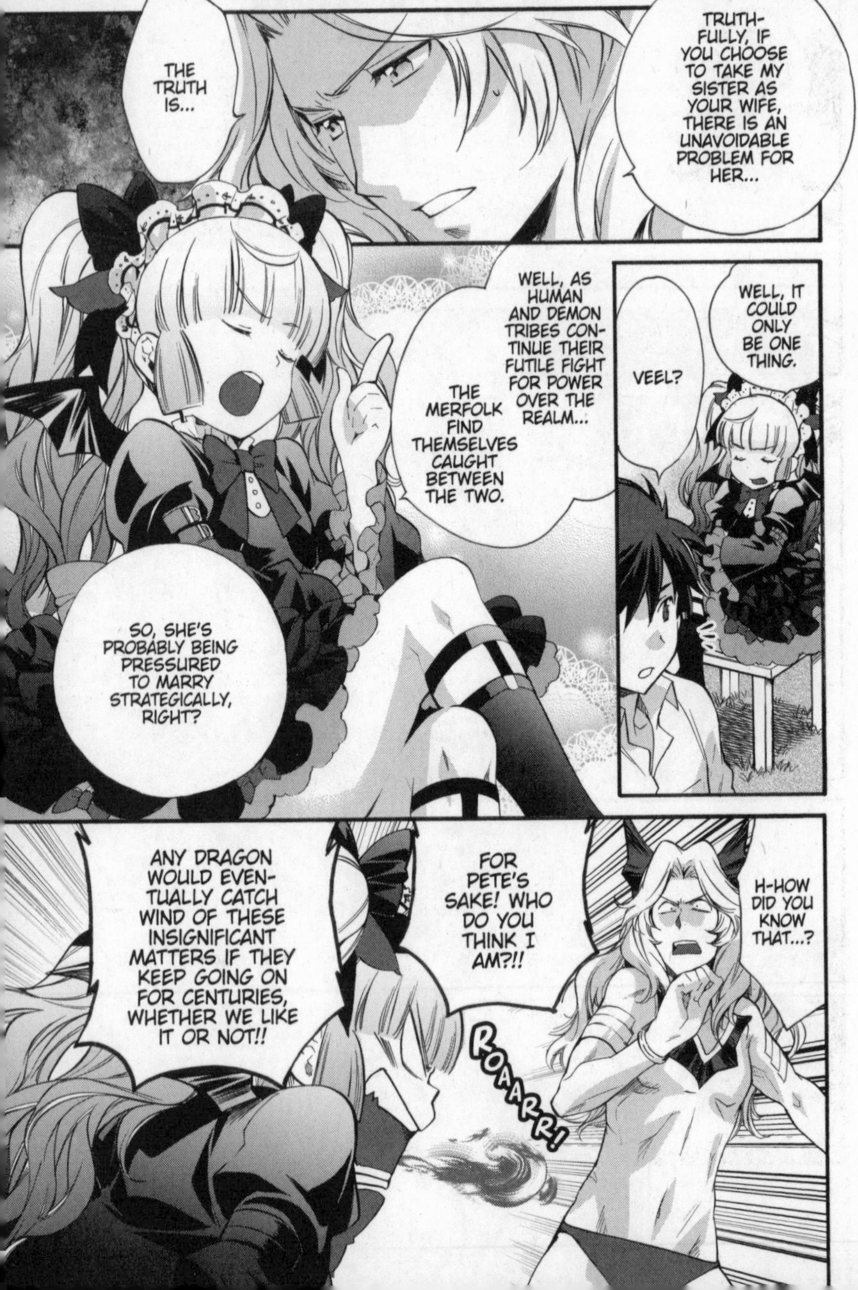
TRUTH-FULLY, IF YOU CHOOSE TO TAKE MY SISTER AS YOUR WIFE, THERE IS AN UNAVOIDABLE PROBLEM FOR HER...
THE TRUTH IS...
WELL, IT COULD ONLY BE ONE THING.
VEEL?
WELL, AS HUMAN AND DEMON TRIBES CON-TINUE THEIR FUTILE FIGHT FOR POWER OVER THE REALM...
THE MERFOLK FIND THEMSELVES CAUGHT BETWEEN THE TWO.
SO, SHE'S PROBABLY BEING PRESSURED TO MARRY STRATEGICALLY, RIGHT?
H-HOW DID YOU KNOW THAT...?
FOR PETE'S SAKE! WHO DO YOU THINK I AM?!!
ANY DRAGON WOULD EVEN-TUALLY CATCH WIND OF THESE INSIGNIFICANT MATTERS IF THEY KEEP GOING ON FOR CENTURIES, WHETHER WE LIKE IT OR NOT!!
ROAAARR!

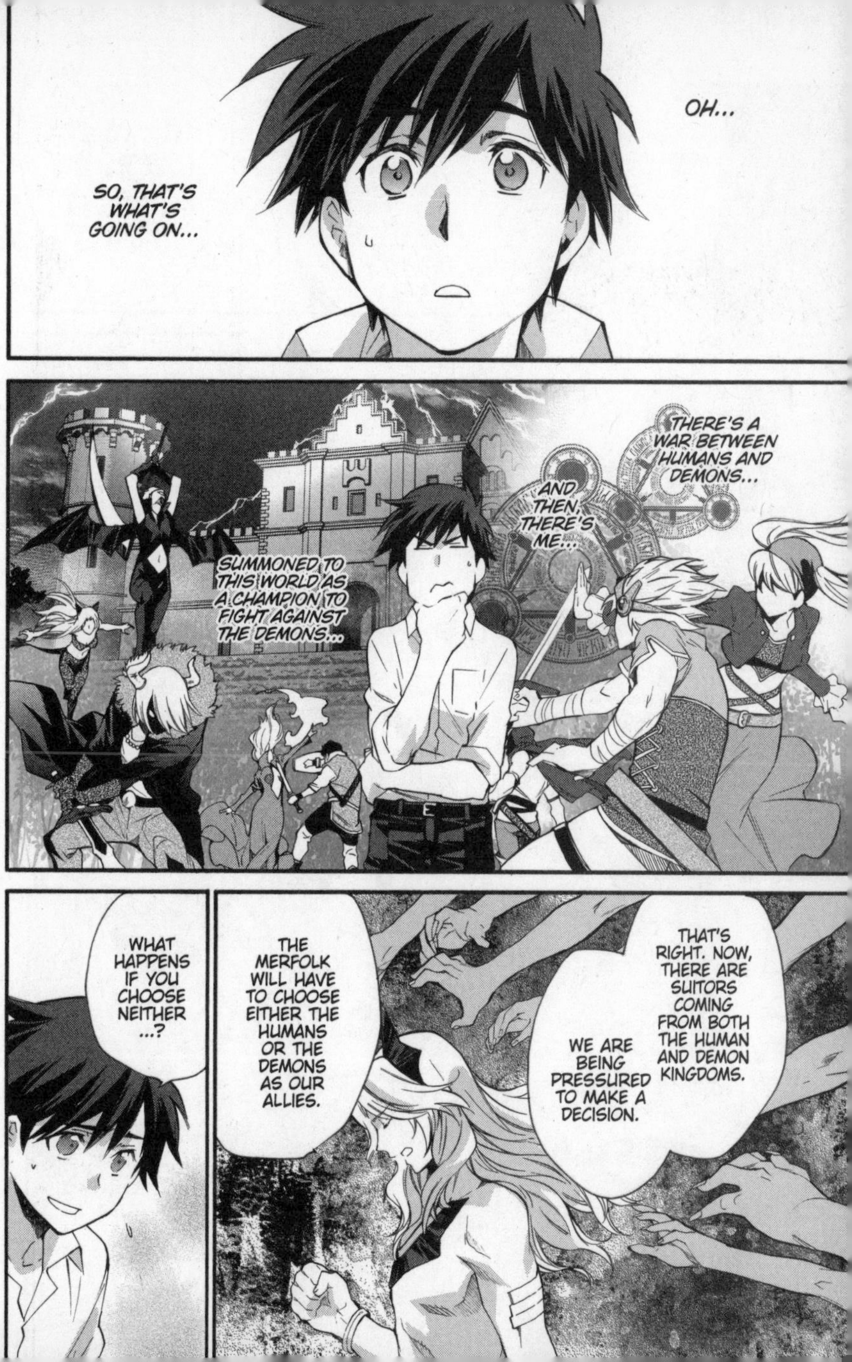
OH...
SO, THAT'S WHAT'S GOING ON...
THERE'S A WAR BETWEEN HUMANS AND DEMONS...
AND THEN, THERE'S ME...
SUMMONED TO THIS WORLD AS A CHAMPION TO FIGHT AGAINST THE DEMONS...
THAT'S RIGHT. NOW, THERE ARE SUITORS COMING FROM BOTH THE HUMAN AND DEMON KINGDOMS.
WE ARE BEING PRESSURED TO MAKE A DECISION.
THE MERFOLK WILL HAVE TO CHOOSE EITHER THE HUMANS OR THE DEMONS AS OUR ALLIES.
WHAT HAPPENS IF YOU CHOOSE NEITHER ...?

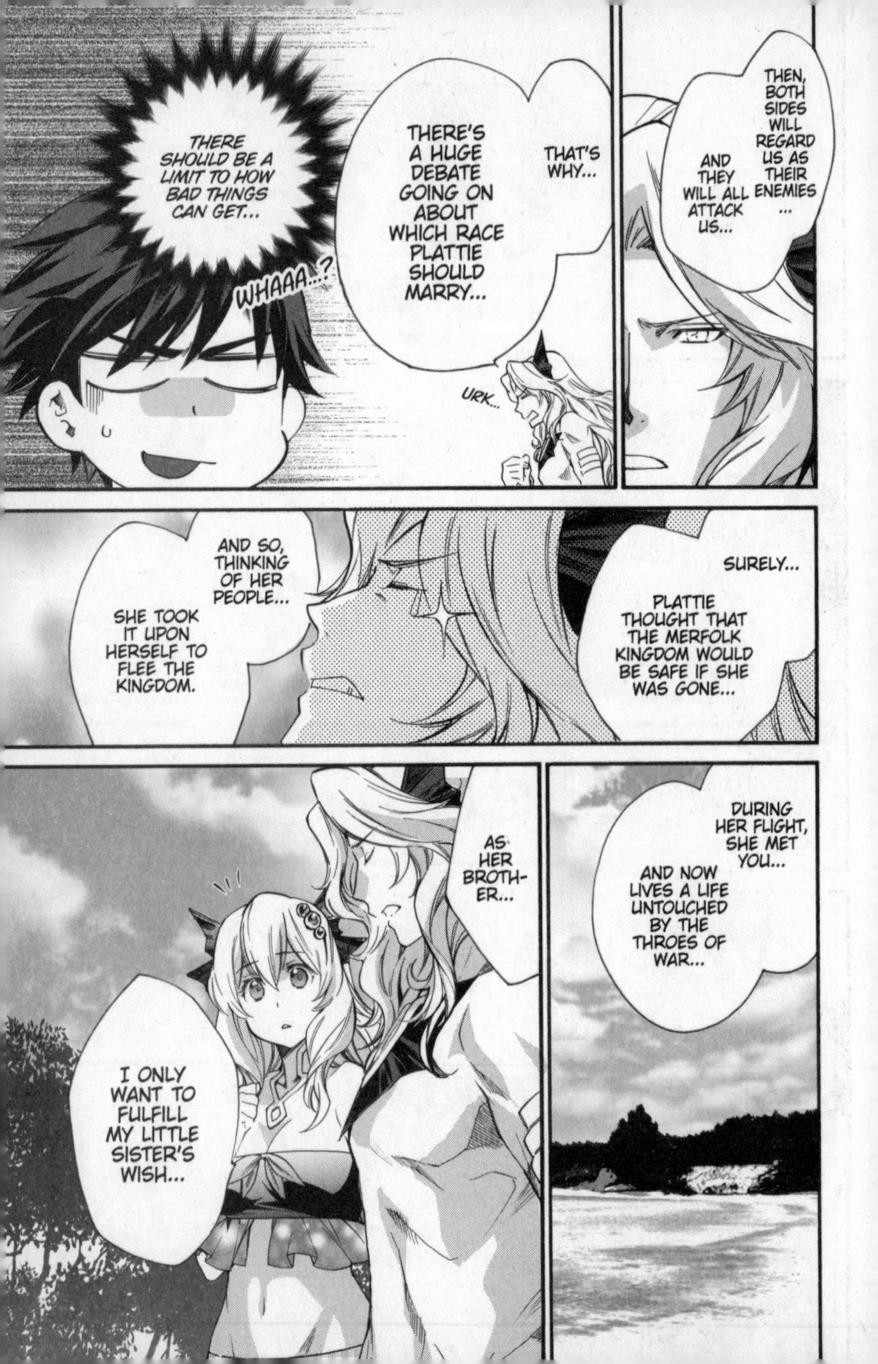
THEN, BOTH SIDES WILL REGARD US AS THEIR ENEMIES...
AND THEY WILL ALL ATTACK US...
THAT'S WHY...
THERE'S A HUGE DEBATE GOING ON ABOUT WHICH RACE PLATTIE SHOULD MARRY...
URK...
WHAAA...?
THERE SHOULD BE A LIMIT TO HOW BAD THINGS CAN GET...
SURELY...
PLATTIE THOUGHT THAT THE MERFOLK KINGDOM WOULD BE SAFE IF SHE WAS GONE...
AND SO, THINKING OF HER PEOPLE...
SHE TOOK IT UPON HERSELF TO FLEE THE KINGDOM.
DURING HER FLIGHT, SHE MET YOU...
AND NOW LIVES A LIFE UNTOUCHED BY THE THROES OF WAR...
AS HER BROTHER-ER...
I ONLY WANT TO FULFILL MY LITTLE SISTER'S WISH...

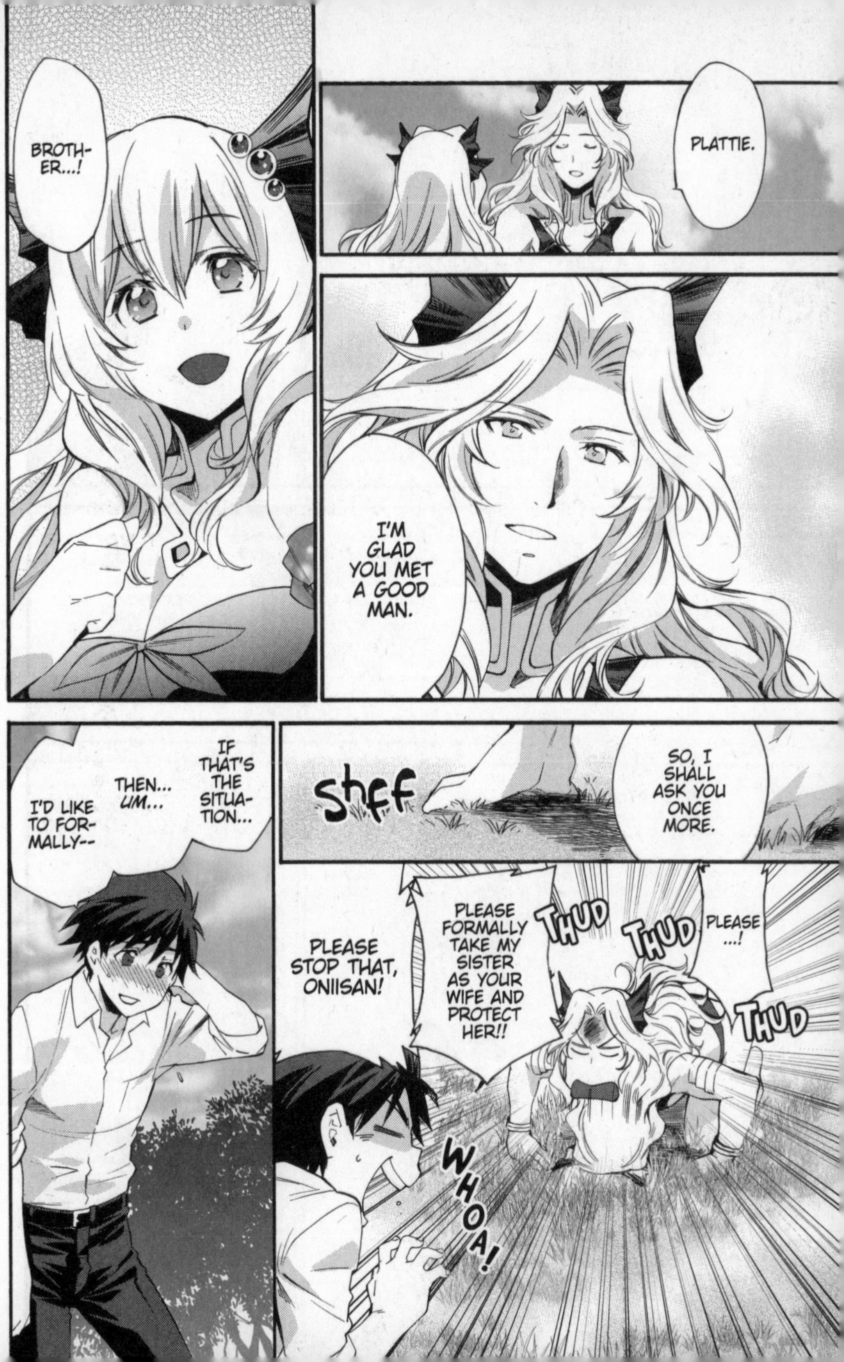
PLATTIE.
I'M GLAD YOU MET A GOOD MAN.
BROTHER...!
SO, I SHALL ASK YOU ONCE MORE.
SHFF
PLEASE ...!
THUD
THUD
PLEASE FORMALLY TAKE MY SISTER AS YOUR WIFE AND PROTECT HER!!
THUD
PLEASE STOP THAT, ONIISAN!
WHOA!
IF THAT'S THE SITUATION...
THEN... UM...
I'D LIKE TO FORMALLY--

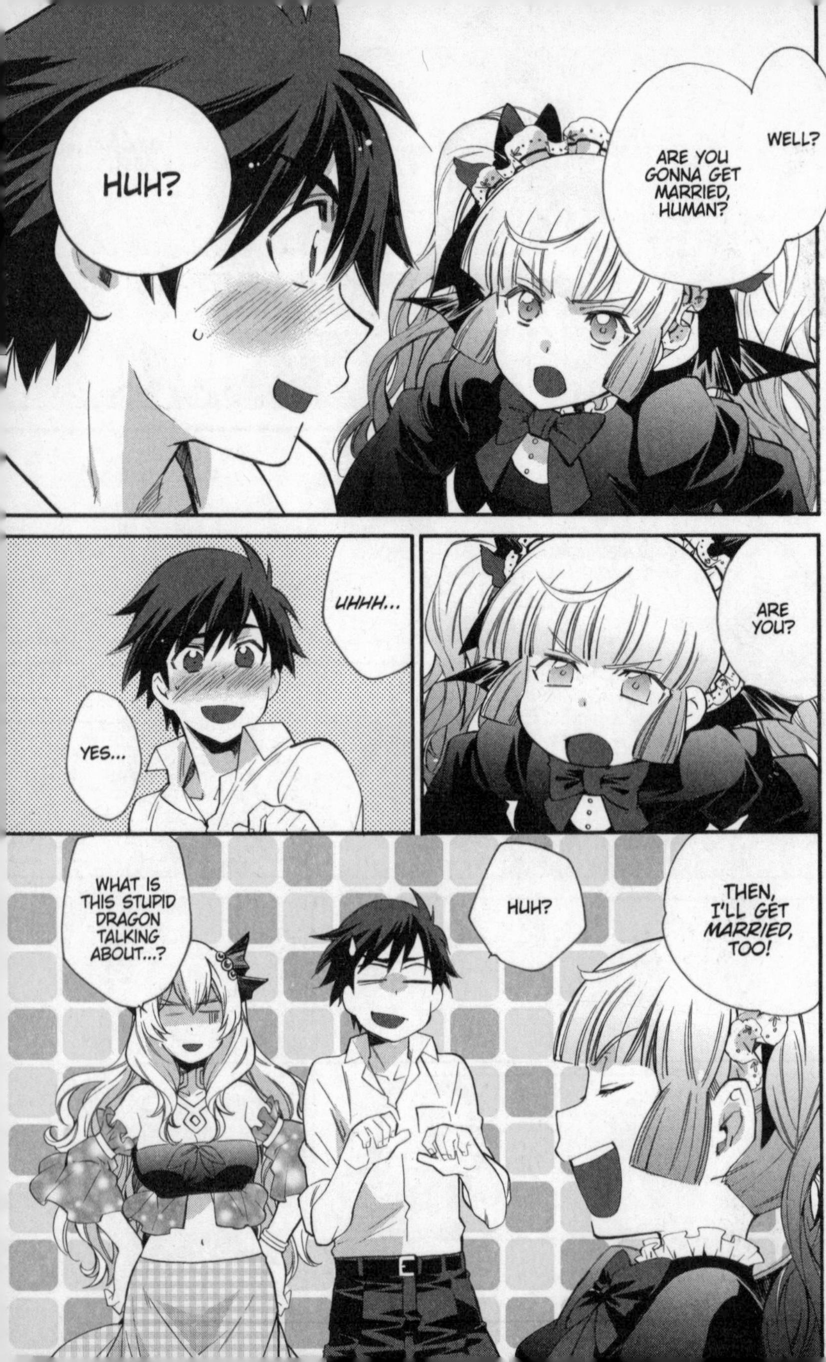
WELL?
ARE YOU GONNA GET MARRIED, HUMAN?
HUH?
ARE YOU?
UHHH...
YES...
THEN, I'LL GET *MARRIED*, TOO!
HUH?
WHAT IS THIS STUPID DRAGON TALKING ABOUT...?

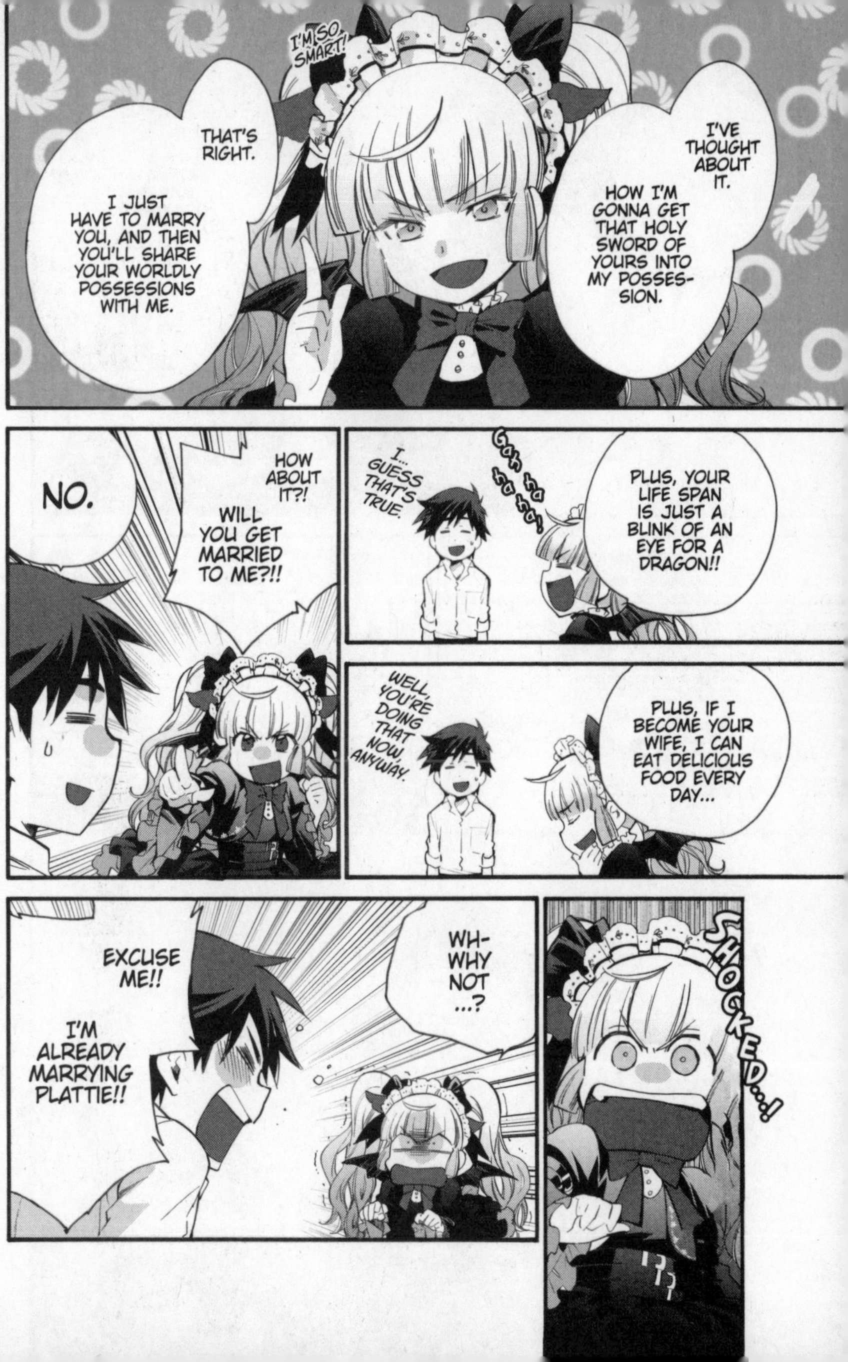
I'VE THOUGHT ABOUT IT.
HOW I'M GONNA GET THAT HOLY SWORD OF YOURS INTO MY POSSESSION.
I'M SO SMART!
THAT'S RIGHT.
I JUST HAVE TO MARRY YOU, AND THEN YOU'LL SHARE YOUR WORLDLY POSSESSIONS WITH ME.
PLUS, YOUR LIFE SPAN IS JUST A BLINK OF AN EYE FOR A DRAGON!!
Gah ha ha ha!
I... GUESS THAT'S TRUE.
PLUS, IF I BECOME YOUR WIFE, I CAN EAT DELICIOUS FOOD EVERY DAY...
WELL, YOU'RE DOING THAT NOW, ANYWAY.
HOW ABOUT IT?!
WILL YOU GET MARRIED TO ME?!!
NO.
SHOCKED...!
WH-WHY NOT ...?
EXCUSE ME!!
I'M ALREADY MARRYING PLATTIE!!

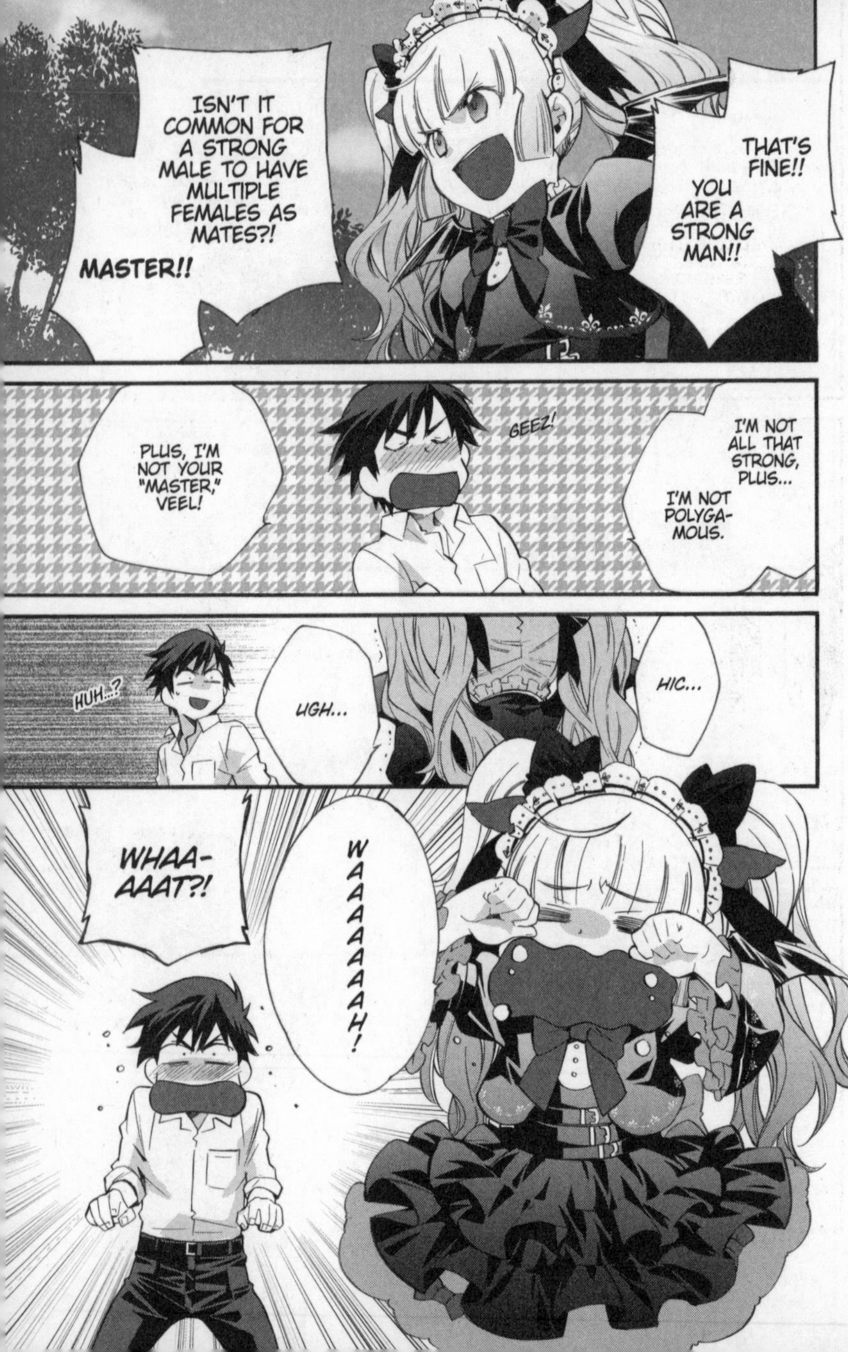
THAT'S FINE!!
YOU ARE A STRONG MAN!!
ISN'T IT COMMON FOR A STRONG MALE TO HAVE MULTIPLE FEMALES AS MATES?!
MASTER!!
I'M NOT ALL THAT STRONG, PLUS...
I'M NOT POLYGA-MOUS.
GEEZ!
PLUS, I'M NOT YOUR "MASTER," VEEL!
HIC...
UGH...
HUH...?
WAAAAAAAAAH!
WHAA-AAAT?!

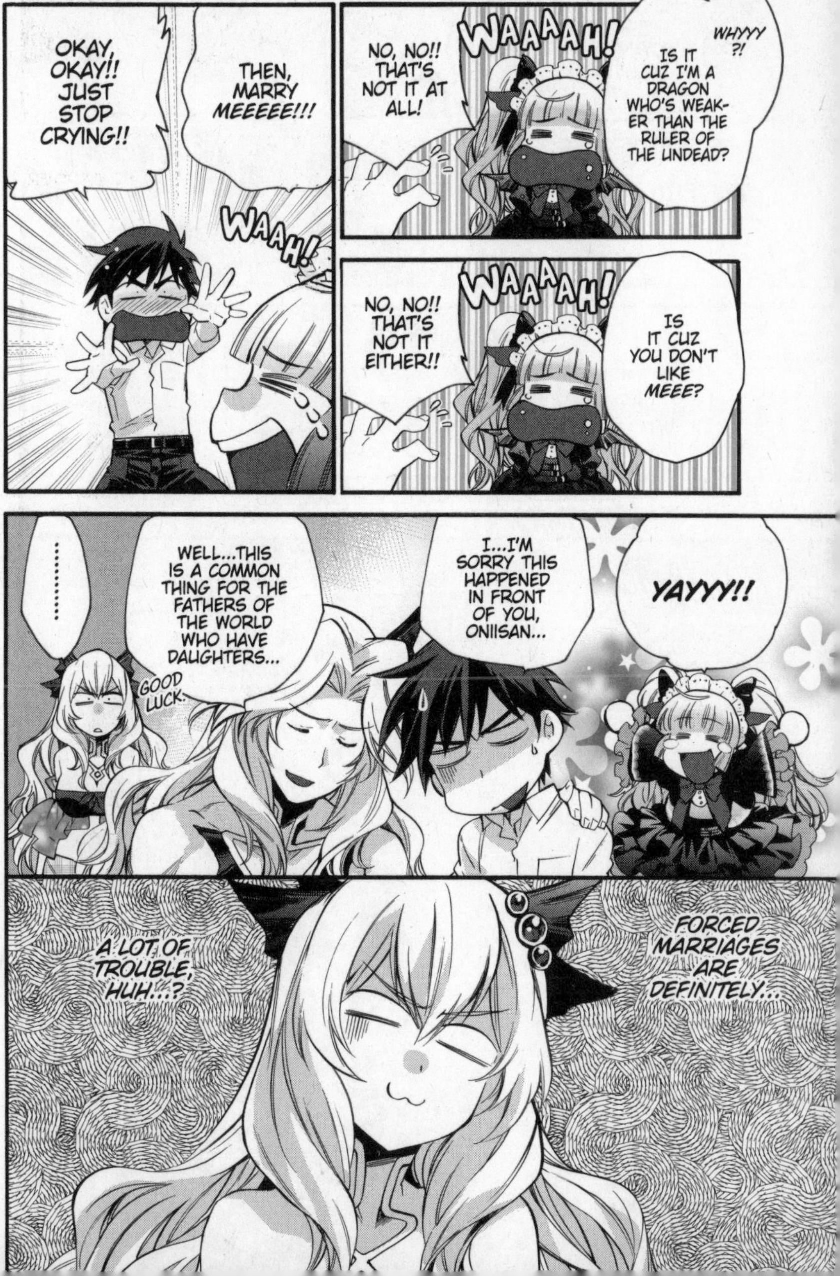
WHYYY ?!
IS IT CUZ I'M A DRAGON WHO'S WEAK-ER THAN THE RULER OF THE UNDEAD?
WAAAAAH!
NO, NO!! THAT'S NOT IT AT ALL!
WAAAAAH!
IS IT CUZ YOU DON'T LIKE MEEE?
NO, NO!! THAT'S NOT IT EITHER!!
THEN, MARRY MEEEEE!!!
OKAY, OKAY!! JUST STOP CRYING!!
WAAAH!
YAYYY!!
I...I'M SORRY THIS HAPPENED IN FRONT OF YOU, ONIISAN...
WELL...THIS IS A COMMON THING FOR THE FATHERS OF THE WORLD WHO HAVE DAUGHTERS...
GOOD LUCK.
....
FORCED MARRIAGES ARE DEFINITELY...
A LOT OF TROUBLE, HUH...?

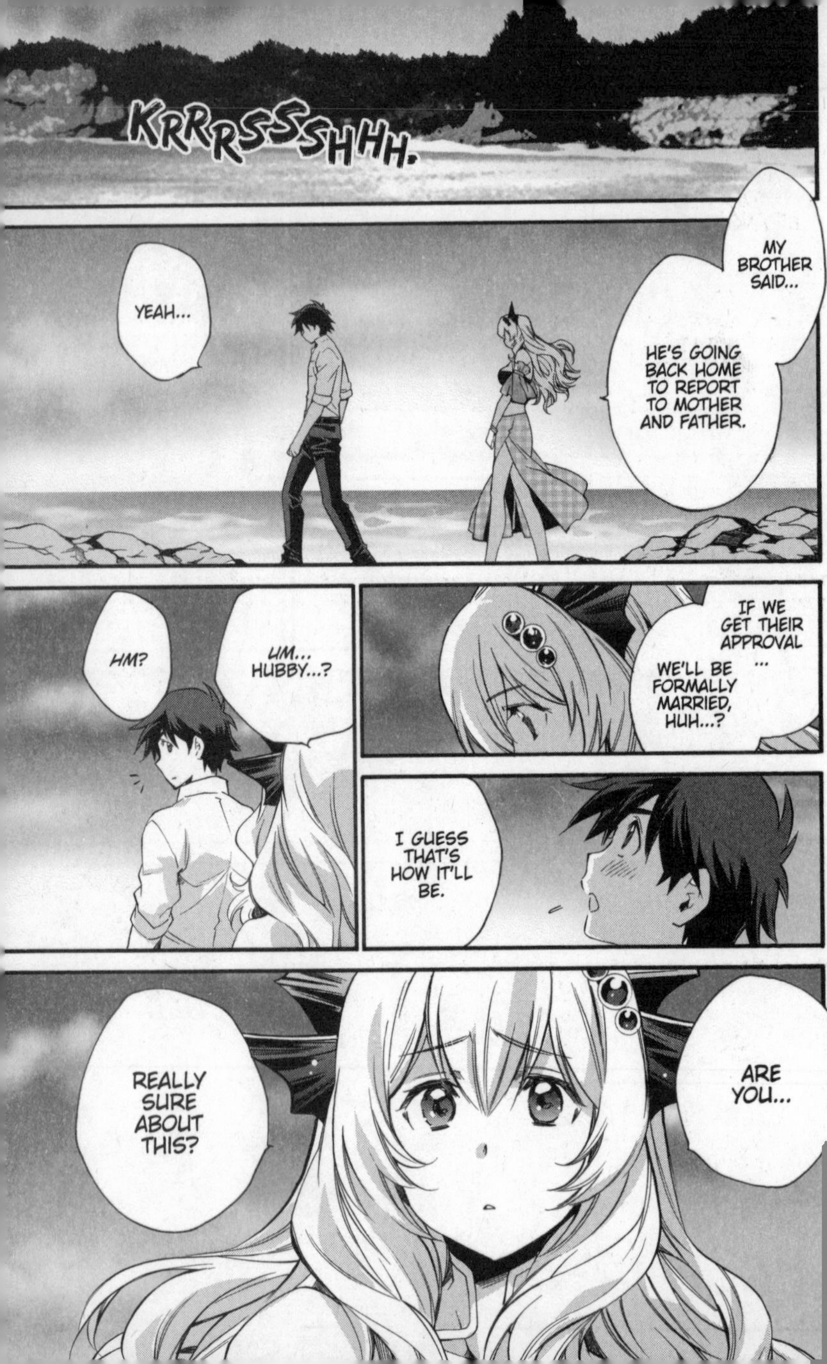
KRRRSSSHHH.
MY BROTHER SAID...
HE'S GOING BACK HOME TO REPORT TO MOTHER AND FATHER.
YEAH...
IF WE GET THEIR APPROVAL...
WE'LL BE FORMALLY MARRIED, HUH...?
I GUESS THAT'S HOW IT'LL BE.
UM... HUBBY...?
HM?
ARE YOU...
REALLY SURE ABOUT THIS?

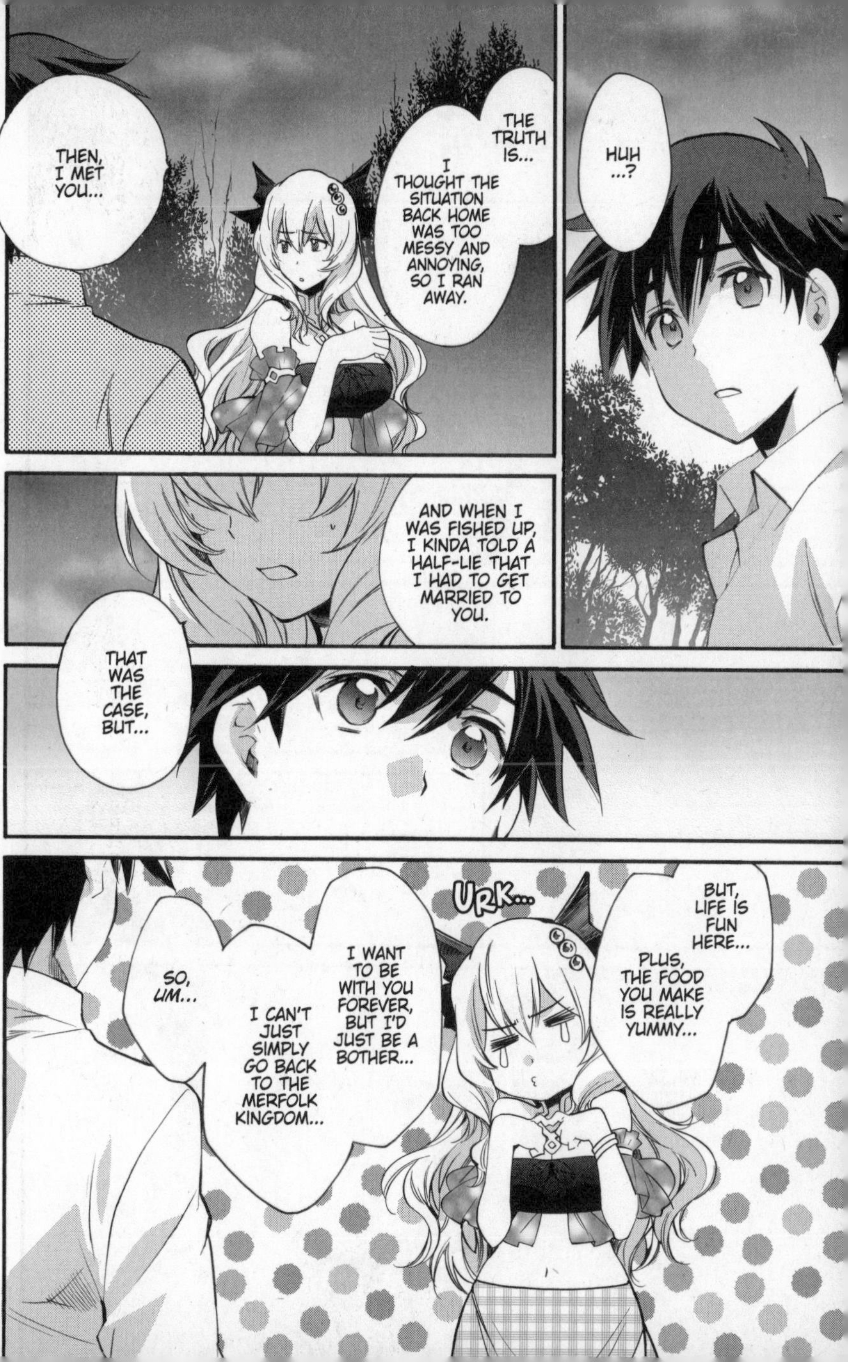
HUH ...?
THE TRUTH IS...
I THOUGHT THE SITUATION BACK HOME WAS TOO MESSY AND ANNOYING, SO I RAN AWAY.
THEN, I MET YOU...
AND WHEN I WAS FISHED UP, I KINDA TOLD A HALF-LIE THAT I HAD TO GET MARRIED TO YOU.
THAT WAS THE CASE, BUT...
BUT, LIFE IS FUN HERE...
PLUS, THE FOOD YOU MAKE IS REALLY YUMMY...
URK...
I WANT TO BE WITH YOU FOREVER, BUT I'D JUST BE A BOTHER...
I CAN'T JUST SIMPLY GO BACK TO THE MERFOLK KINGDOM...
SO, UM...

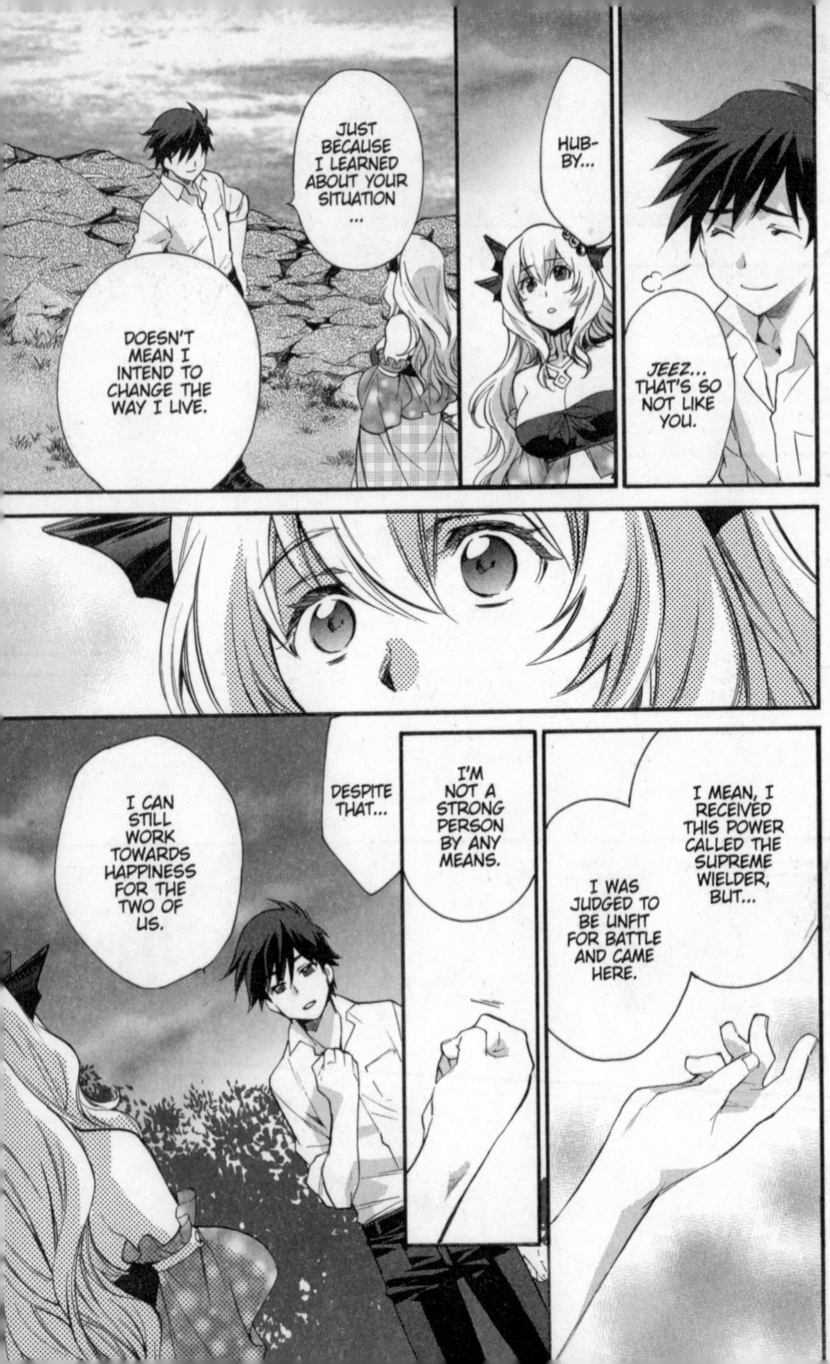
JEEZ... THAT'S SO NOT LIKE YOU.
HUB-BY...
JUST BECAUSE I LEARNED ABOUT YOUR SITUATION ...
DOESN'T MEAN I INTEND TO CHANGE THE WAY I LIVE.
I MEAN, I RECEIVED THIS POWER CALLED THE SUPREME WIELDER, BUT...
I WAS JUDGED TO BE UNFIT FOR BATTLE AND CAME HERE.
I'M NOT A STRONG PERSON BY ANY MEANS.
DESPITE THAT...
I CAN STILL WORK TOWARDS HAPPINESS FOR THE TWO OF US.

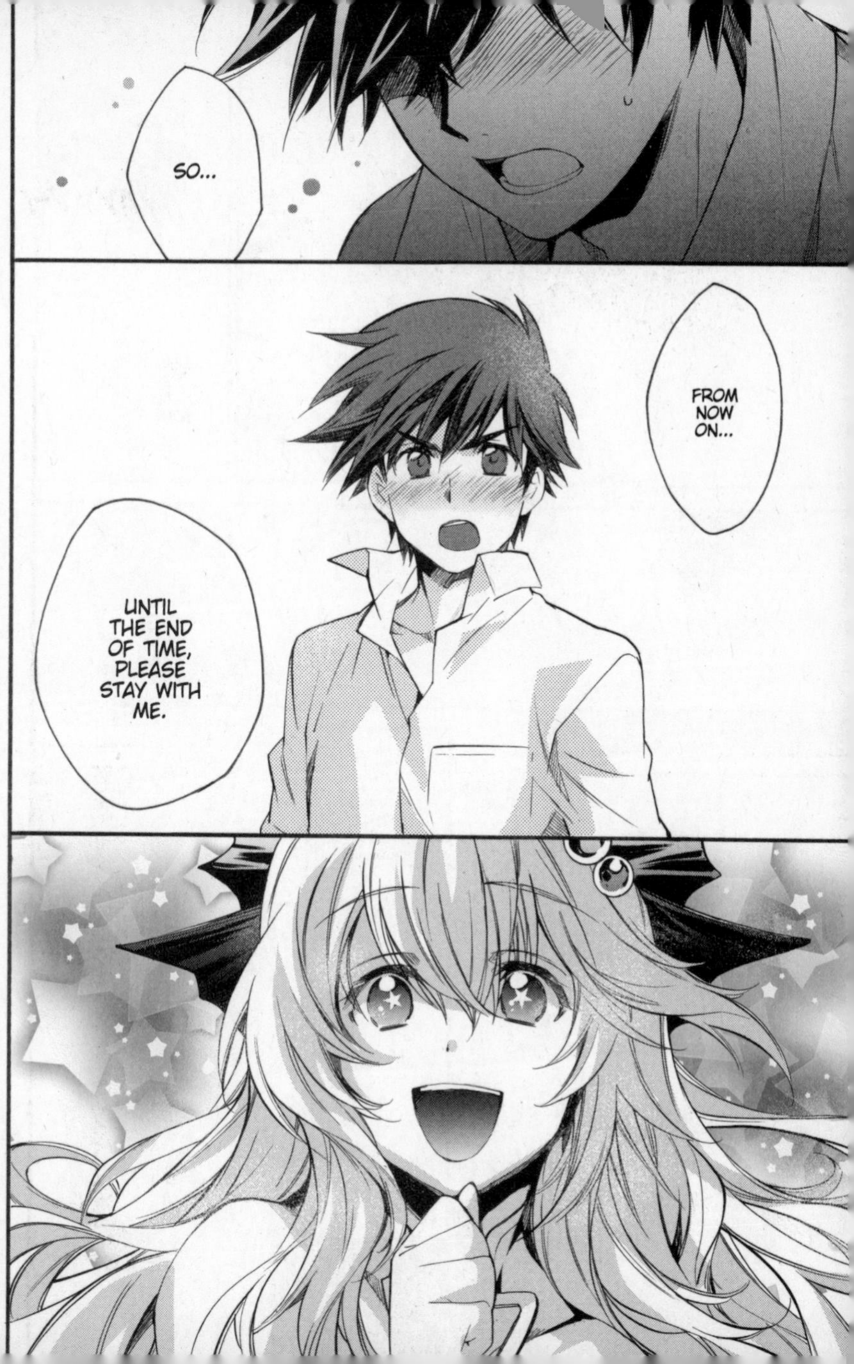
SO...
FROM NOW ON...
UNTIL THE END OF TIME, PLEASE STAY WITH ME.

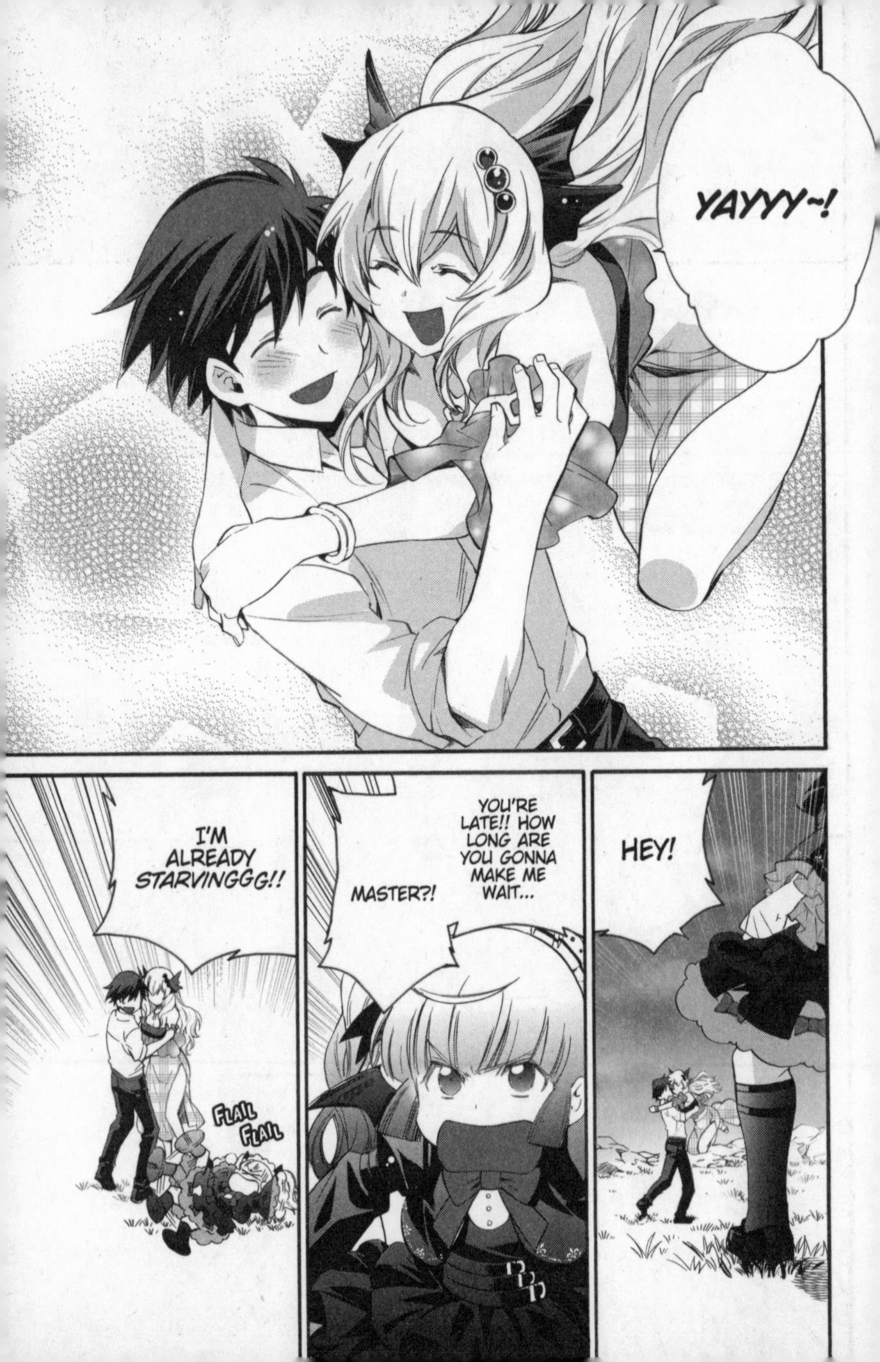
YAYYY~!
HEY!
YOU'RE LATE!! HOW LONG ARE YOU GONNA MAKE ME WAIT...
MASTER?!
I'M ALREADY STARVINGGG!!
FLAIL FLAIL

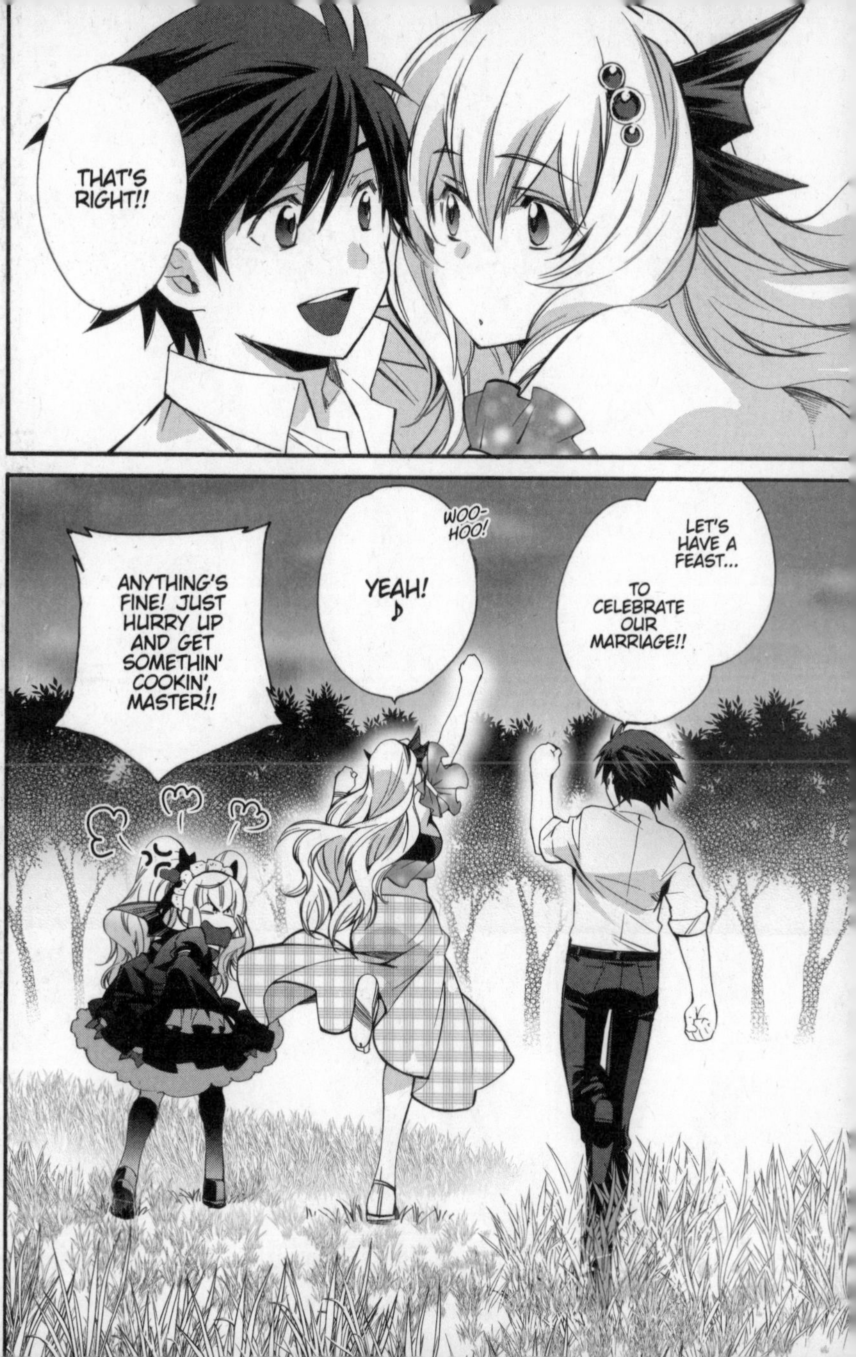
THAT'S RIGHT!!
LET'S HAVE A FEAST...
TO CELEBRATE OUR MARRIAGE!!
WOO-HOO!
YEAH! ♪
ANYTHING'S FINE! JUST HURRY UP AND GET SOMETHIN' COOKIN', MASTER!!

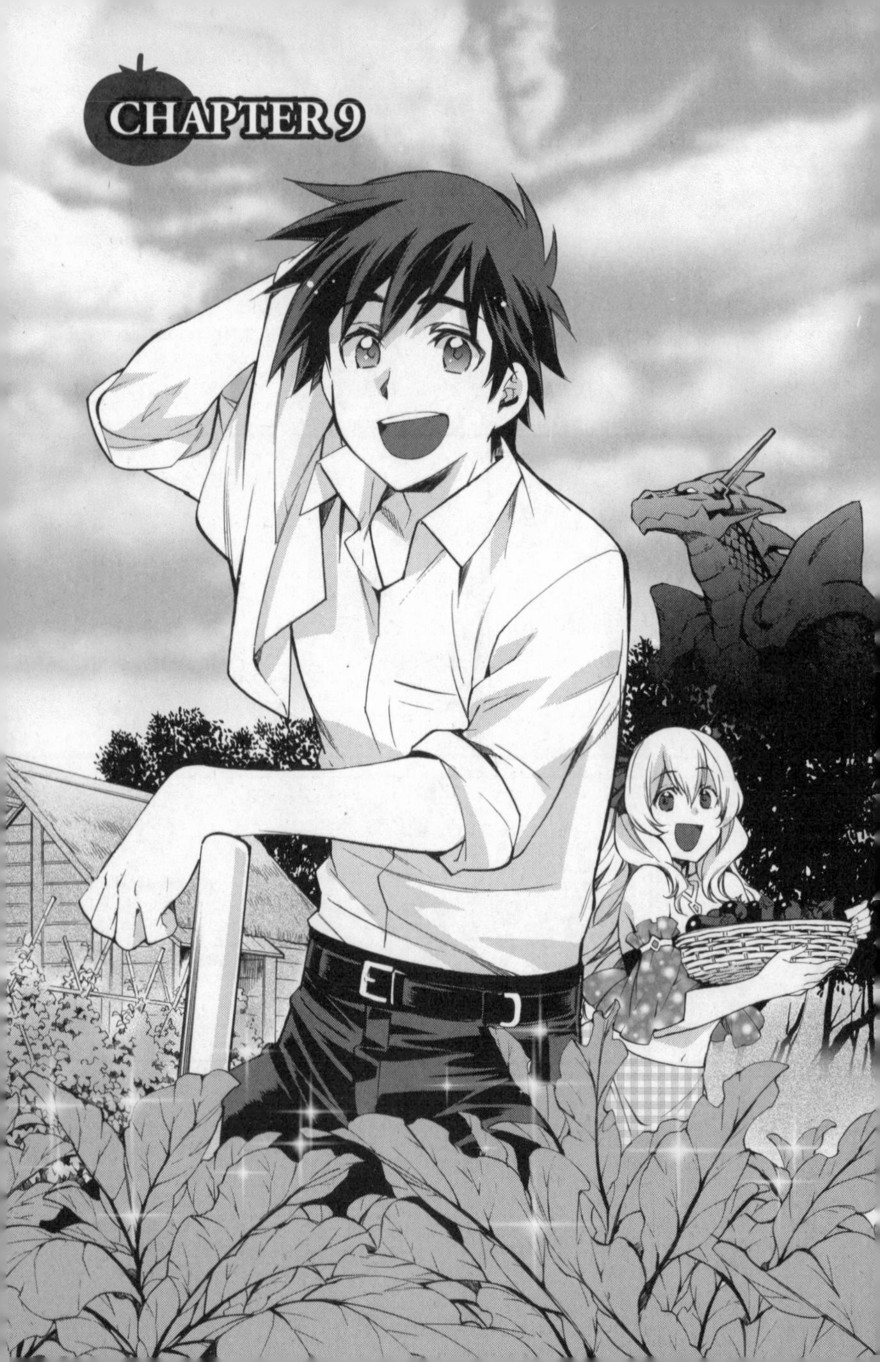
CHAPTER 9

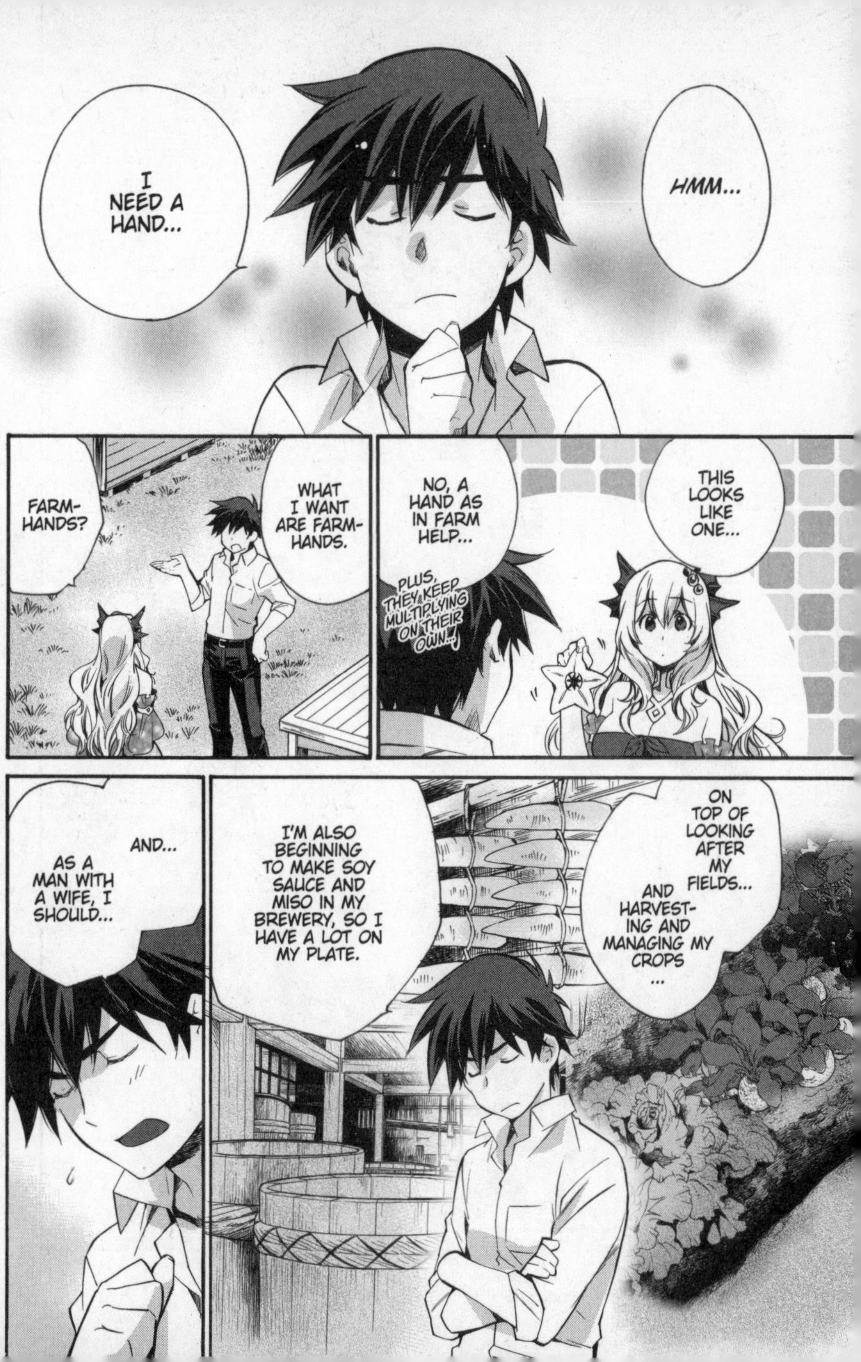
HMM...
I NEED A HAND...
THIS LOOKS LIKE ONE...
NO, A HAND AS IN FARM HELP...
PLUS, THEY KEEP MULTIPLYING ON THEIR OWN...!
WHAT I WANT ARE FARM-HANDS.
FARM-HANDS?
ON TOP OF LOOKING AFTER MY FIELDS...
AND HARVEST-ING AND MANAGING MY CROPS ...
I'M ALSO BEGINNING TO MAKE SOY SAUCE AND MISO IN MY BREWERY, SO I HAVE A LOT ON MY PLATE.
AND...
AS A MAN WITH A WIFE, I SHOULD...

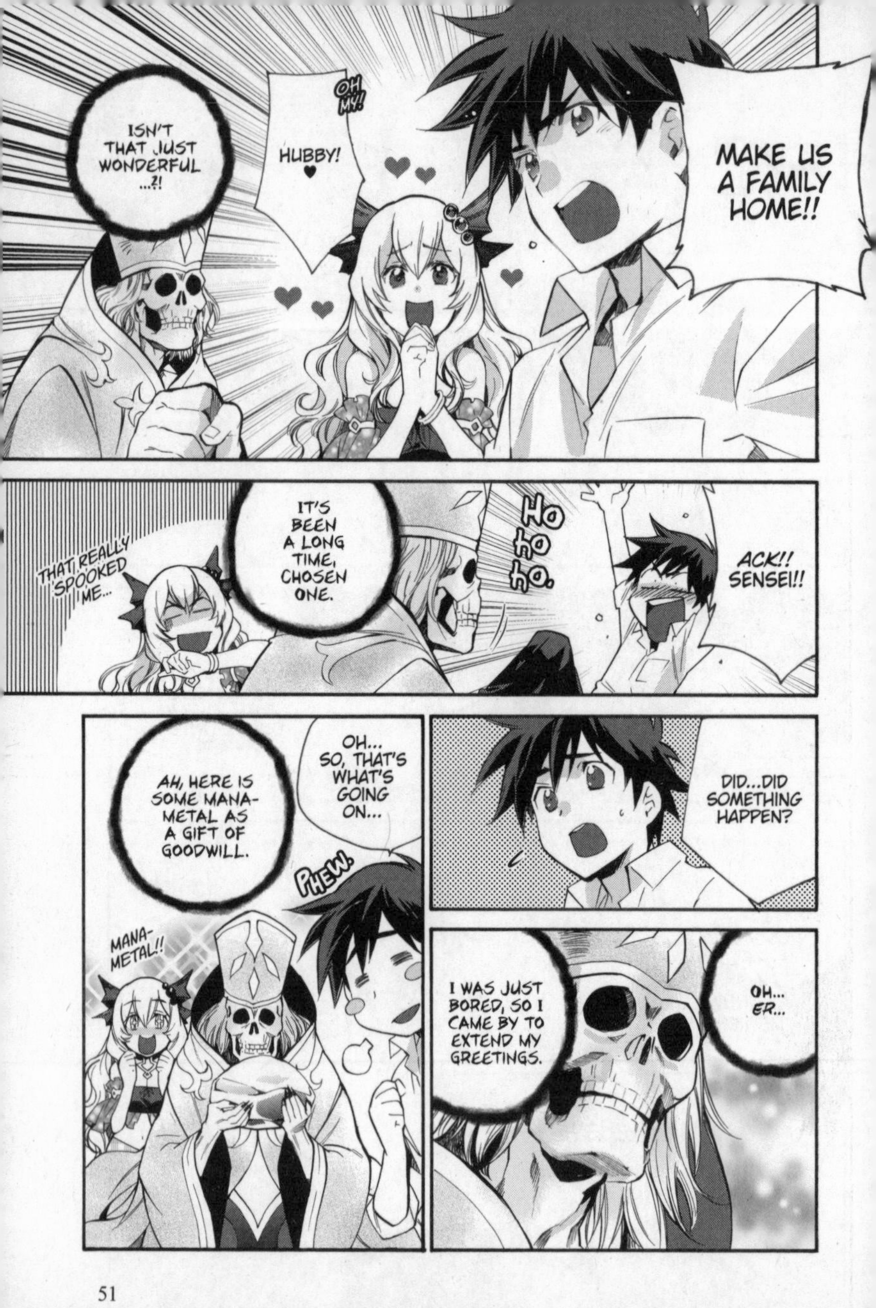
MAKE US A FAMILY HOME!!
OH MY!
HUBBY! ♥
ISN'T THAT JUST WONDERFUL ...?!
ACK!! SENSEI!!
Ho ho ho.
IT'S BEEN A LONG TIME, CHOSEN ONE.
THAT REALLY SPOOKED ME...
DID...DID SOMETHING HAPPEN?
OH... ER...
I WAS JUST BORED, SO I CAME BY TO EXTEND MY GREETINGS.
OH... SO, THAT'S WHAT'S GOING ON...
AH, HERE IS SOME MANA-METAL AS A GIFT OF GOODWILL.
PHEW.
MANA-METAL!!

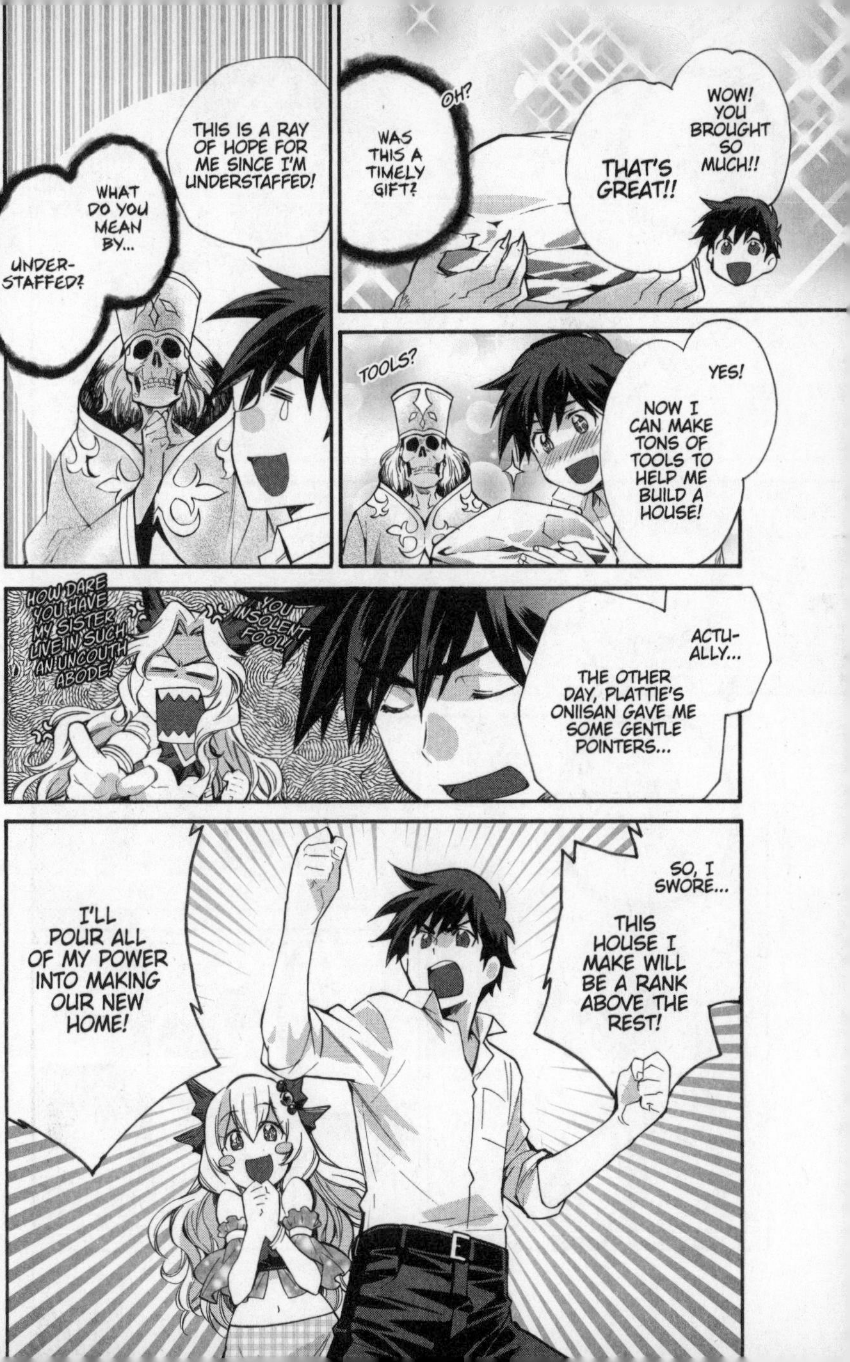
WOW! YOU BROUGHT SO MUCH!!
THAT'S GREAT!!
OH?
WAS THIS A TIMELY GIFT?
YES!
NOW I CAN MAKE TONS OF TOOLS TO HELP ME BUILD A HOUSE!
TOOLS?
THIS IS A RAY OF HOPE FOR ME SINCE I'M UNDERSTAFFED!
WHAT DO YOU MEAN BY... UNDER-STAFFED?
ACTU-ALLY...
THE OTHER DAY, PLATTIE'S ONIISAN GAVE ME SOME GENTLE POINTERS...
YOU INSOLENT FOOL!
HOW DARE YOU HAVE MY SISTER LIVE IN SUCH AN UNCOUTH ABODE!
SO, I SWORE...
THIS HOUSE I MAKE WILL BE A RANK ABOVE THE REST!
I'LL POUR ALL OF MY POWER INTO MAKING OUR NEW HOME!

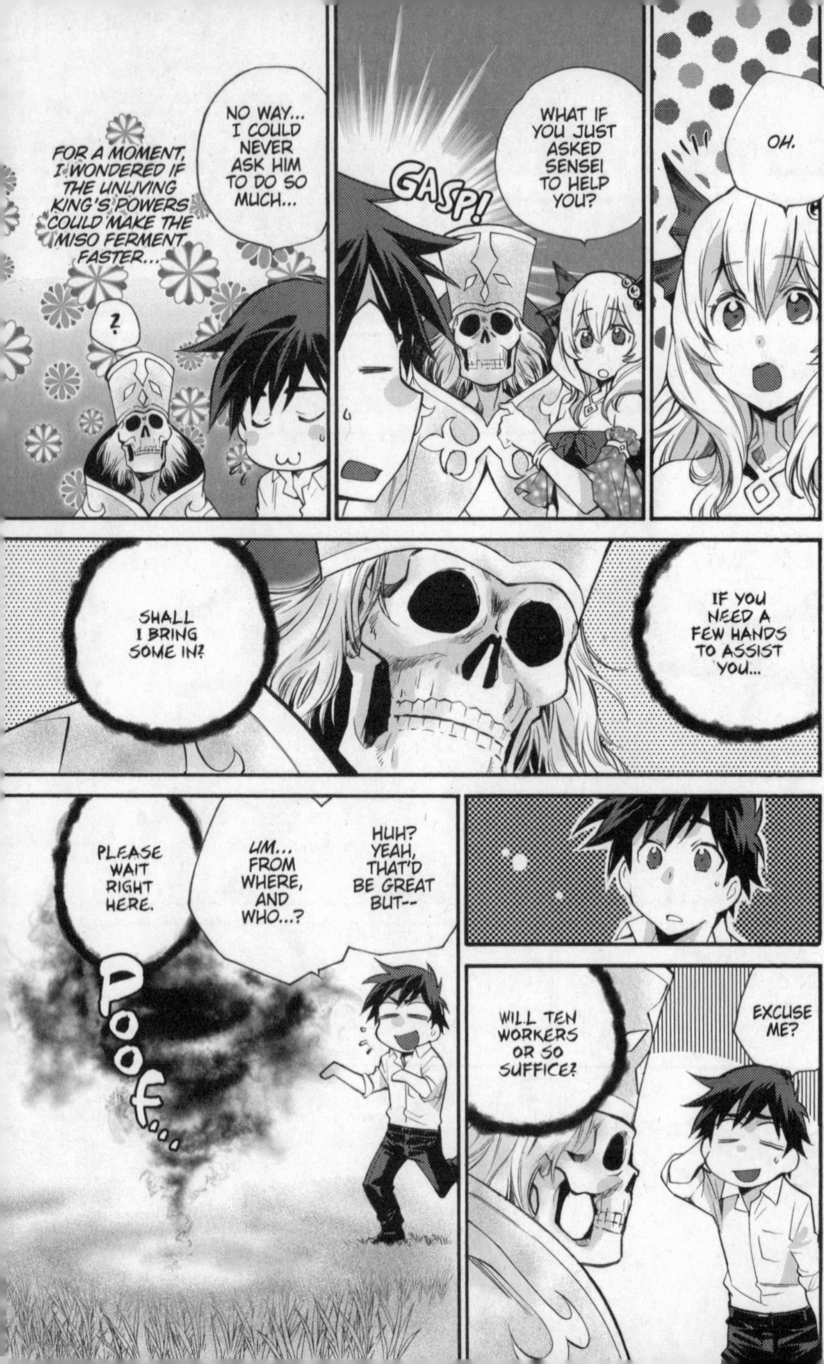
OH.
WHAT IF YOU JUST ASKED SENSEI TO HELP YOU?
GASP!
NO WAY... I COULD NEVER ASK HIM TO DO SO MUCH...
FOR A MOMENT, I WONDERED IF THE UNLIVING KING'S POWERS COULD MAKE THE MISO FERMENT FASTER...
?
IF YOU NEED A FEW HANDS TO ASSIST YOU...
SHALL I BRING SOME IN?
EXCUSE ME?
WILL TEN WORKERS OR SO SUFFICE?
HUH? YEAH, THAT'D BE GREAT BUT--
UM... FROM WHERE, AND WHO...?
PLEASE WAIT RIGHT HERE.
POOF...

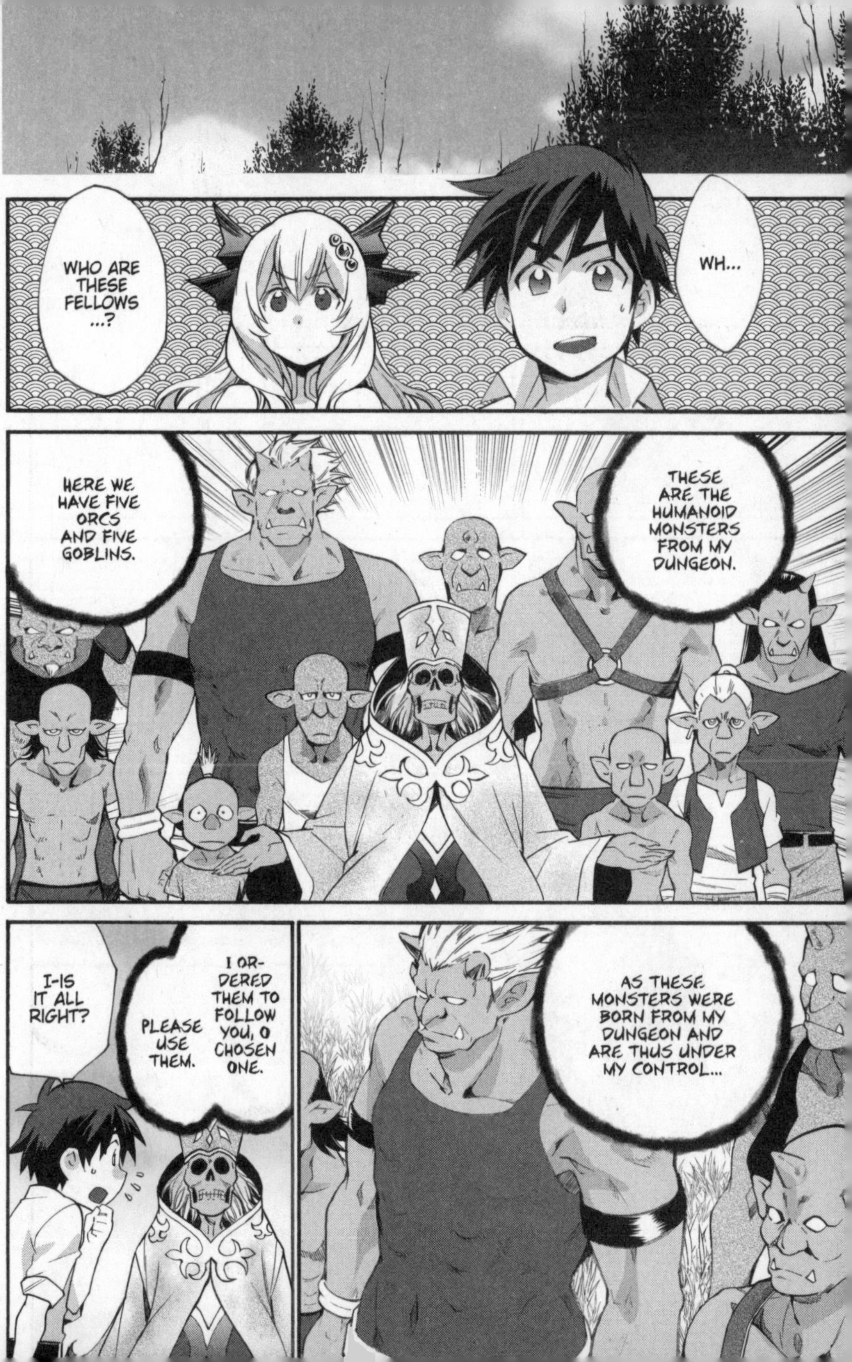
WH...
WHO ARE THESE FELLOWS ...?
THESE ARE THE HUMANOID MONSTERS FROM MY DUNGEON.
HERE WE HAVE FIVE ORCS AND FIVE GOBLINS.
AS THESE MONSTERS WERE BORN FROM MY DUNGEON AND ARE THUS UNDER MY CONTROL...
I OR-DERED THEM TO FOLLOW YOU, O CHOSEN ONE.
PLEASE USE THEM.
I-IS IT ALL RIGHT?

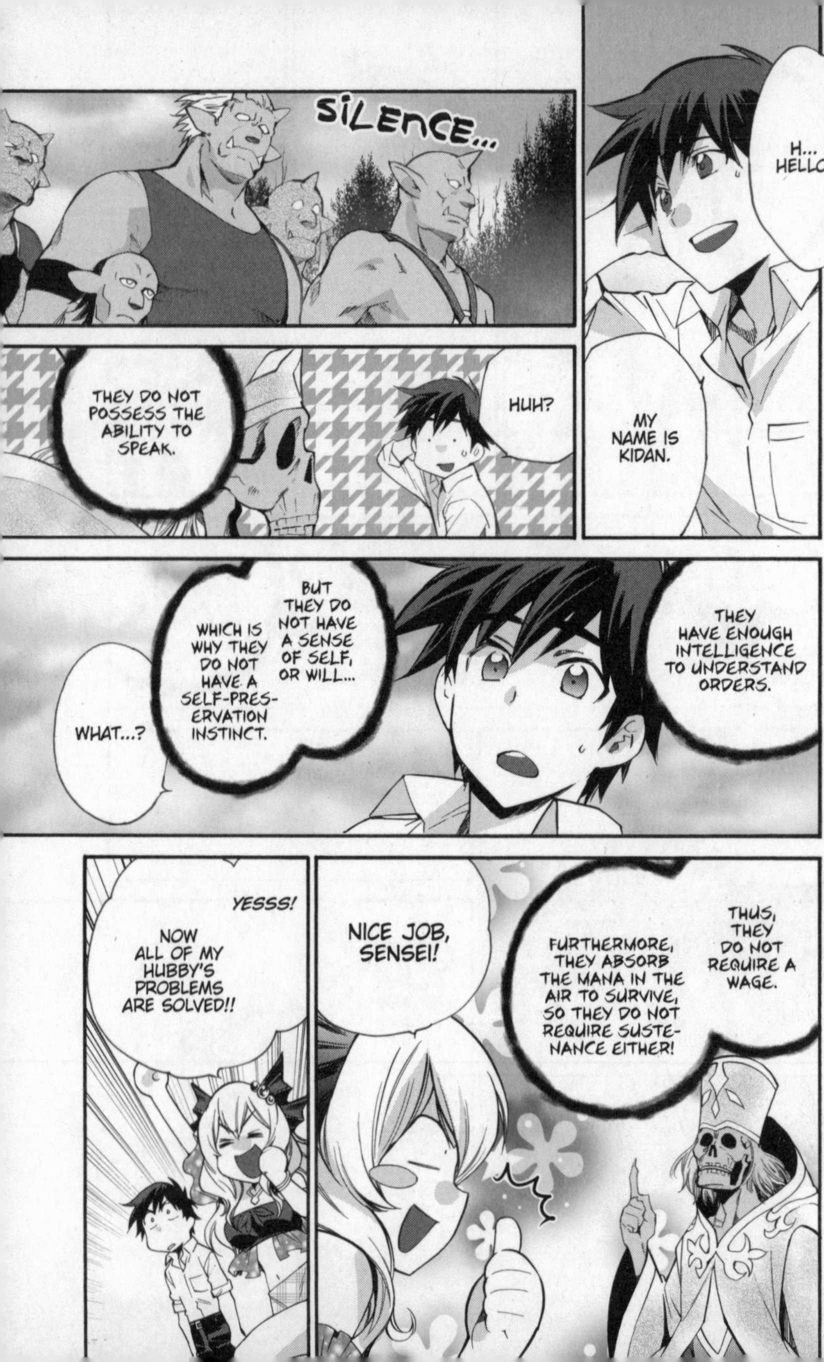
H... HELLO.
MY NAME IS KIDAN.
SILENCE...
HUH?
THEY DO NOT POSSESS THE ABILITY TO SPEAK.
THEY HAVE ENOUGH INTELLIGENCE TO UNDERSTAND ORDERS.
BUT THEY DO NOT HAVE A SENSE OF SELF, OR WILL...
WHICH IS WHY THEY DO NOT HAVE A SELF-PRESERVATION INSTINCT.
WHAT...?
THUS, THEY DO NOT REQUIRE A WAGE.
FURTHERMORE, THEY ABSORB THE MANA IN THE AIR TO SURVIVE, SO THEY DO NOT REQUIRE SUSTENANCE EITHER!
NICE JOB, SENSEI!
YESSS!
NOW ALL OF MY HUBBY'S PROBLEMS ARE SOLVED!!

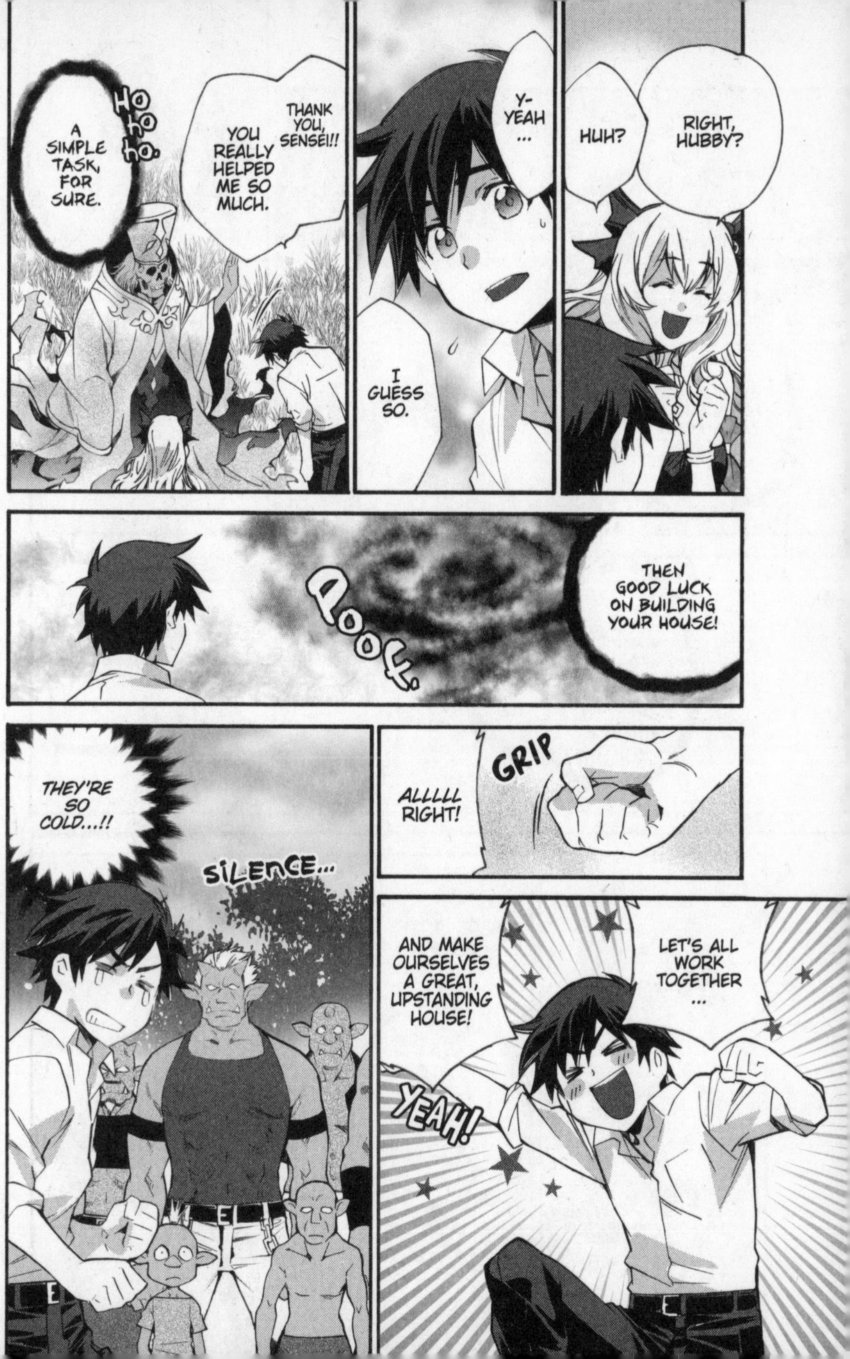
RIGHT, HUBBY?
HUH?
Y-YEAH ...
I GUESS SO.
THANK YOU, SENSEI!!
YOU REALLY HELPED ME SO MUCH.
HO HO HO.
A SIMPLE TASK, FOR SURE.
THEN GOOD LUCK ON BUILDING YOUR HOUSE!
POOF.
GRIP
ALLLLL RIGHT!
LET'S ALL WORK TOGETHER ...
AND MAKE OURSELVES A GREAT, UPSTANDING HOUSE!
YEAH!
THEY'RE SO COLD...!!
SILENCE...

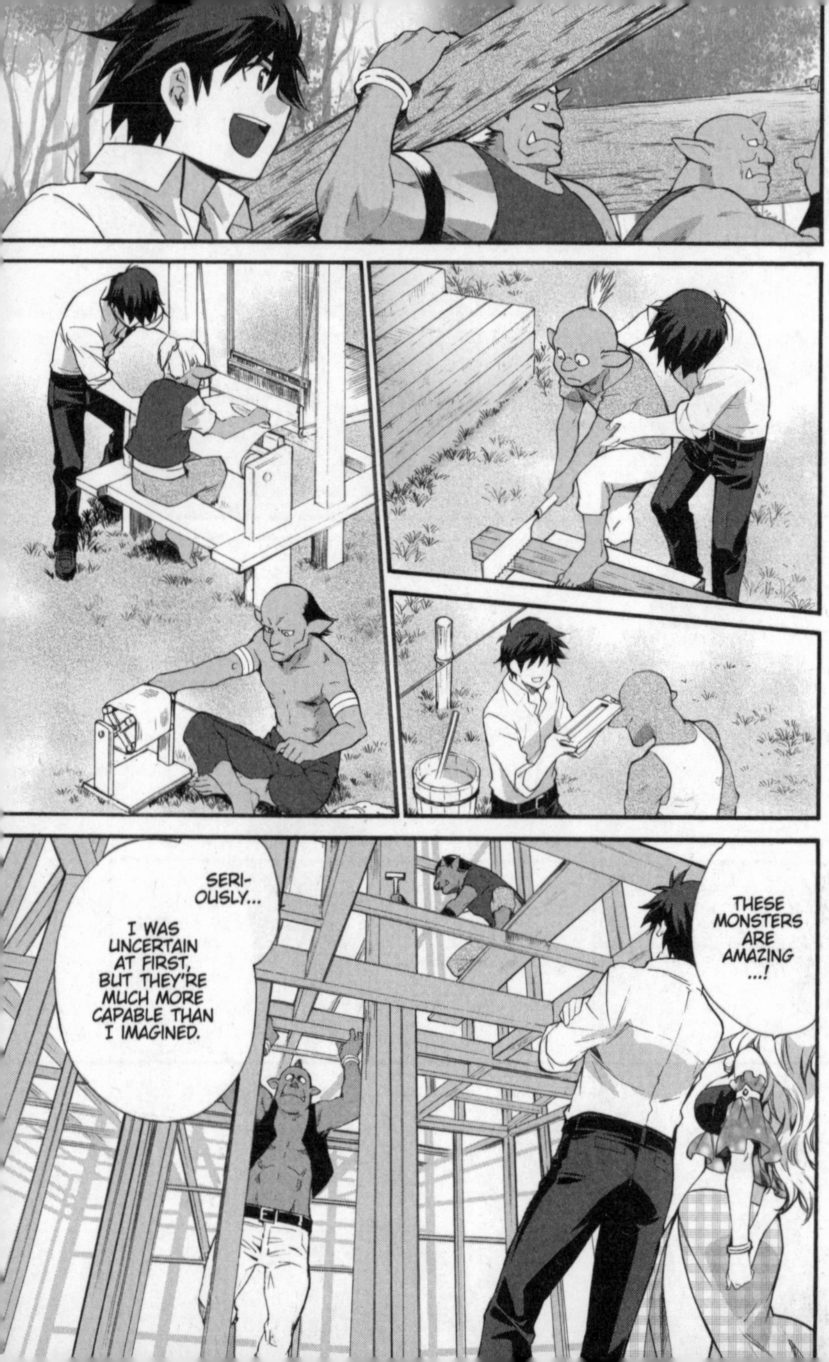
THESE MONSTERS ARE AMAZING ...!
SERI-OUSLY...
I WAS UNCERTAIN AT FIRST, BUT THEY'RE MUCH MORE CAPABLE THAN I IMAGINED.

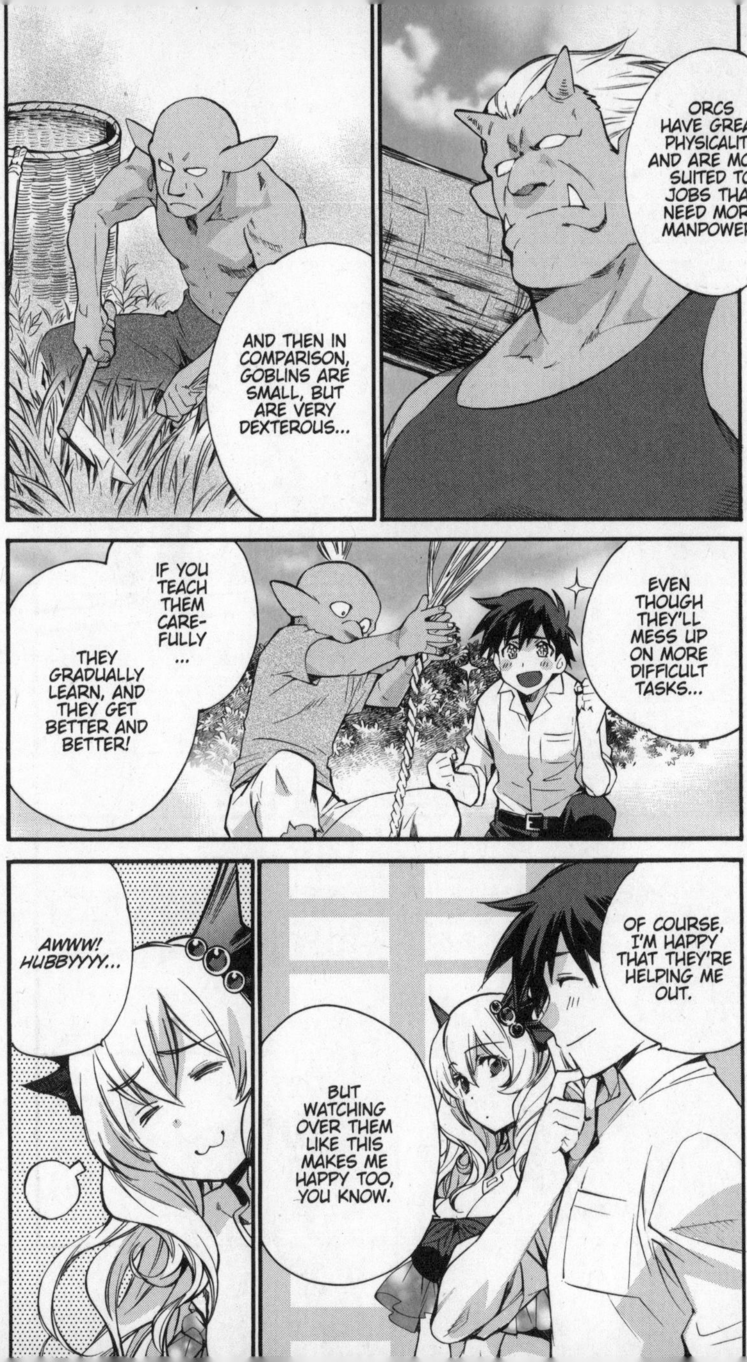
ORCS HAVE GREAT PHYSICALITY AND ARE MORE SUITED TO JOBS THAT NEED MORE MANPOWER.
AND THEN IN COMPARISON, GOBLINS ARE SMALL, BUT ARE VERY DEXTEROUS...
EVEN THOUGH THEY'LL MESS UP ON MORE DIFFICULT TASKS...
IF YOU TEACH THEM CARE-FULLY ...
THEY GRADUALLY LEARN, AND THEY GET BETTER AND BETTER!
OF COURSE, I'M HAPPY THAT THEY'RE HELPING ME OUT.
BUT WATCHING OVER THEM LIKE THIS MAKES ME HAPPY TOO, YOU KNOW.
AWWW! HUBBYYYY...

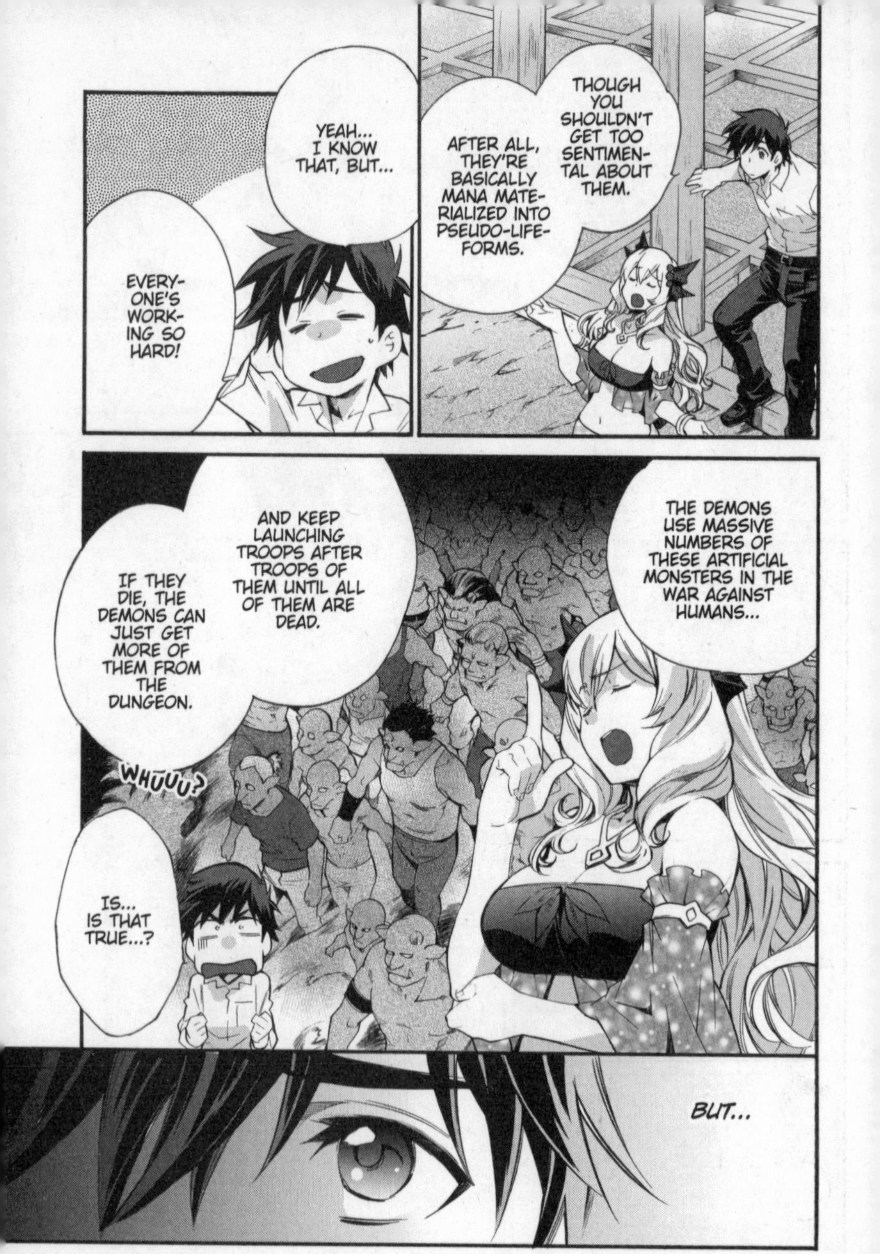
THOUGH YOU SHOULDN'T GET TOO SENTIMENTAL ABOUT THEM.
AFTER ALL, THEY'RE BASICALLY MANA MATERIALIZED INTO PSEUDO-LIFE-FORMS.
YEAH... I KNOW THAT, BUT...
EVERYONE'S WORKING SO HARD!
THE DEMONS USE MASSIVE NUMBERS OF THESE ARTIFICIAL MONSTERS IN THE WAR AGAINST HUMANS...
AND KEEP LAUNCHING TROOPS AFTER TROOPS OF THEM UNTIL ALL OF THEM ARE DEAD.
IF THEY DIE, THE DEMONS CAN JUST GET MORE OF THEM FROM THE DUNGEON.
WHUUU?
IS... IS THAT TRUE...?
BUT...

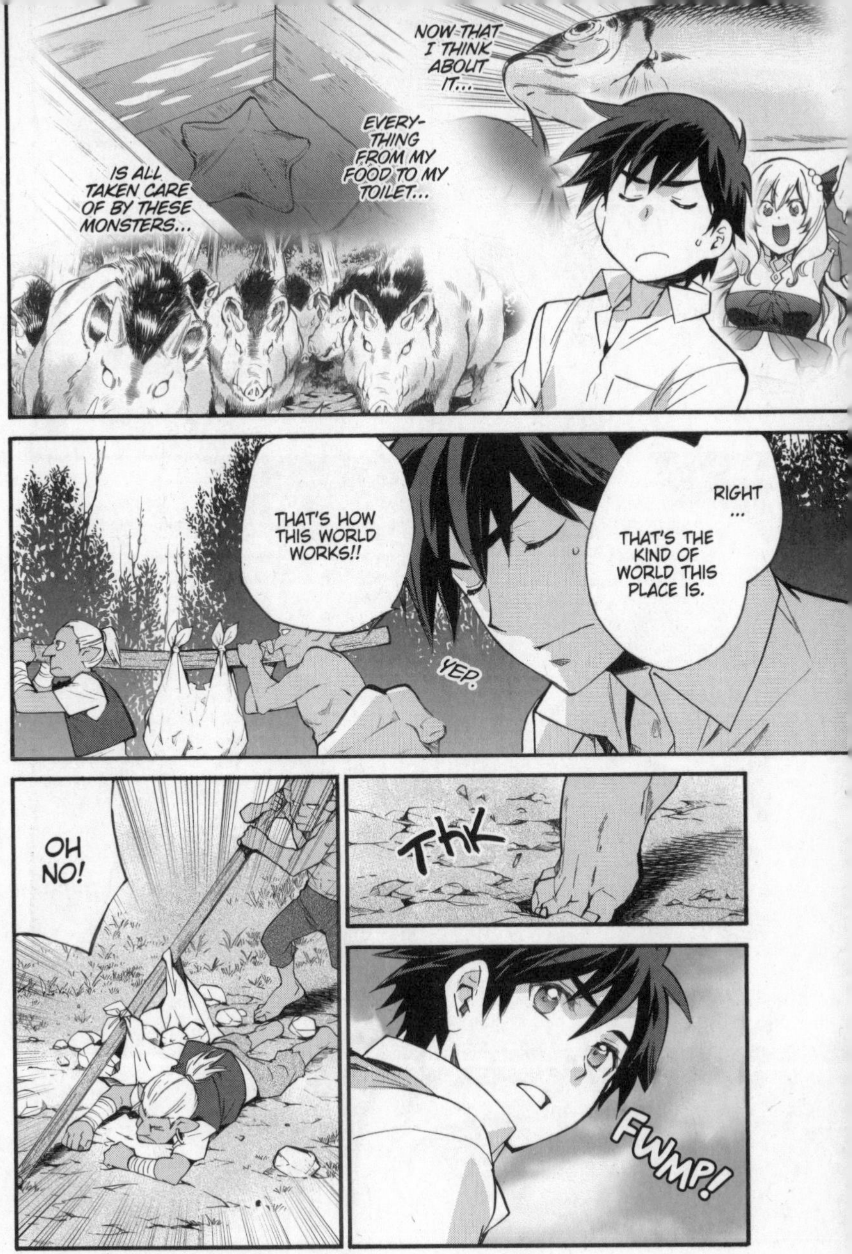
NOW THAT I THINK ABOUT IT...
EVERY-THING FROM MY FOOD TO MY TOILET...
IS ALL TAKEN CARE OF BY THESE MONSTERS...
RIGHT ... THAT'S THE KIND OF WORLD THIS PLACE IS.
THAT'S HOW THIS WORLD WORKS!!
YEP.
THK
FWMP!
OH NO!

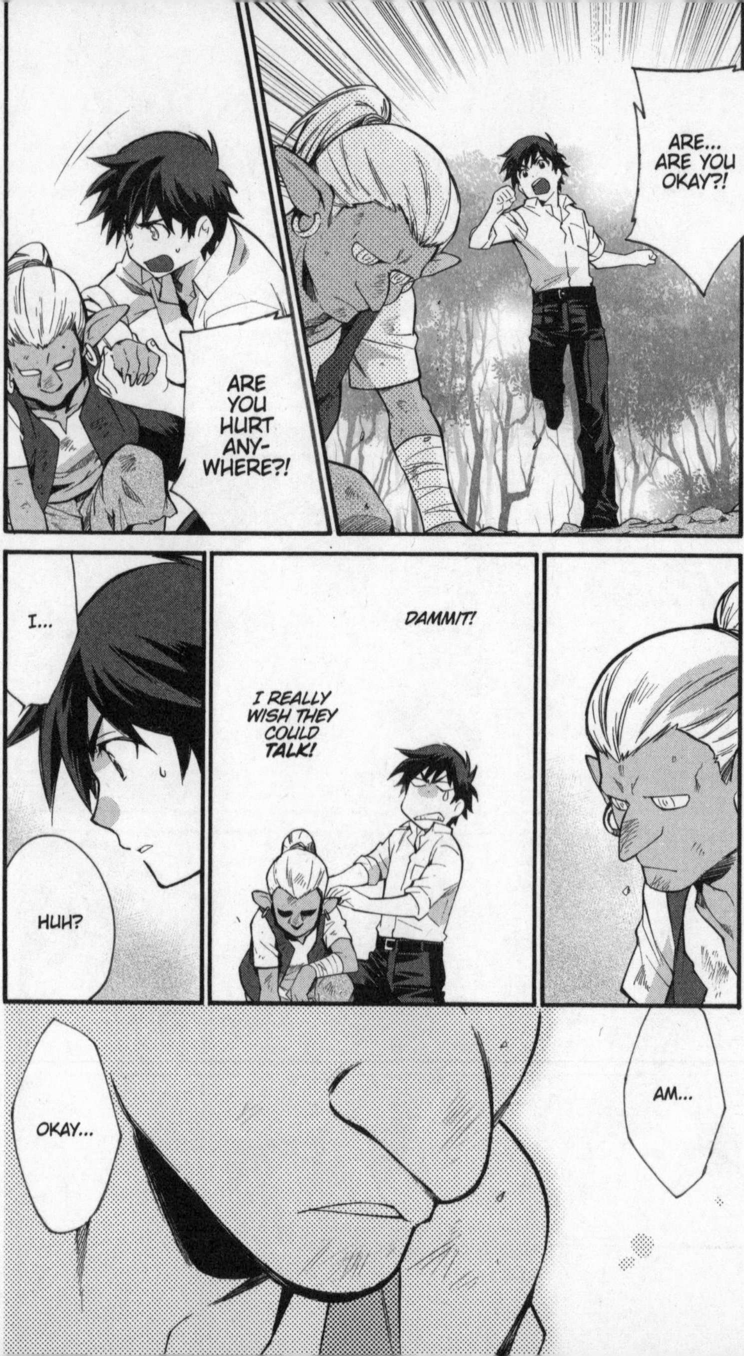
ARE... ARE YOU OKAY?!
ARE YOU HURT ANY-WHERE?!
DAMMIT!
I REALLY WISH THEY COULD TALK!
I...
HUH?
AM...
OKAY...

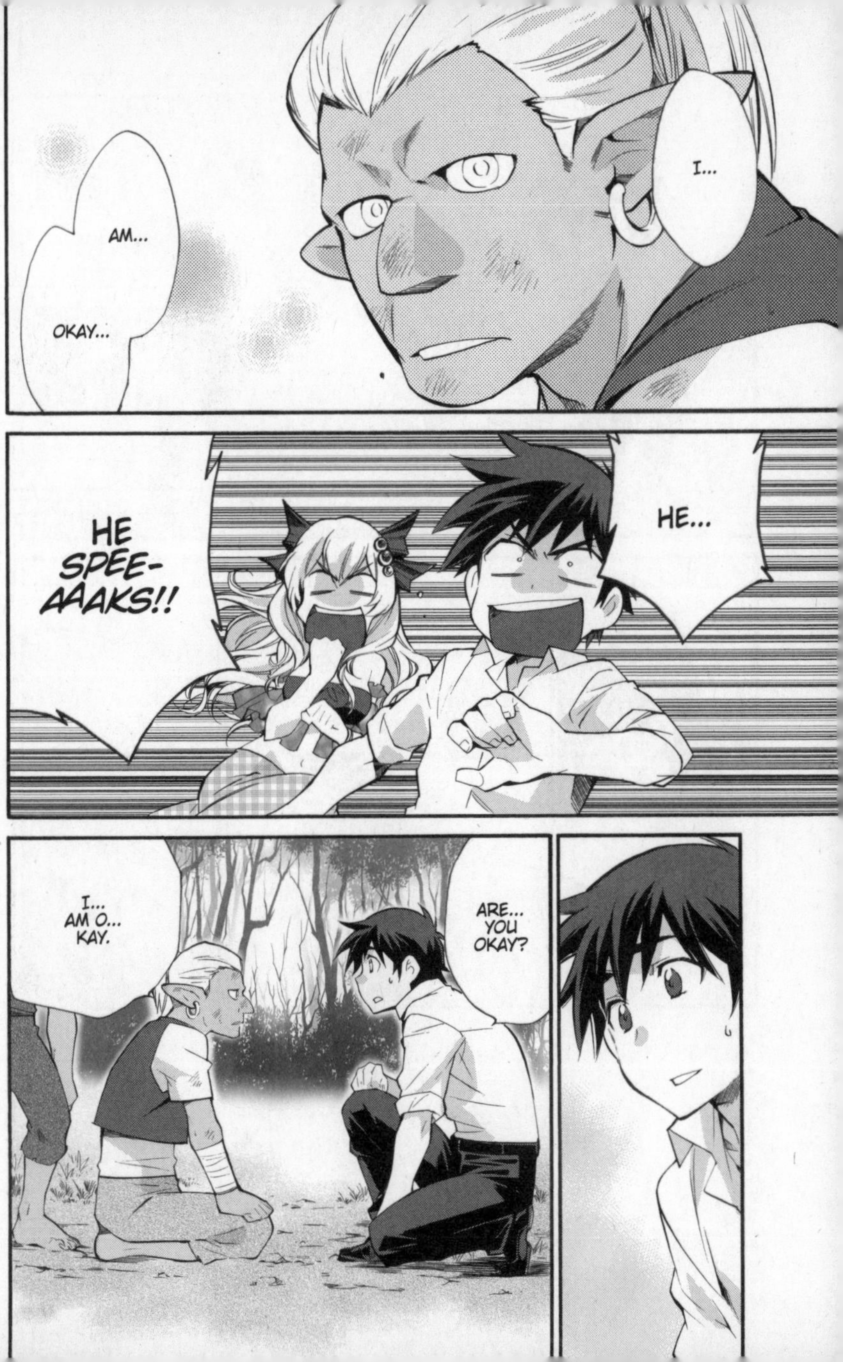
I...
AM... OKAY...
HE...
HE SPEE-AAAKS!!
ARE... YOU OKAY?
I... AM O... KAY.

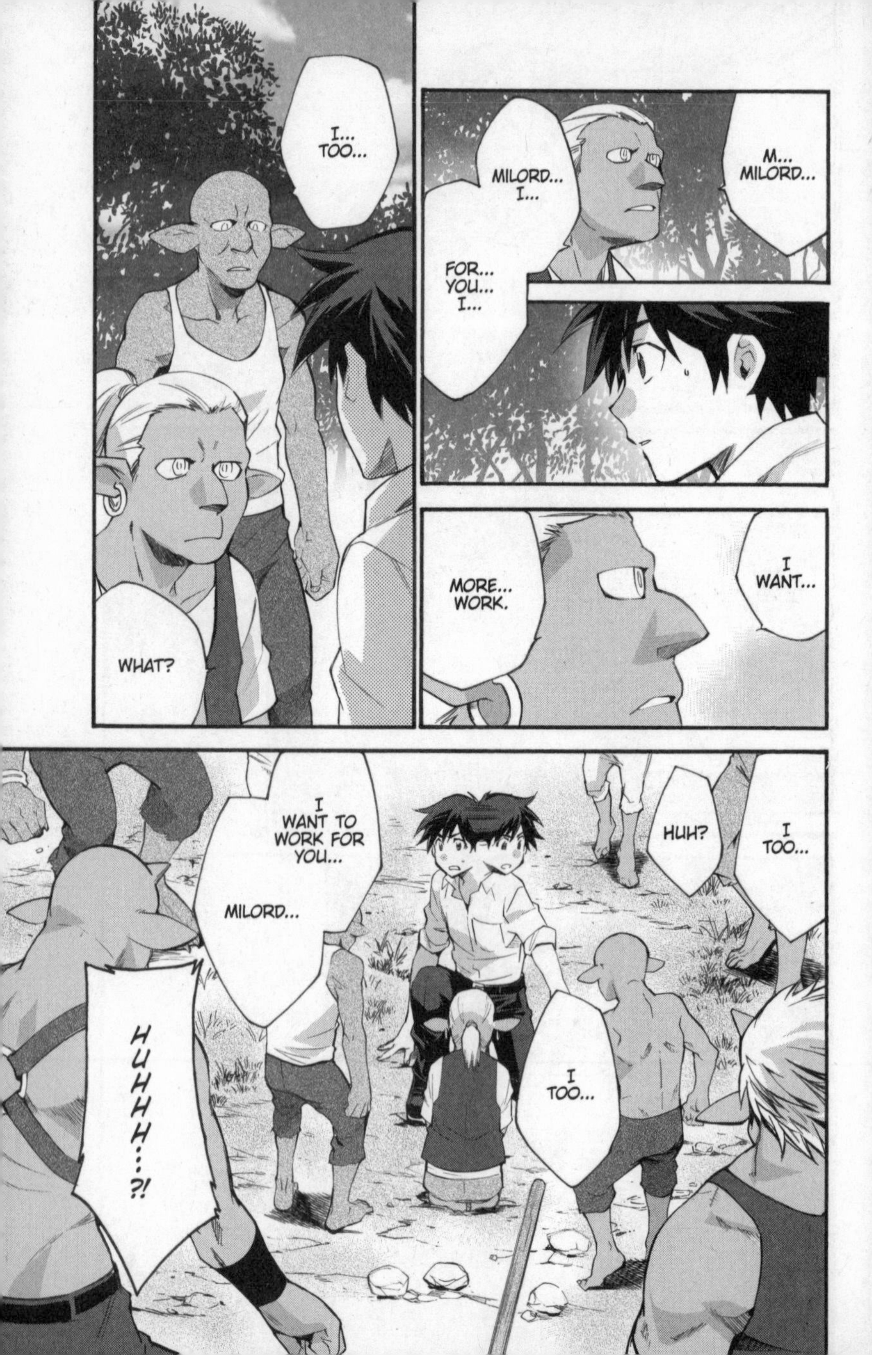
M... MILORD...
MILORD... I...
FOR... YOU... I...
I WANT...
MORE... WORK.
I... TOO...
WHAT?
I TOO...
HUH?
I WANT TO WORK FOR YOU...
MILORD...
I TOO...
HUHHH...?!

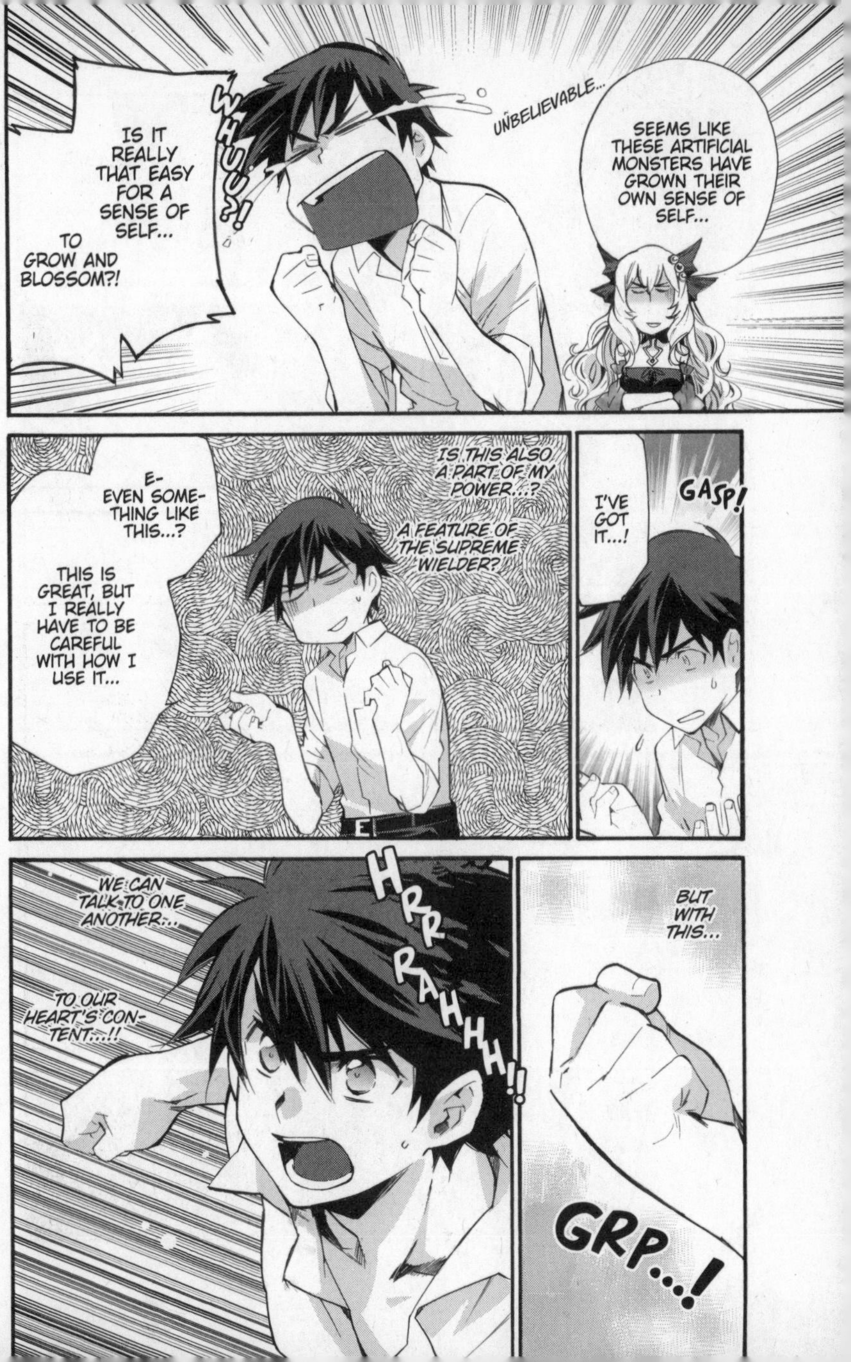
SEEMS LIKE THESE ARTIFICIAL MONSTERS HAVE GROWN THEIR OWN SENSE OF SELF...
UNBELIEVABLE...
WHUU?!
IS IT REALLY THAT EASY FOR A SENSE OF SELF...
TO GROW AND BLOSSOM?!
GASP!
I'VE GOT IT...!
IS THIS ALSO A PART OF MY POWER...?
A FEATURE OF THE SUPREME WIELDER?
E- EVEN SOMETHING LIKE THIS...?
THIS IS GREAT, BUT I REALLY HAVE TO BE CAREFUL WITH HOW I USE IT...
BUT WITH THIS...
GRP...!
HRRRAHHHH!!
WE CAN TALK TO ONE ANOTHER...
TO OUR HEART'S CON- TENT...!!

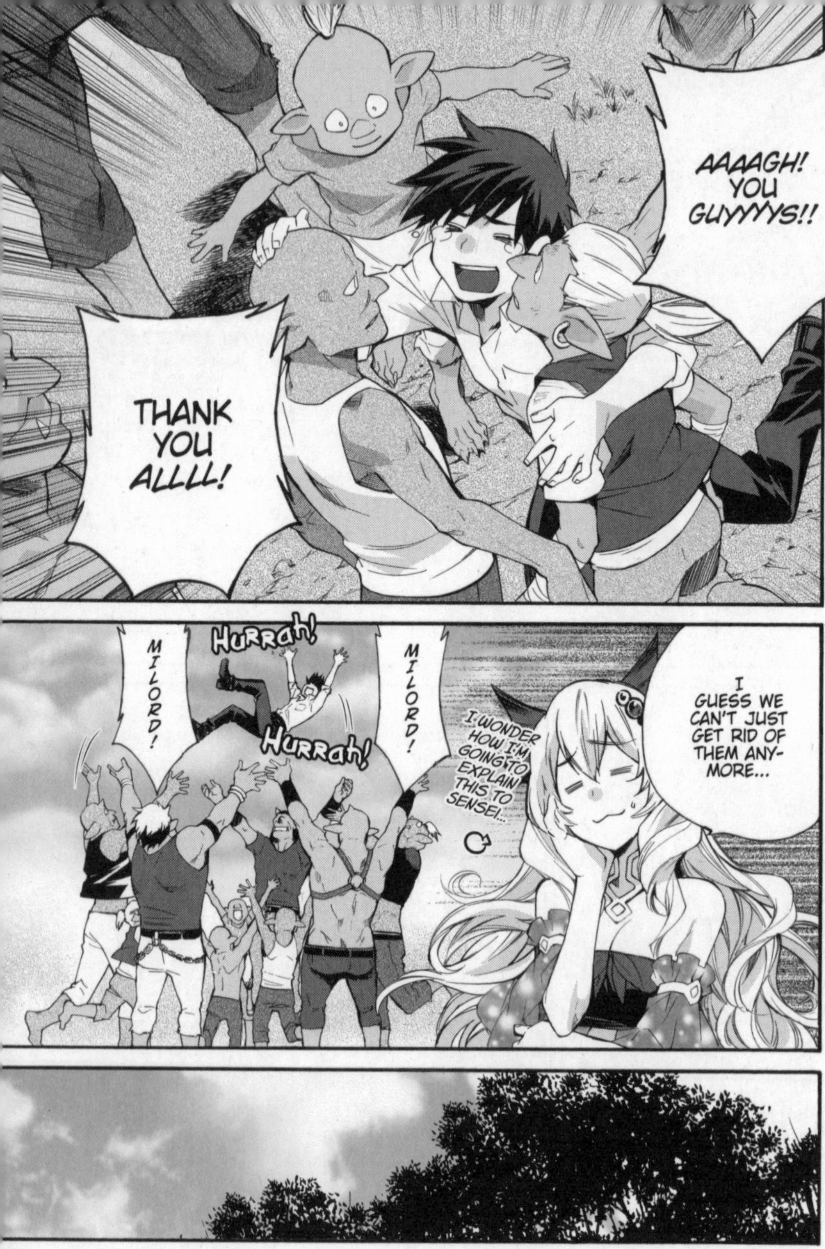
AAAAGH! YOU GUYYYYS!!
THANK YOU ALLLL!
I GUESS WE CAN'T JUST GET RID OF THEM ANY-MORE...
I WONDER HOW I'M GOING TO EXPLAIN THIS TO SENSEI...
MILORD!
Hurrah!
Hurrah!
MILORD!

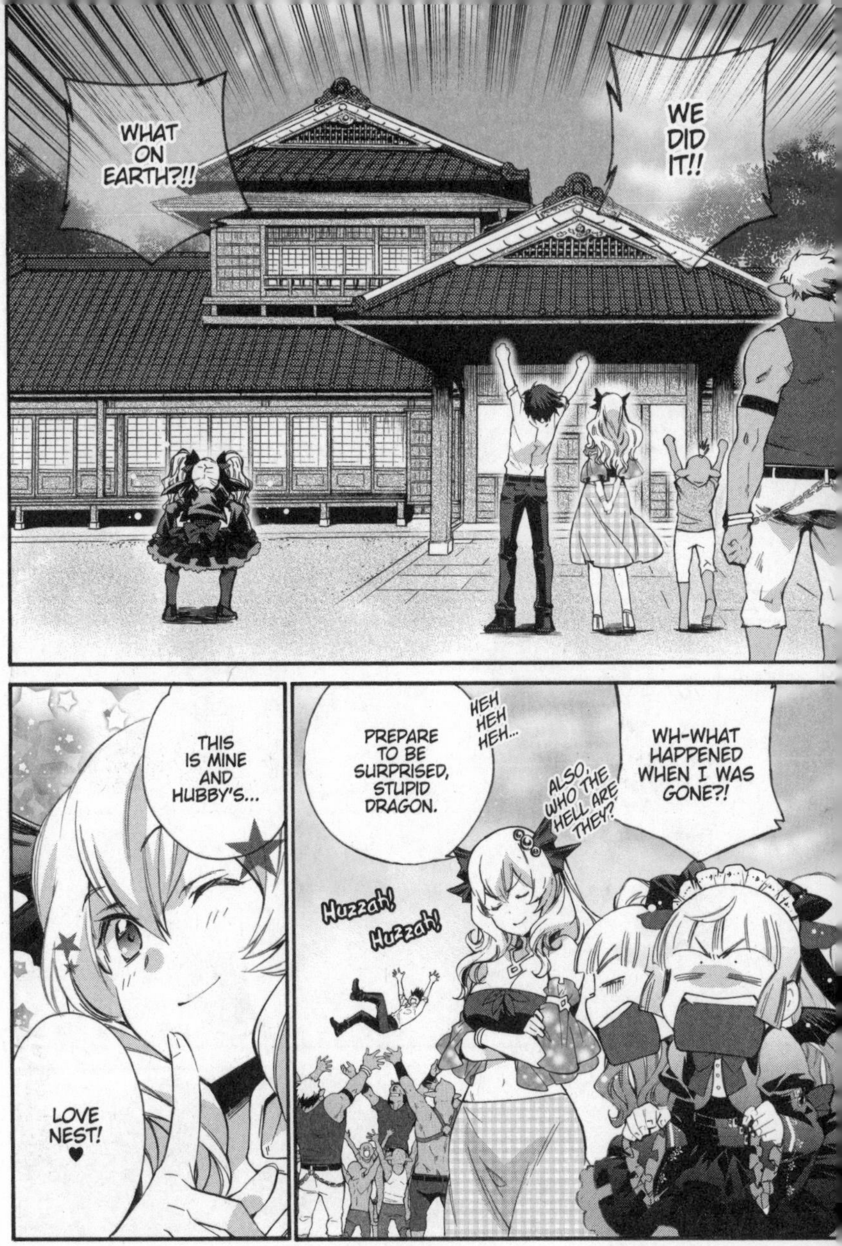
WE DID IT!!
WHAT ON EARTH?!!
WH-WHAT HAPPENED WHEN I WAS GONE?!
ALSO, WHO THE HELL ARE THEY?
HEH HEH HEH...
PREPARE TO BE SURPRISED, STUPID DRAGON.
Huzzah!
Huzzah!
THIS IS MINE AND HUBBY'S...
LOVE NEST! ♥

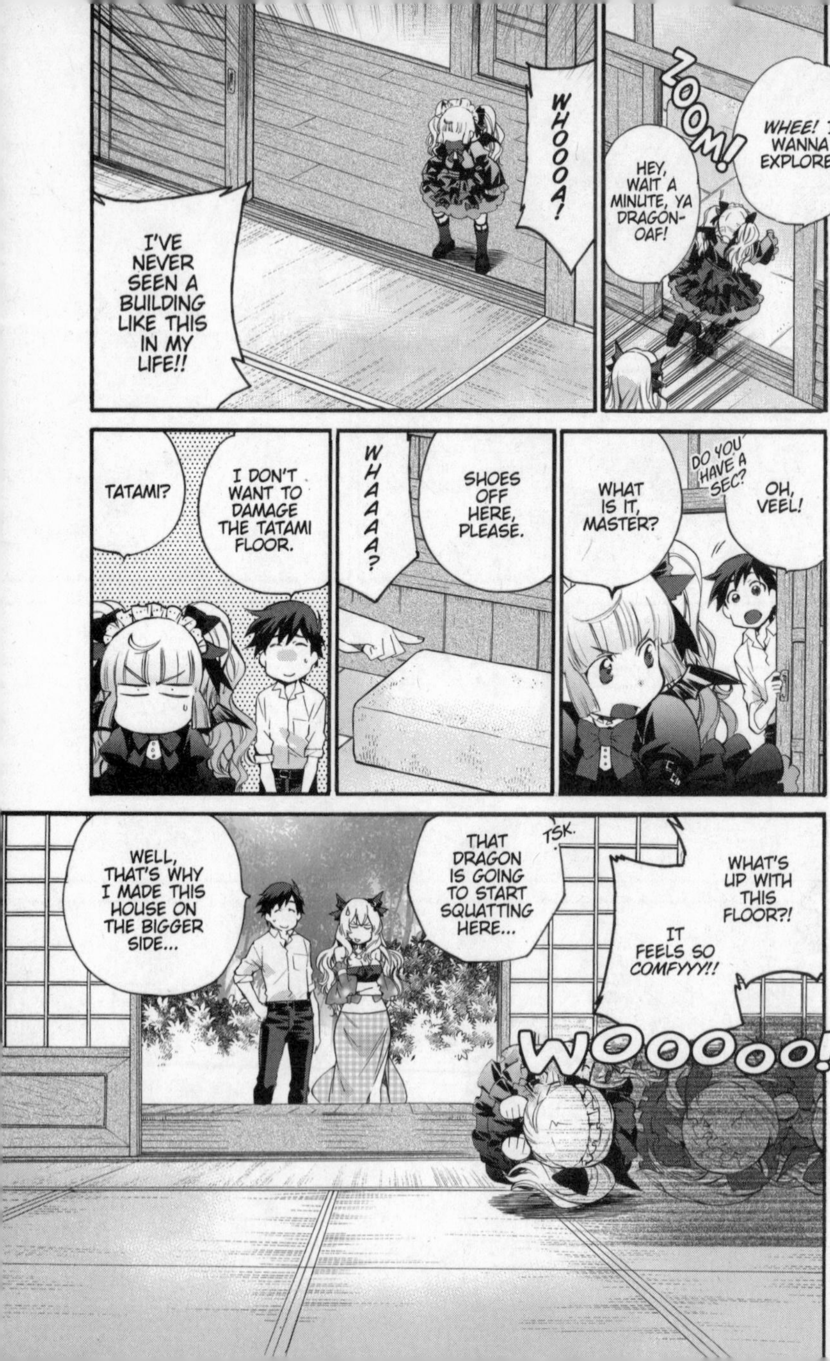
WHEE! I WANNA EXPLORE!
ZOOM!
HEY, WAIT A MINUTE, YA DRAGON-OAF!
WHOOOA!
I'VE NEVER SEEN A BUILDING LIKE THIS IN MY LIFE!!
OH, VEEL!
DO YOU HAVE A SEC?
WHAT IS IT, MASTER?
SHOES OFF HERE, PLEASE.
WHAAAAA?
I DON'T WANT TO DAMAGE THE TATAMI FLOOR.
TATAMI?
WHAT'S UP WITH THIS FLOOR?!
IT FEELS SO COMFYYY!!
WOOOOO!
TSK.
THAT DRAGON IS GOING TO START SQUATTING HERE...
WELL, THAT'S WHY I MADE THIS HOUSE ON THE BIGGER SIDE...

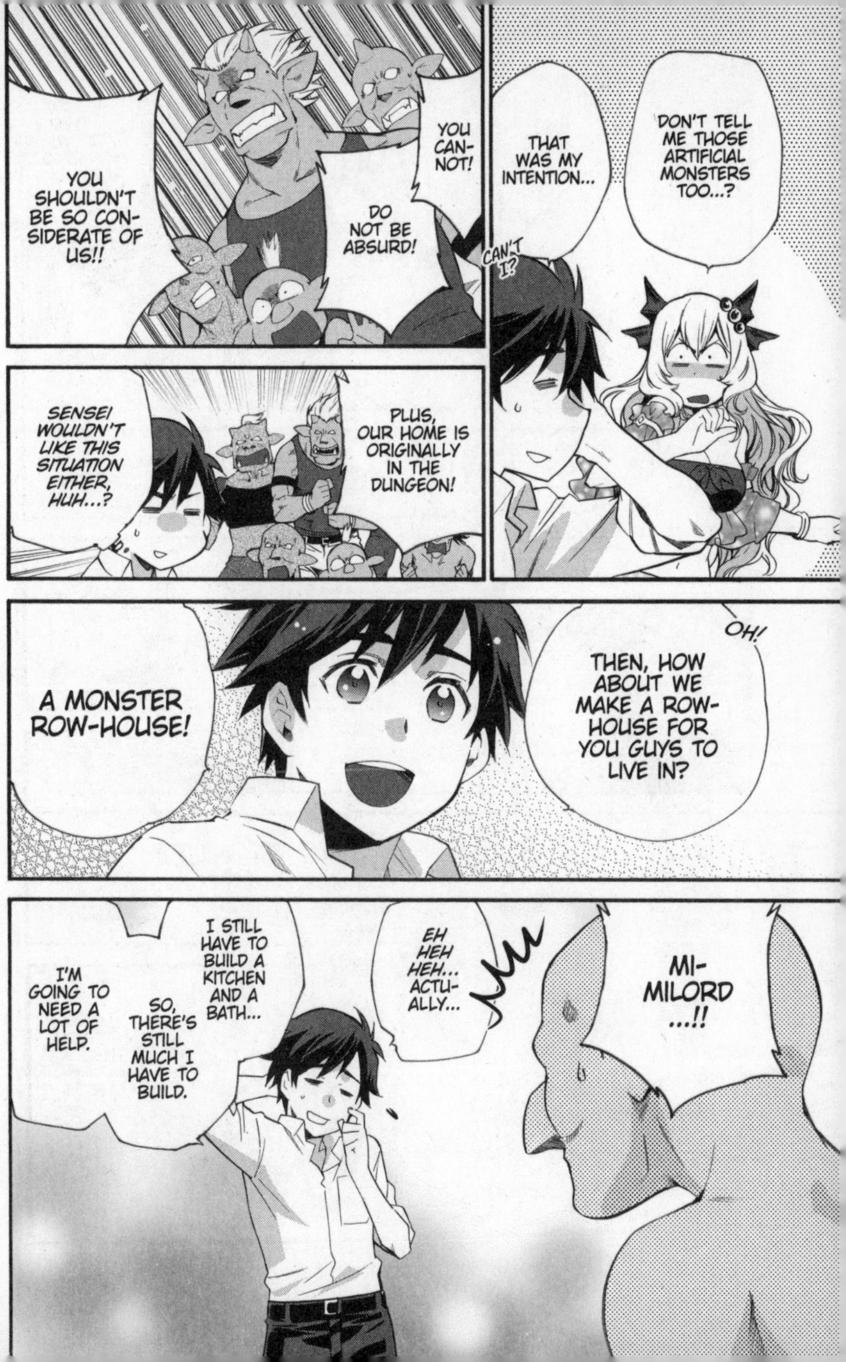
DON'T TELL ME THOSE ARTIFICIAL MONSTERS TOO...?
THAT WAS MY INTENTION...
CAN'T I?
YOU CAN-NOT!
DO NOT BE ABSURD!
YOU SHOULDN'T BE SO CON-SIDERATE OF US!!
PLUS, OUR HOME IS ORIGINALLY IN THE DUNGEON!
SENSEI WOULDN'T LIKE THIS SITUATION EITHER, HUH...?
OH!
THEN, HOW ABOUT WE MAKE A ROW-HOUSE FOR YOU GUYS TO LIVE IN?
A MONSTER ROW-HOUSE!
MI-MILORD ...!!
EH HEH HEH... ACTU-ALLY...
I STILL HAVE TO BUILD A KITCHEN AND A BATH...
SO, THERE'S STILL MUCH I HAVE TO BUILD.
I'M GOING TO NEED A LOT OF HELP.

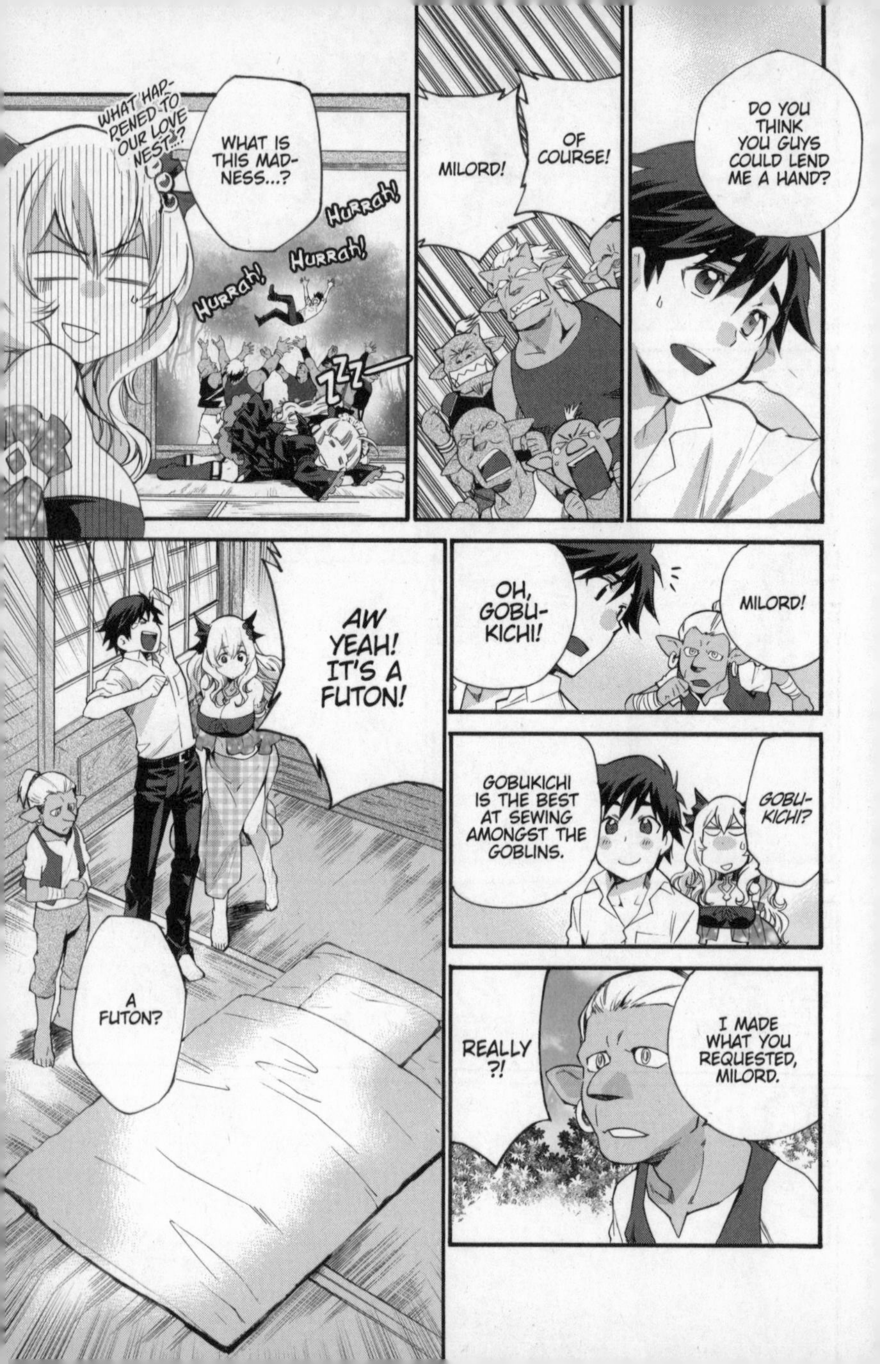
DO YOU THINK YOU GUYS COULD LEND ME A HAND?
OF COURSE!
MILORD!
WHAT IS THIS MADNESS...?
WHAT HAPPENED TO OUR LOVE NEST...?
Hurrah!
Hurrah!
Hurrah!
ZZZ
MILORD!
OH, GOBUKICHI!
GOBUKICHI?
GOBUKICHI IS THE BEST AT SEWING AMONGST THE GOBLINS.
I MADE WHAT YOU REQUESTED, MILORD.
REALLY?!
AW YEAH! IT'S A FUTON!
A FUTON?

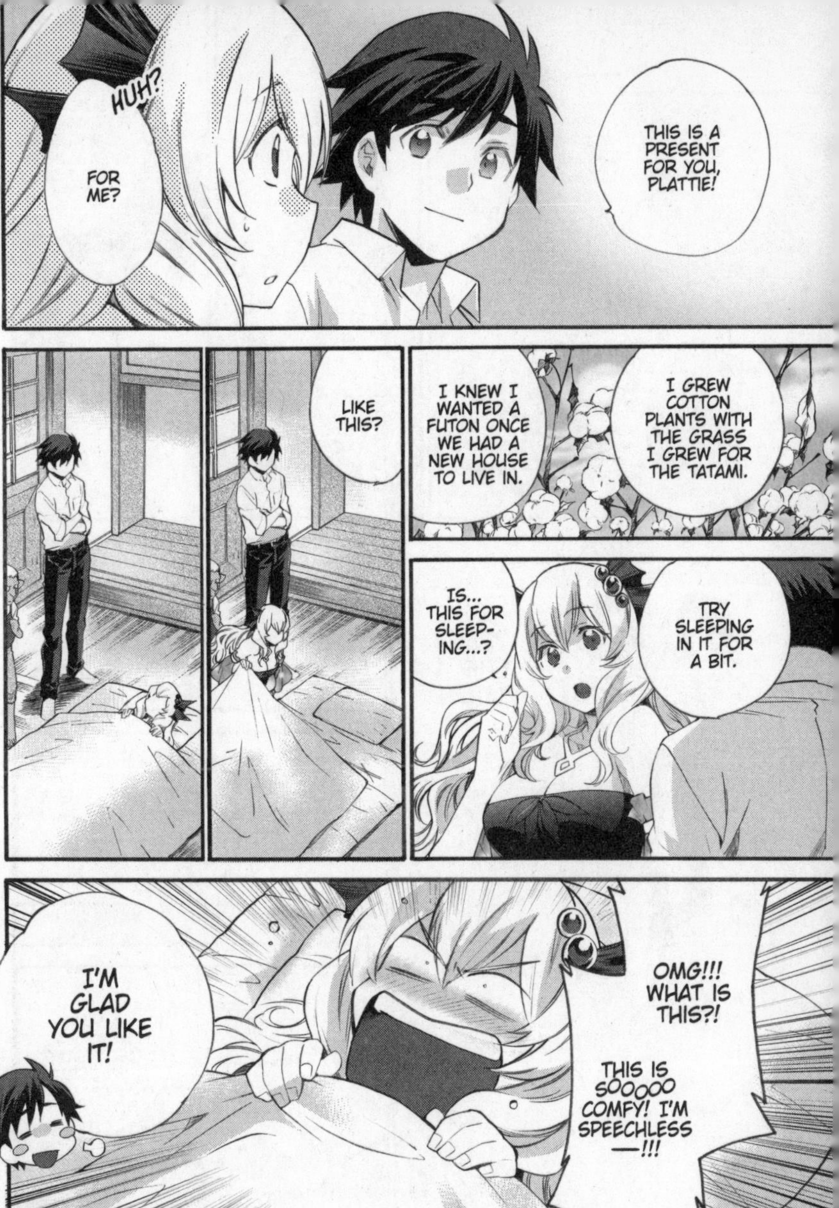
THIS IS A PRESENT FOR YOU, PLATTIE!
HUH?
FOR ME?
I GREW COTTON PLANTS WITH THE GRASS I GREW FOR THE TATAMI.
I KNEW I WANTED A FUTON ONCE WE HAD A NEW HOUSE TO LIVE IN.
TRY SLEEPING IN IT FOR A BIT.
IS... THIS FOR SLEEP-ING...?
LIKE THIS?
OMG!!! WHAT IS THIS?!
THIS IS SOOOOOO COMFY! I'M SPEECHLESS—!!!
I'M GLAD YOU LIKE IT!

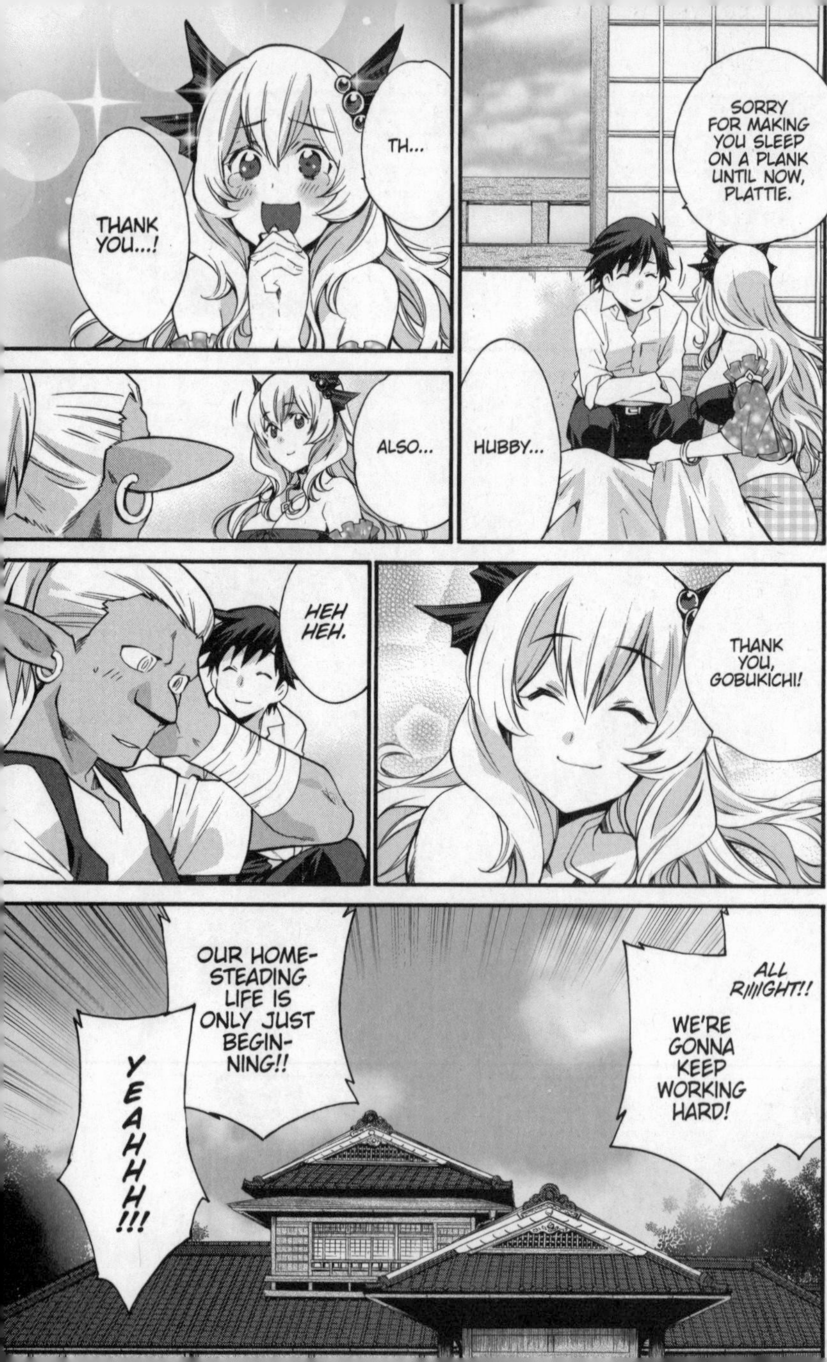
SORRY FOR MAKING YOU SLEEP ON A PLANK UNTIL NOW, PLATTIE.
HUBBY...
TH...
THANK YOU...!
ALSO...
THANK YOU, GOBUKICHI!
HEH HEH.
ALL RIIIGHT!!
WE'RE GONNA KEEP WORKING HARD!
OUR HOME-STEADING LIFE IS ONLY JUST BEGIN-NING!!
YEAHHH!!!

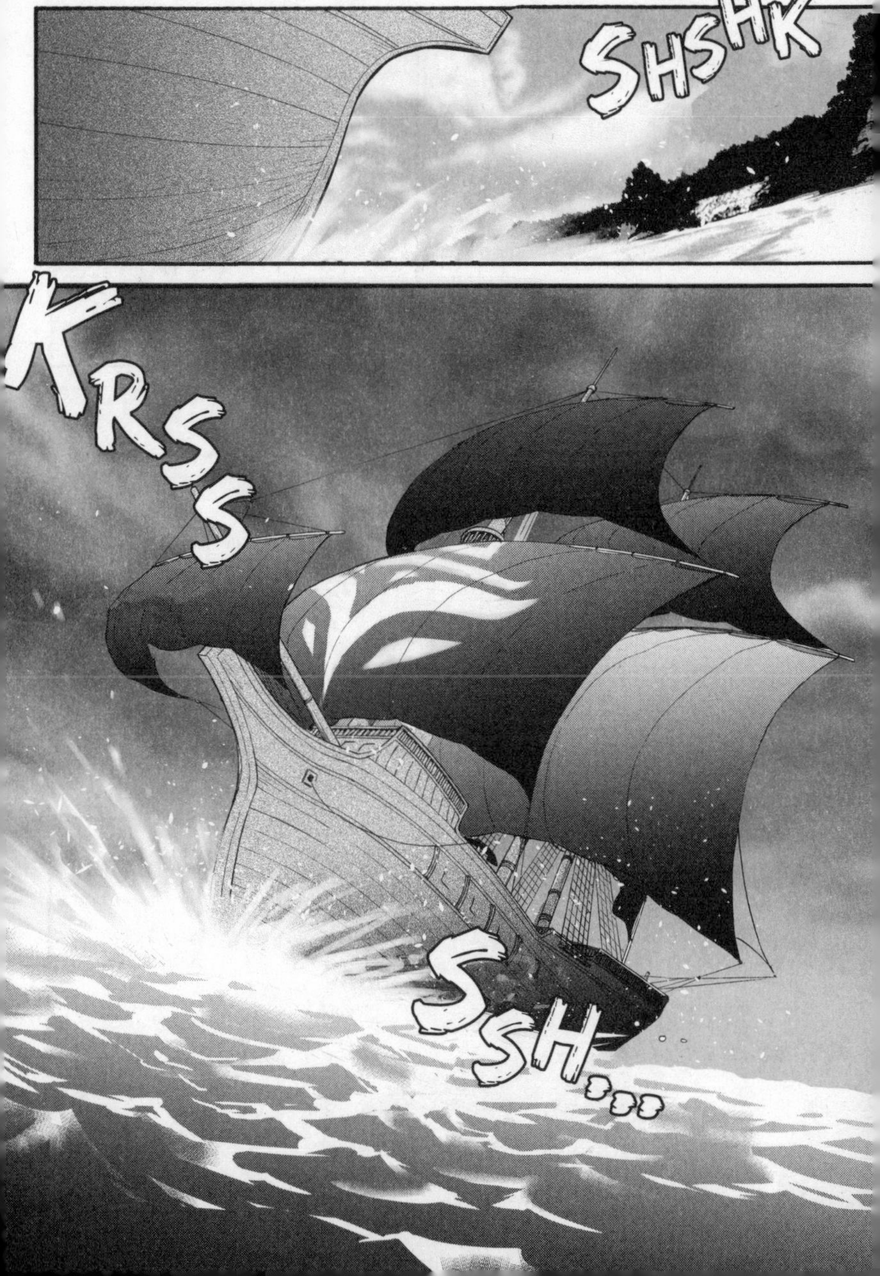
SHSHK
KRSS
SSH...

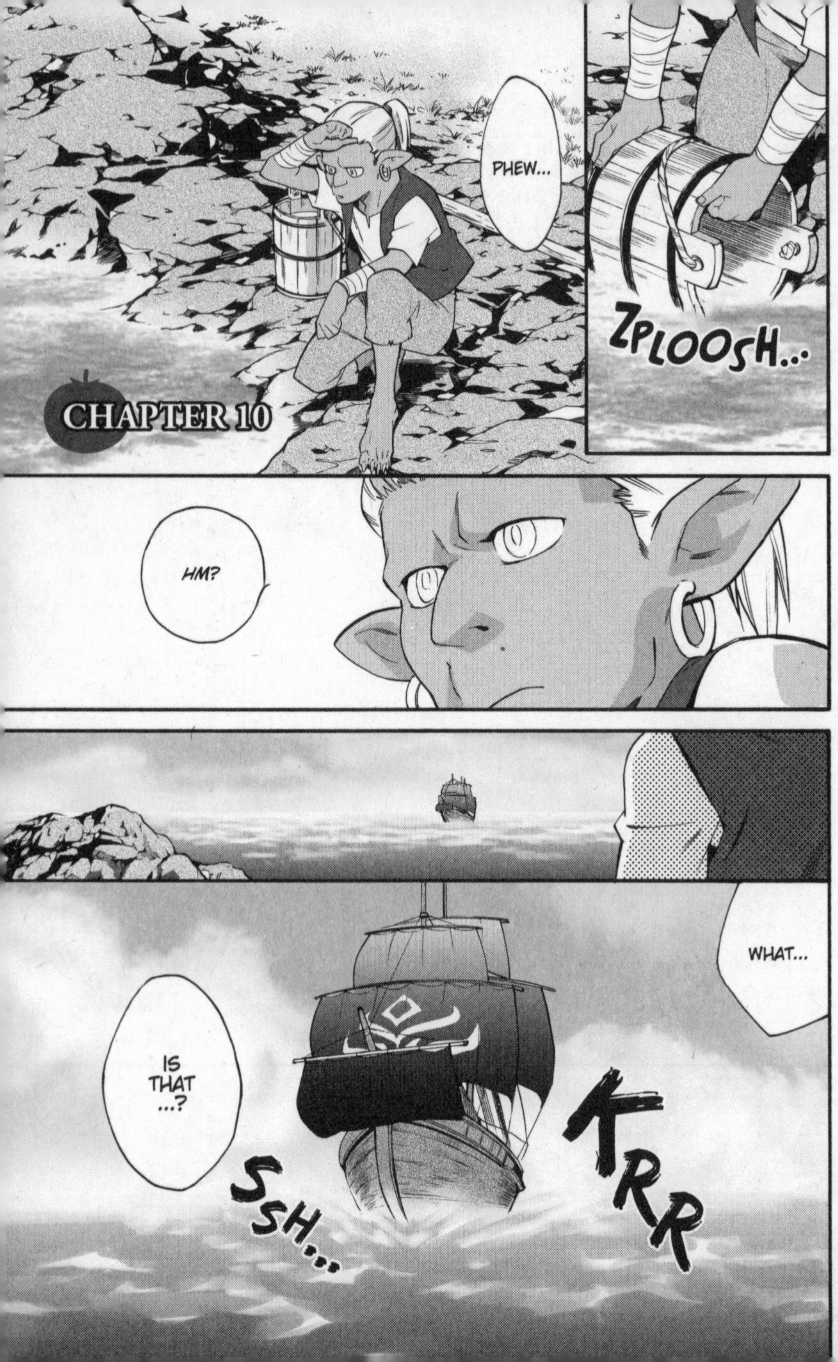
ZPLOOSH...
PHEW...
CHAPTER 10
HM?
WHAT...
IS THAT ...?
KRR
SSH...

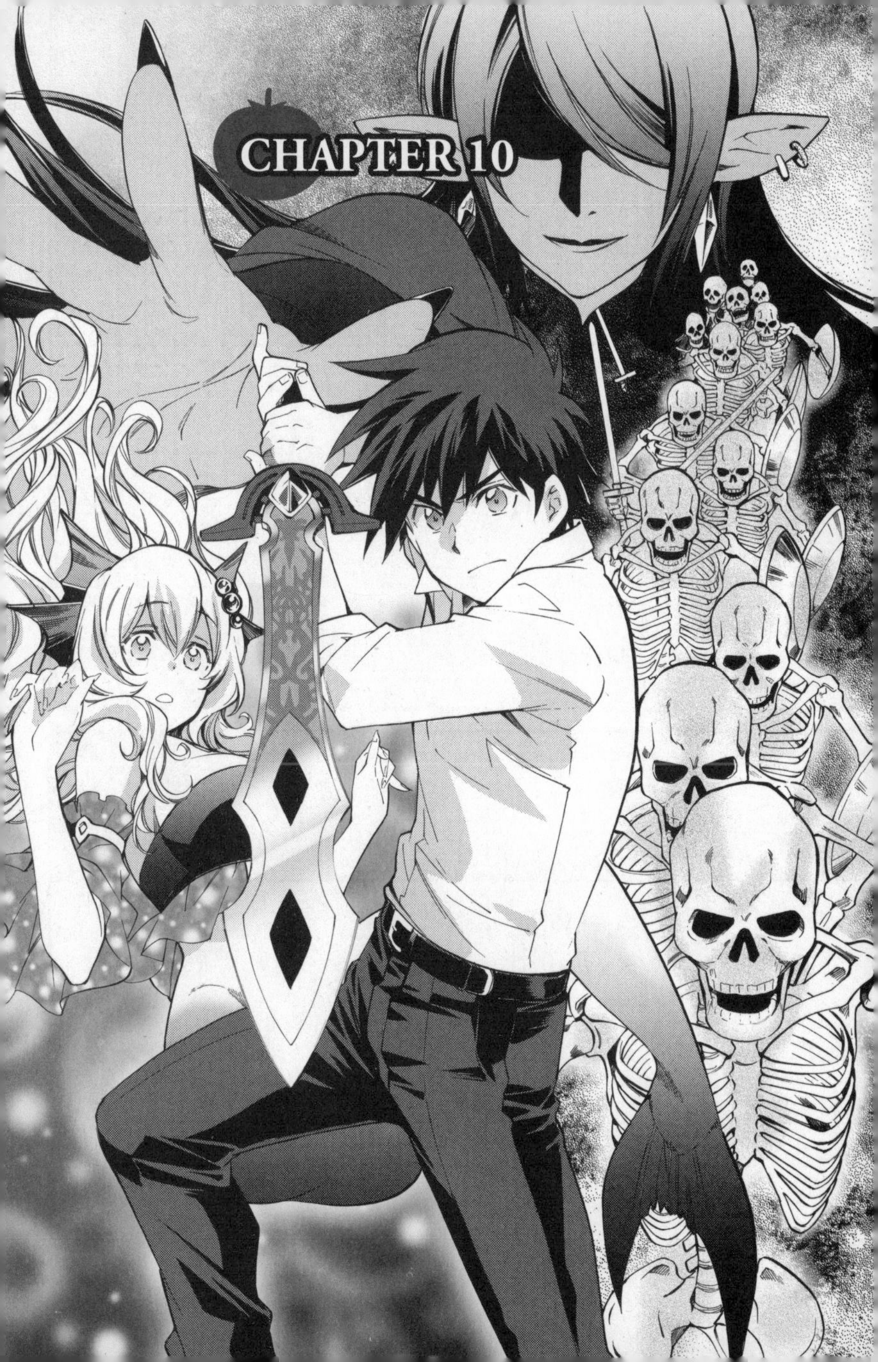
CHAPTER 10

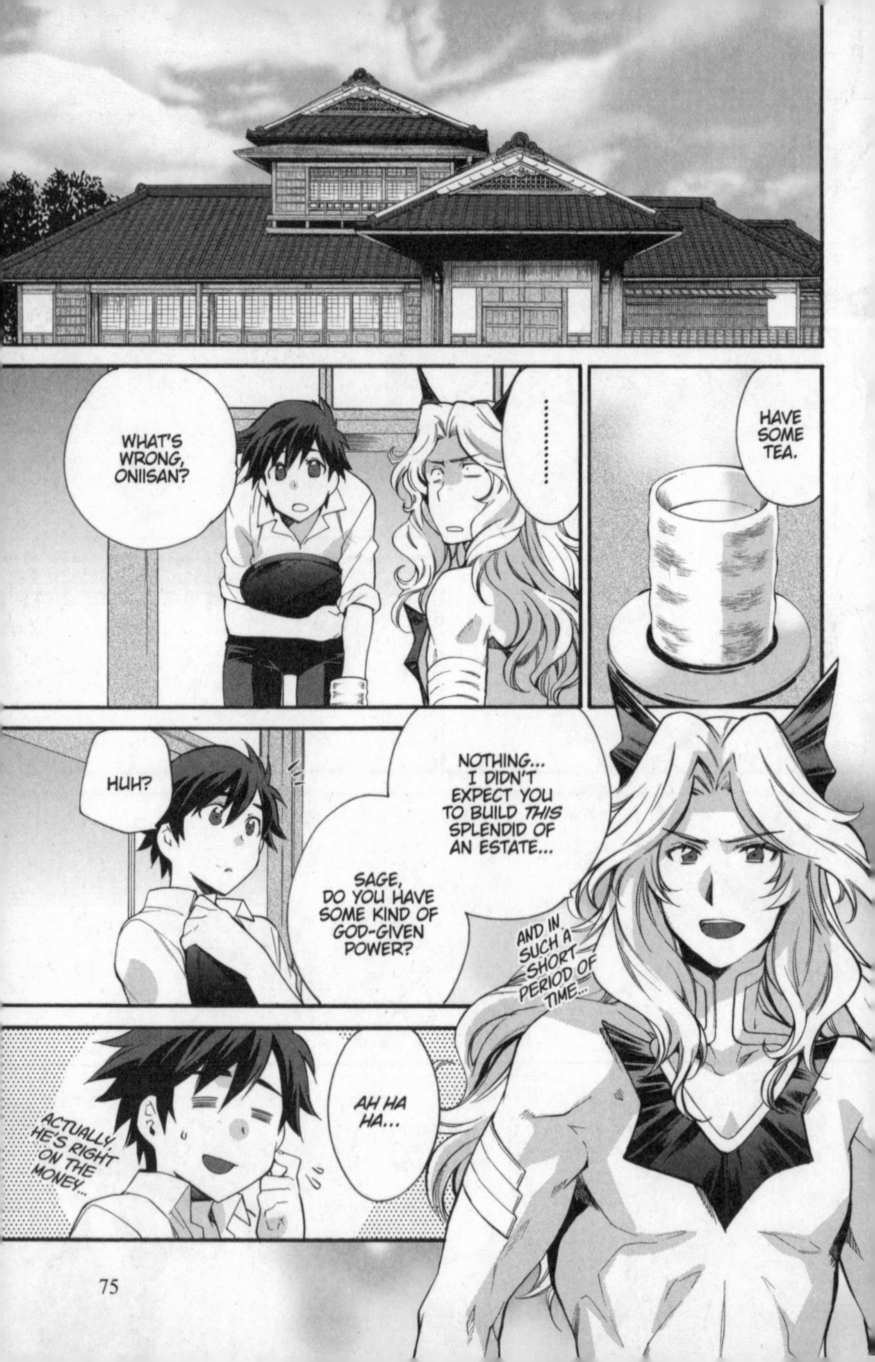
HAVE SOME TEA.
......
WHAT'S WRONG, ONIISAN?
NOTHING... I DIDN'T EXPECT YOU TO BUILD *THIS* SPLENDID OF AN ESTATE...
AND IN SUCH A SHORT PERIOD OF TIME...
SAGE, DO YOU HAVE SOME KIND OF GOD-GIVEN POWER?
HUH?
AH HA HA...
ACTUALLY, HE'S RIGHT ON THE MONEY...

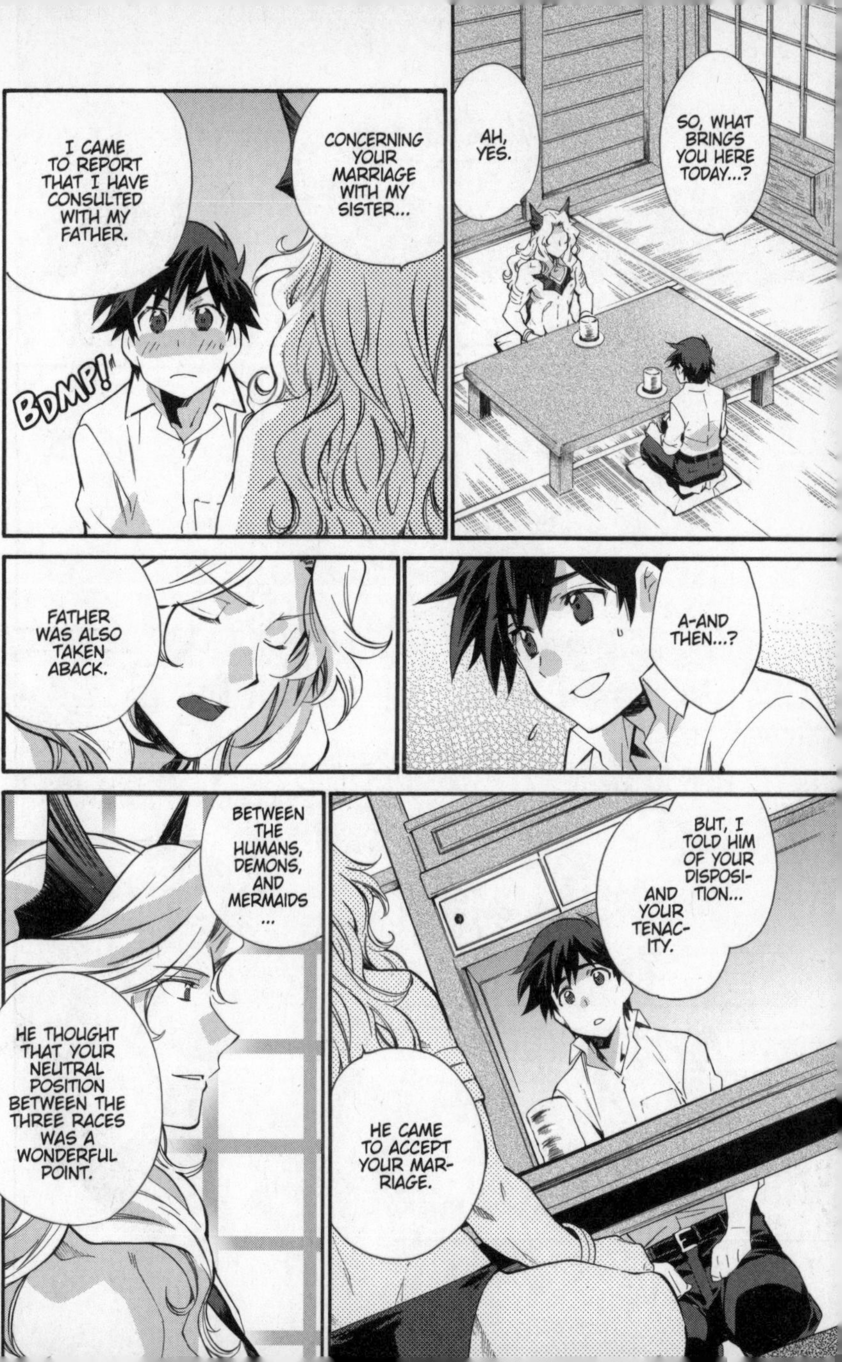
SO, WHAT BRINGS YOU HERE TODAY...?
AH, YES.
CONCERNING YOUR MARRIAGE WITH MY SISTER...
I CAME TO REPORT THAT I HAVE CONSULTED WITH MY FATHER.
BDMP!
A-AND THEN...?
FATHER WAS ALSO TAKEN ABACK.
BUT, I TOLD HIM OF YOUR DISPOSITION...
AND YOUR TENACITY.
HE CAME TO ACCEPT YOUR MARRIAGE.
BETWEEN THE HUMANS, DEMONS, AND MERMAIDS...
HE THOUGHT THAT YOUR NEUTRAL POSITION BETWEEN THE THREE RACES WAS A WONDERFUL POINT.

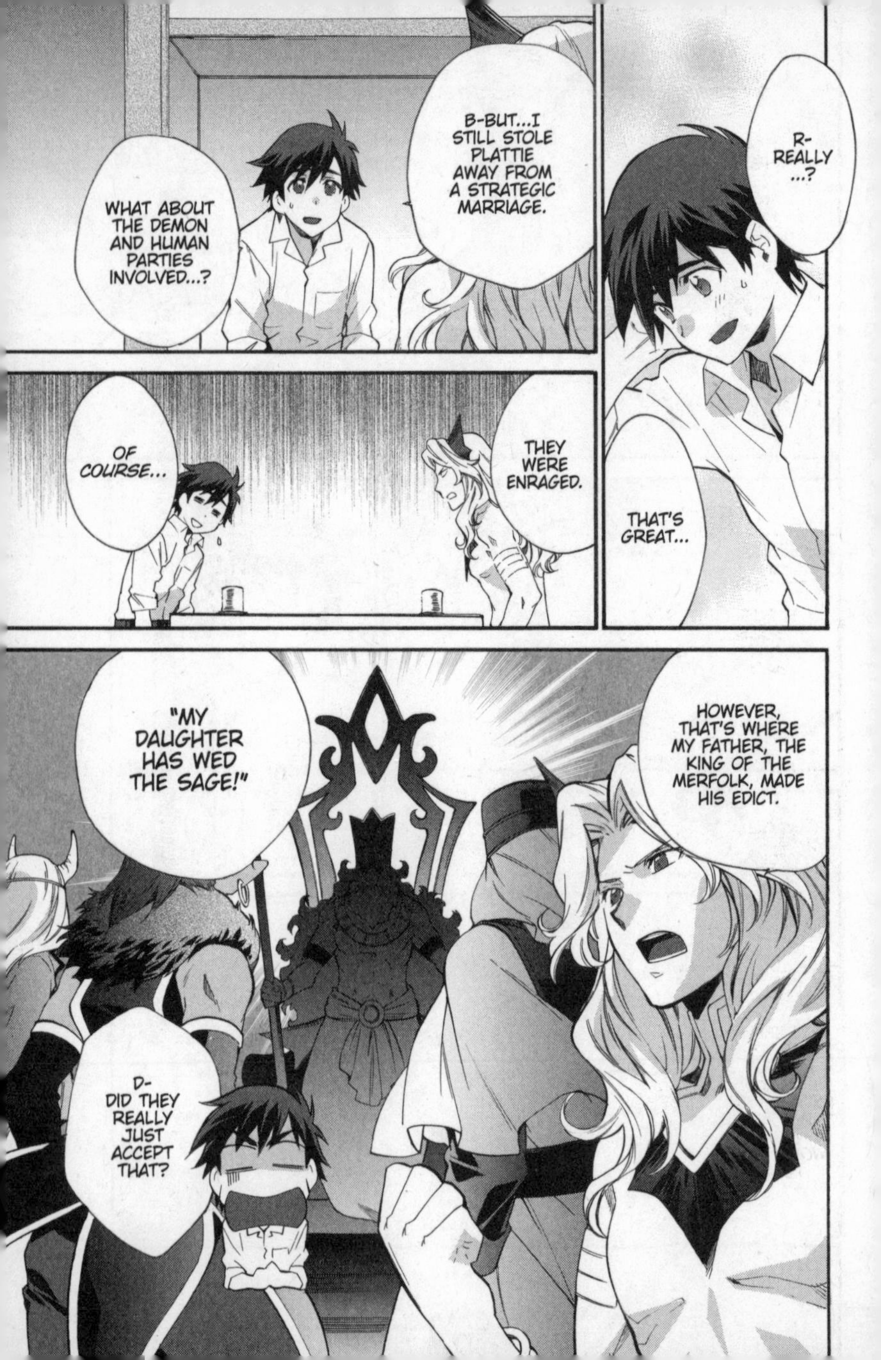
R-REALLY ...?
THAT'S GREAT...
B-BUT...I STILL STOLE PLATTIE AWAY FROM A STRATEGIC MARRIAGE.
WHAT ABOUT THE DEMON AND HUMAN PARTIES INVOLVED...?
THEY WERE ENRAGED.
OF COURSE...
HOWEVER, THAT'S WHERE MY FATHER, THE KING OF THE MERFOLK, MADE HIS EDICT.
"MY DAUGHTER HAS WED THE SAGE!"
D-DID THEY REALLY JUST ACCEPT THAT?

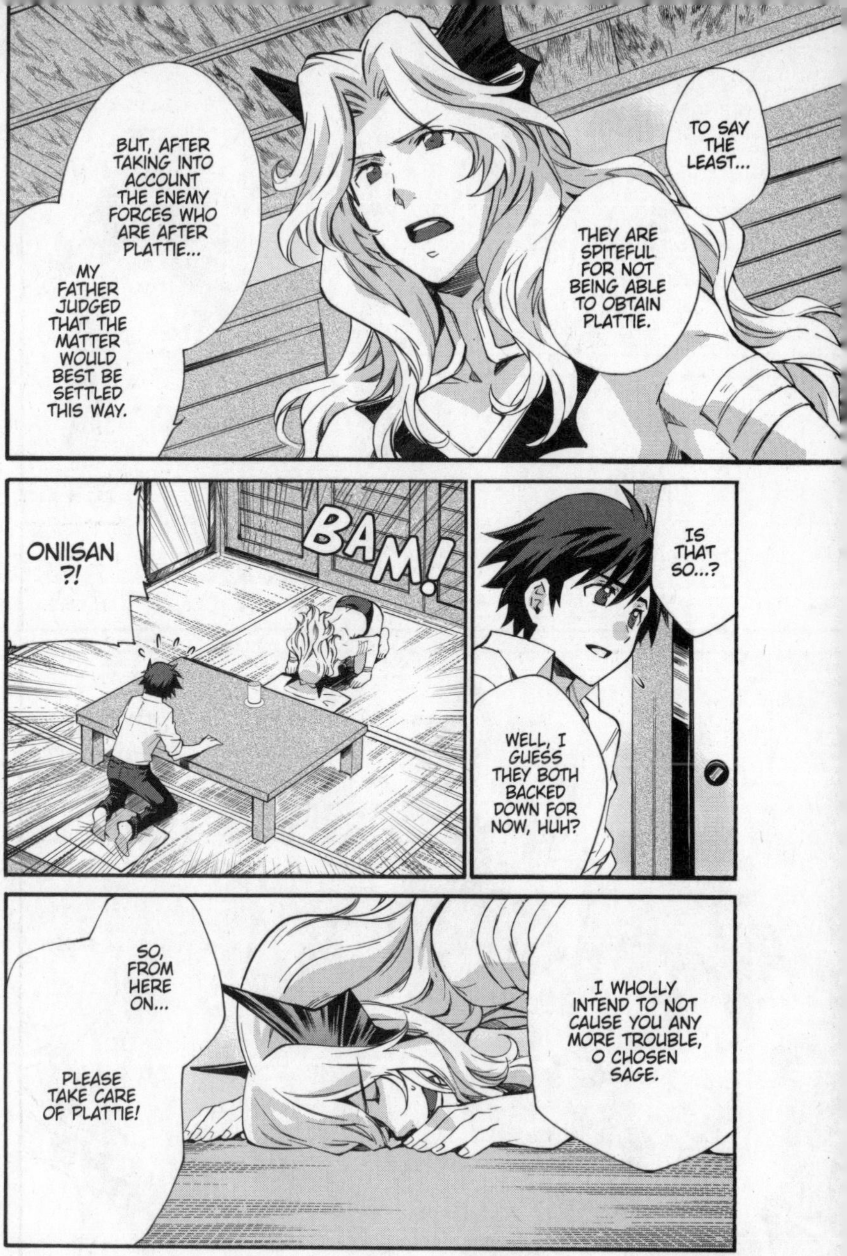
TO SAY THE LEAST...
THEY ARE SPITEFUL FOR NOT BEING ABLE TO OBTAIN PLATTIE.
BUT, AFTER TAKING INTO ACCOUNT THE ENEMY FORCES WHO ARE AFTER PLATTIE...
MY FATHER JUDGED THAT THE MATTER WOULD BEST BE SETTLED THIS WAY.
IS THAT SO...?
WELL, I GUESS THEY BOTH BACKED DOWN FOR NOW, HUH?
BAM!
ONIISAN ?!
I WHOLLY INTEND TO NOT CAUSE YOU ANY MORE TROUBLE, O CHOSEN SAGE.
SO, FROM HERE ON...
PLEASE TAKE CARE OF PLATTIE!

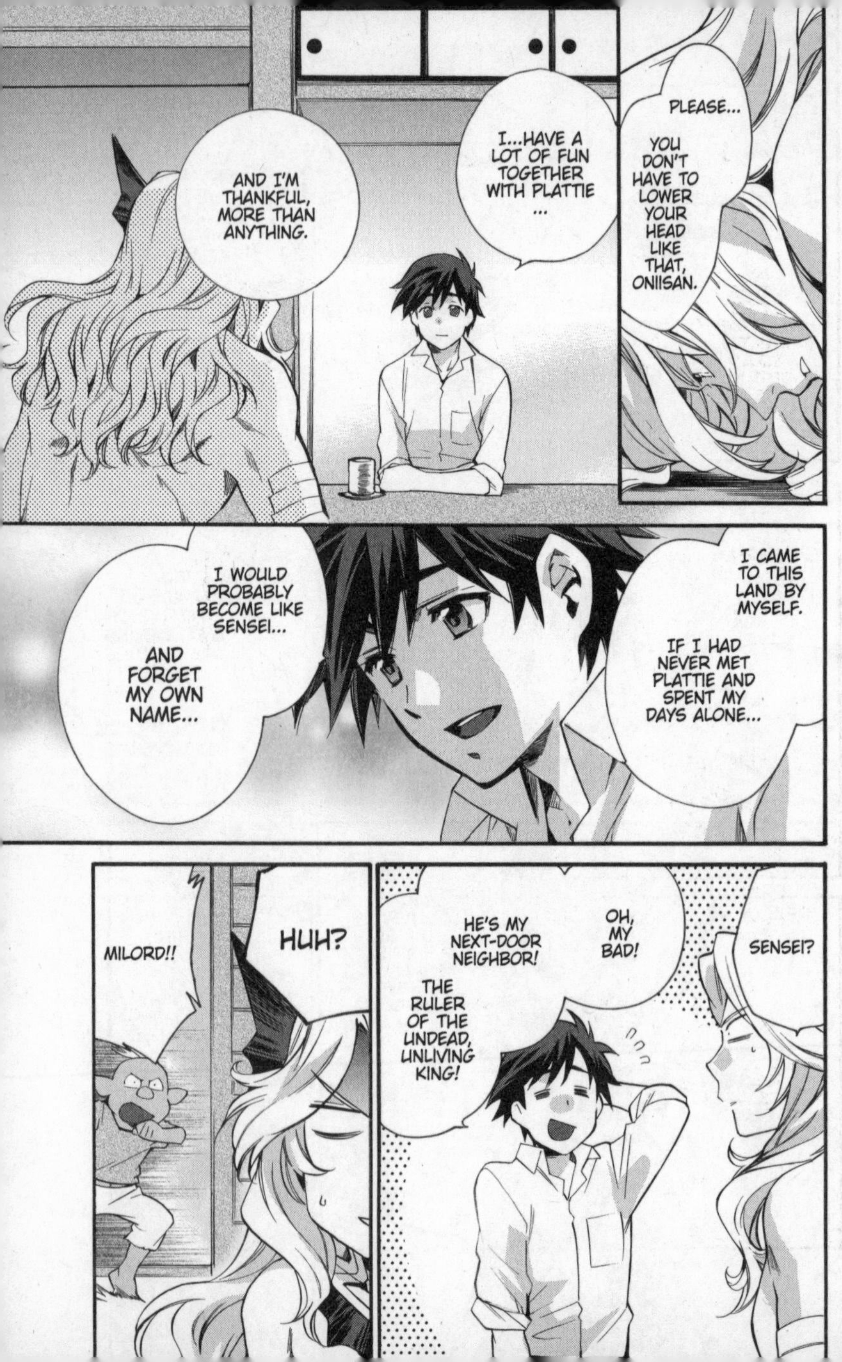
PLEASE...
YOU DON'T HAVE TO LOWER YOUR HEAD LIKE THAT, ONIISAN.
I...HAVE A LOT OF FUN TOGETHER WITH PLATTIE ...
AND I'M THANKFUL, MORE THAN ANYTHING.
I CAME TO THIS LAND BY MYSELF.
IF I HAD NEVER MET PLATTIE AND SPENT MY DAYS ALONE...
I WOULD PROBABLY BECOME LIKE SENSEI...
AND FORGET MY OWN NAME...
SENSEI?
OH, MY BAD!
HE'S MY NEXT-DOOR NEIGHBOR!
THE RULER OF THE UNDEAD, UNLIVING KING!
HUH?
MILORD!!

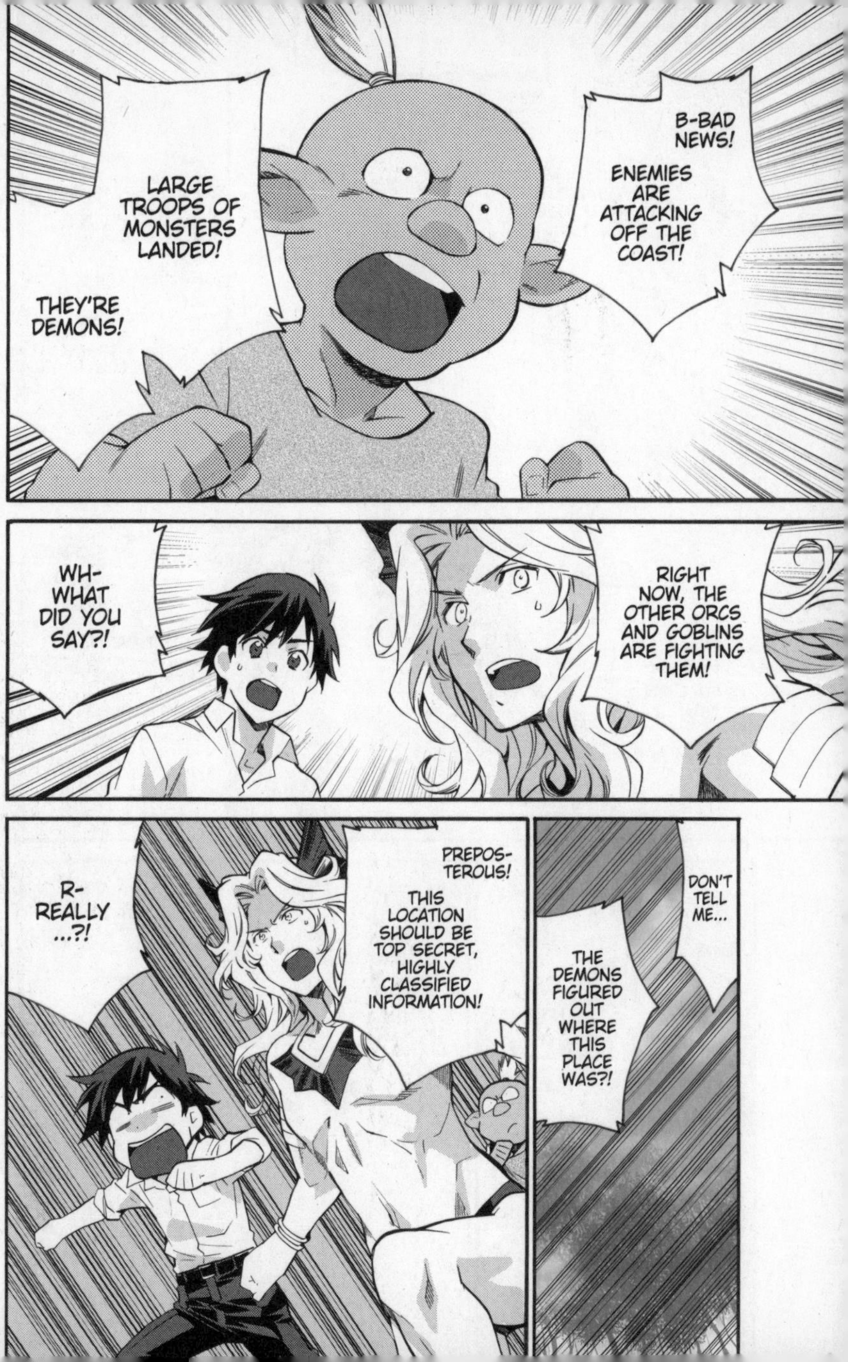
B-BAD NEWS!
ENEMIES ARE ATTACKING OFF THE COAST!
LARGE TROOPS OF MONSTERS LANDED!
THEY'RE DEMONS!
RIGHT NOW, THE OTHER ORCS AND GOBLINS ARE FIGHTING THEM!
WH-WHAT DID YOU SAY?!
DON'T TELL ME...
THE DEMONS FIGURED OUT WHERE THIS PLACE WAS?!
PREPOS-TEROUS!
THIS LOCATION SHOULD BE TOP SECRET, HIGHLY CLASSIFIED INFORMATION!
R-REALLY ...?!

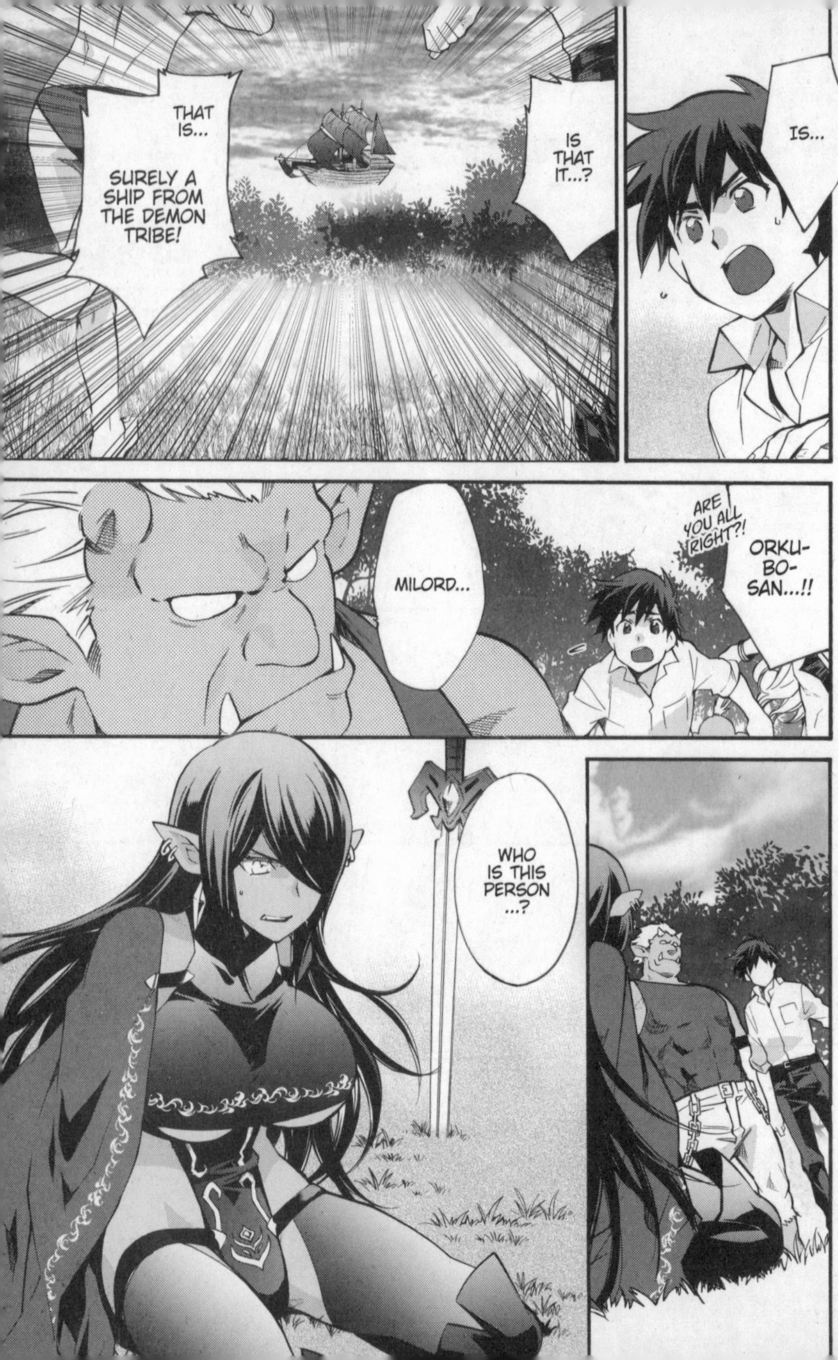
IS...
IS THAT IT...?
THAT IS...
SURELY A SHIP FROM THE DEMON TRIBE!
ORKU-BO-SAN...!!
ARE YOU ALL RIGHT?!
MILORD...
WHO IS THIS PERSON ...?

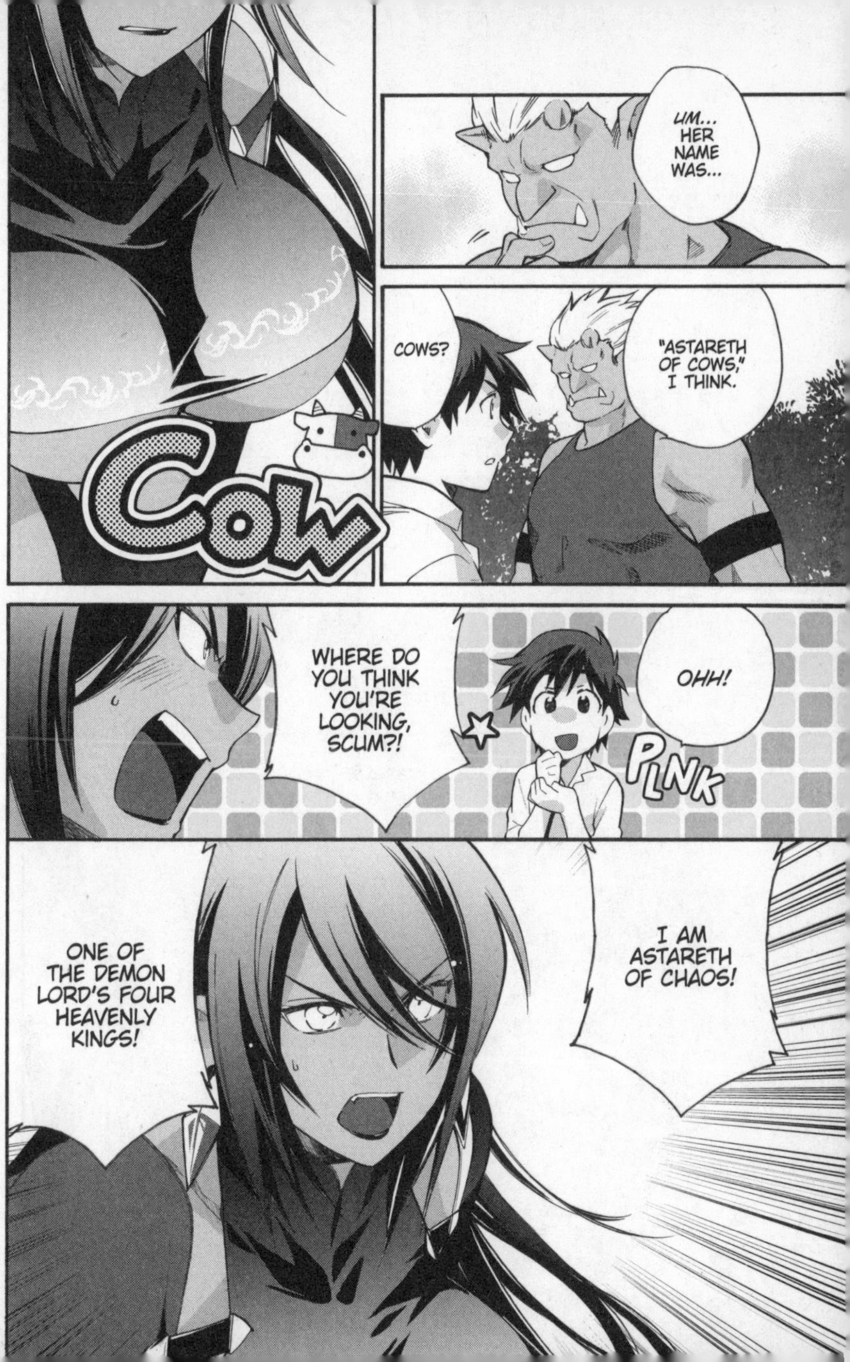
UM... HER NAME WAS...
"ASTARETH OF COWS," I THINK.
COWS?
Cow
OHH!
PLNK
WHERE DO YOU THINK YOU'RE LOOKING, SCUM?!
I AM ASTARETH OF CHAOS!
ONE OF THE DEMON LORD'S FOUR HEAVENLY KINGS!

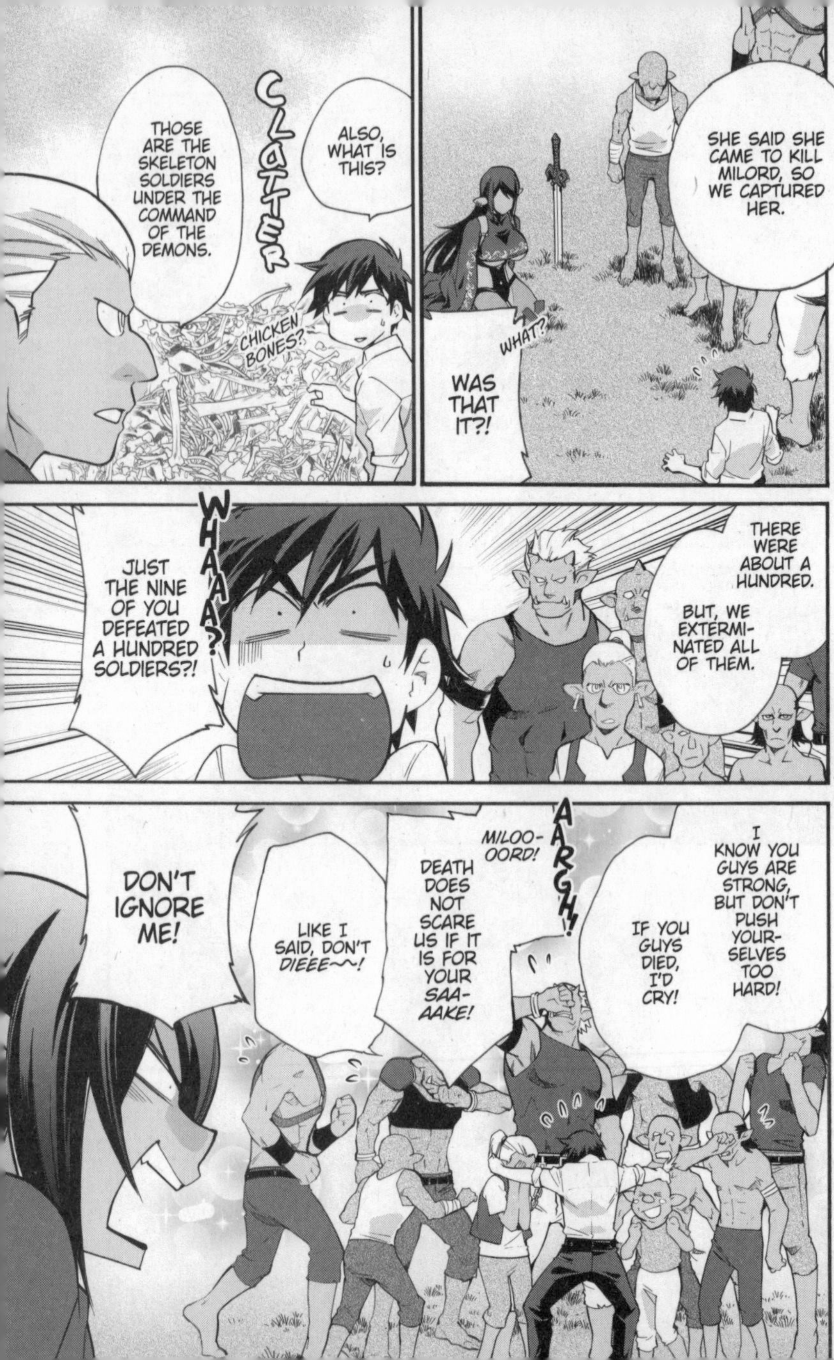
SHE SAID SHE CAME TO KILL MILORD, SO WE CAPTURED HER.
WHAT?
WAS THAT IT?!
ALSO, WHAT IS THIS?
CLATTER
THOSE ARE THE SKELETON SOLDIERS UNDER THE COMMAND OF THE DEMONS.
CHICKEN BONES?
THERE WERE ABOUT A HUNDRED.
BUT, WE EXTERMINATED ALL OF THEM.
WHAAAA?
JUST THE NINE OF YOU DEFEATED A HUNDRED SOLDIERS?!
I KNOW YOU GUYS ARE STRONG, BUT DON'T PUSH YOURSELVES TOO HARD!
IF YOU GUYS DIED, I'D CRY!
AARGH!!
MILOOOORD!
DEATH DOES NOT SCARE US IF IT IS FOR YOUR SAAAAKE!
LIKE I SAID, DON'T DIEEE~~!
DON'T IGNORE ME!

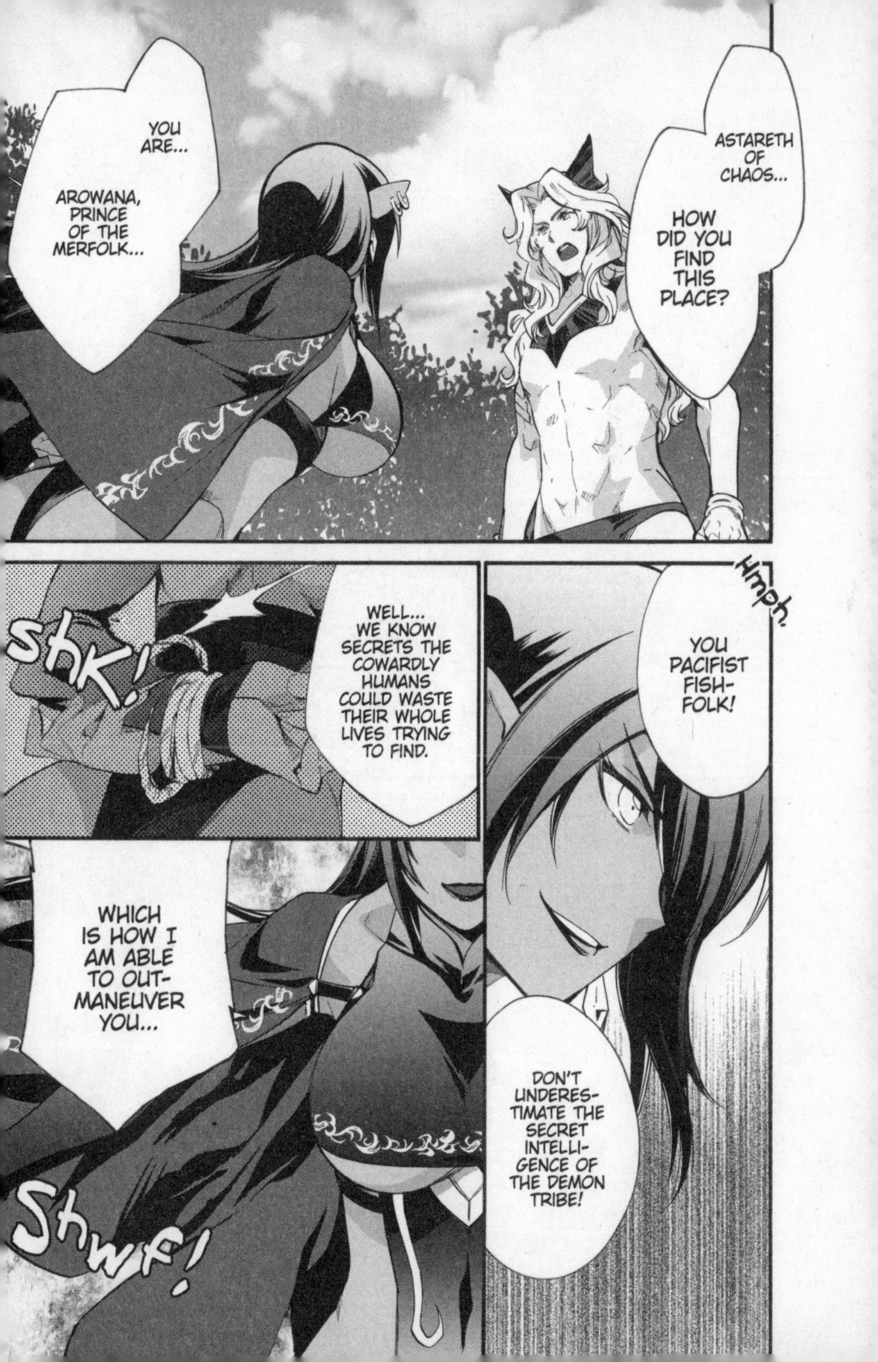
ASTARETH OF CHAOS... HOW DID YOU FIND THIS PLACE?
YOU ARE... AROWANA, PRINCE OF THE MERFOLK...
Hmph.
YOU PACIFIST FISH-FOLK!
DON'T UNDERESTIMATE THE SECRET INTELLIGENCE OF THE DEMON TRIBE!
shk!
WELL... WE KNOW SECRETS THE COWARDLY HUMANS COULD WASTE THEIR WHOLE LIVES TRYING TO FIND.
WHICH IS HOW I AM ABLE TO OUT-MANEUVER YOU...
Shwf!

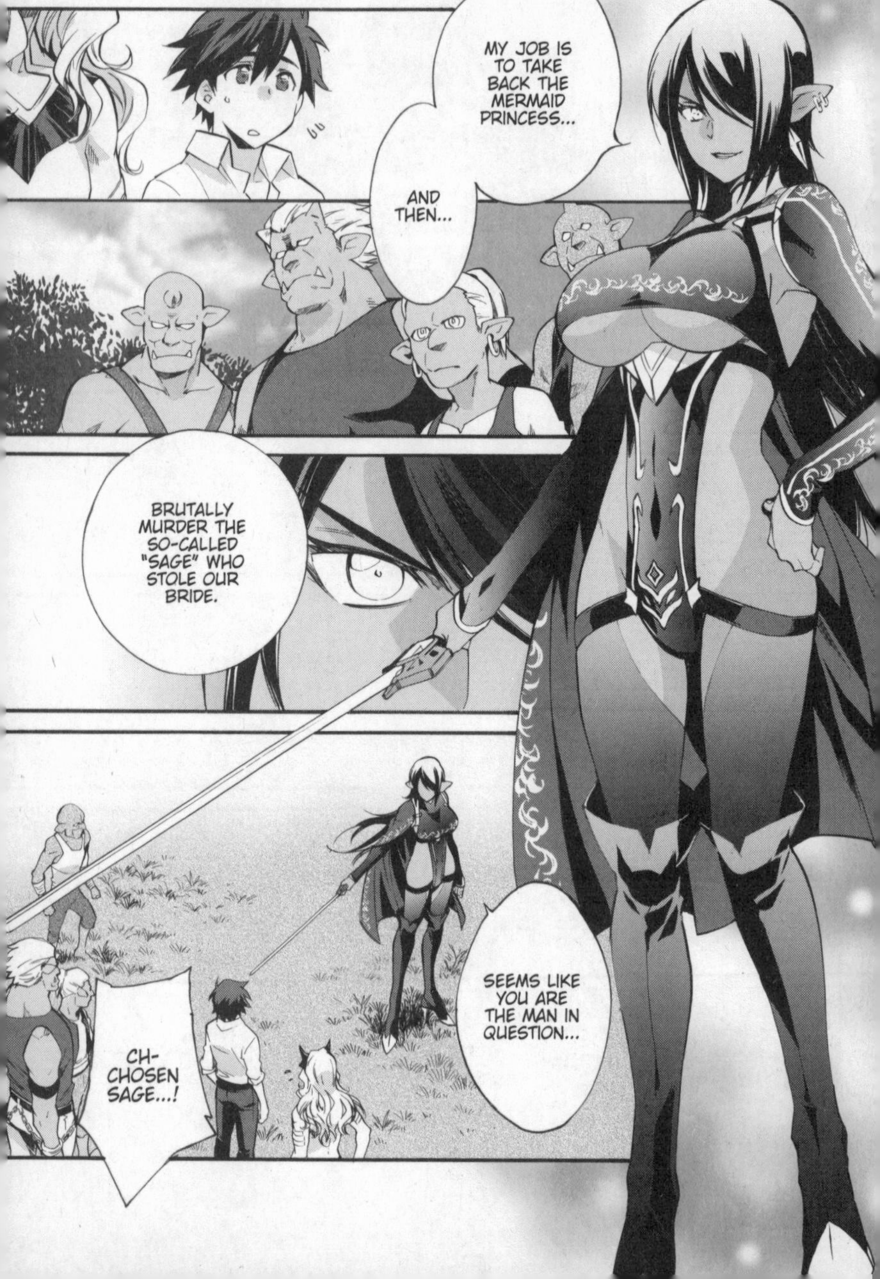
MY JOB IS TO TAKE BACK THE MERMAID PRINCESS...
AND THEN...
BRUTALLY MURDER THE SO-CALLED "SAGE" WHO STOLE OUR BRIDE.
SEEMS LIKE YOU ARE THE MAN IN QUESTION...
CH-CHOSEN SAGE...!

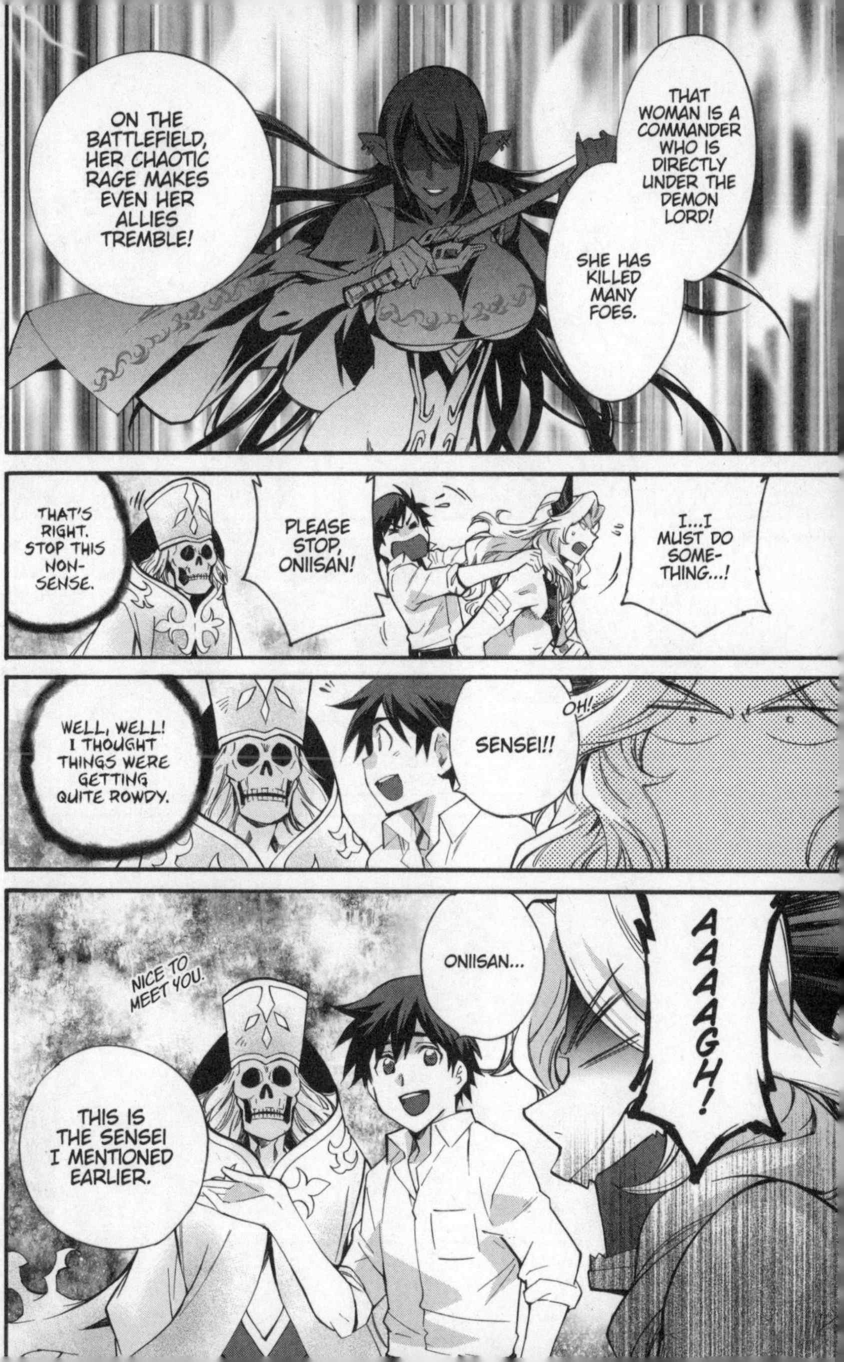
THAT WOMAN IS A COMMANDER WHO IS DIRECTLY UNDER THE DEMON LORD!
SHE HAS KILLED MANY FOES.
ON THE BATTLEFIELD, HER CHAOTIC RAGE MAKES EVEN HER ALLIES TREMBLE!
I...I MUST DO SOME-THING...!
PLEASE STOP, ONIISAN!
THAT'S RIGHT. STOP THIS NON-SENSE.
OH!
SENSEI!!
WELL, WELL! I THOUGHT THINGS WERE GETTING QUITE ROWDY.
AAAAGH!
ONIISAN...
NICE TO MEET YOU.
THIS IS THE SENSEI I MENTIONED EARLIER.

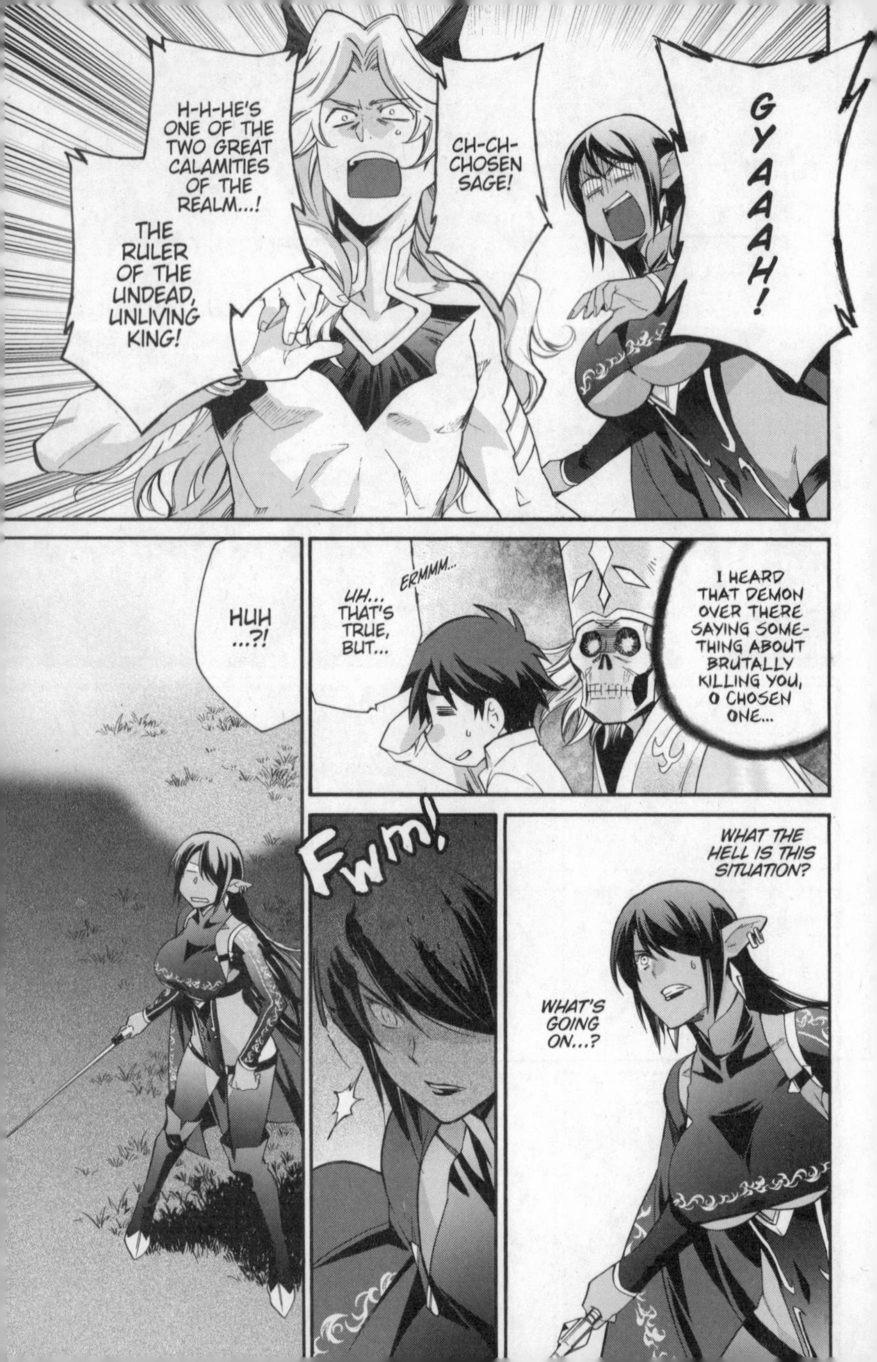
GYAAAAH!
CH-CH-CHOSEN SAGE!
H-H-HE'S ONE OF THE TWO GREAT CALAMITIES OF THE REALM...!
THE RULER OF THE UNDEAD, UNLIVING KING!
I HEARD THAT DEMON OVER THERE SAYING SOME-THING ABOUT BRUTALLY KILLING YOU, O CHOSEN ONE...
ERMMM...
UH... THAT'S TRUE, BUT...
WHAT THE HELL IS THIS SITUATION?
WHAT'S GOING ON...?
Fwm!
HUH ...?!

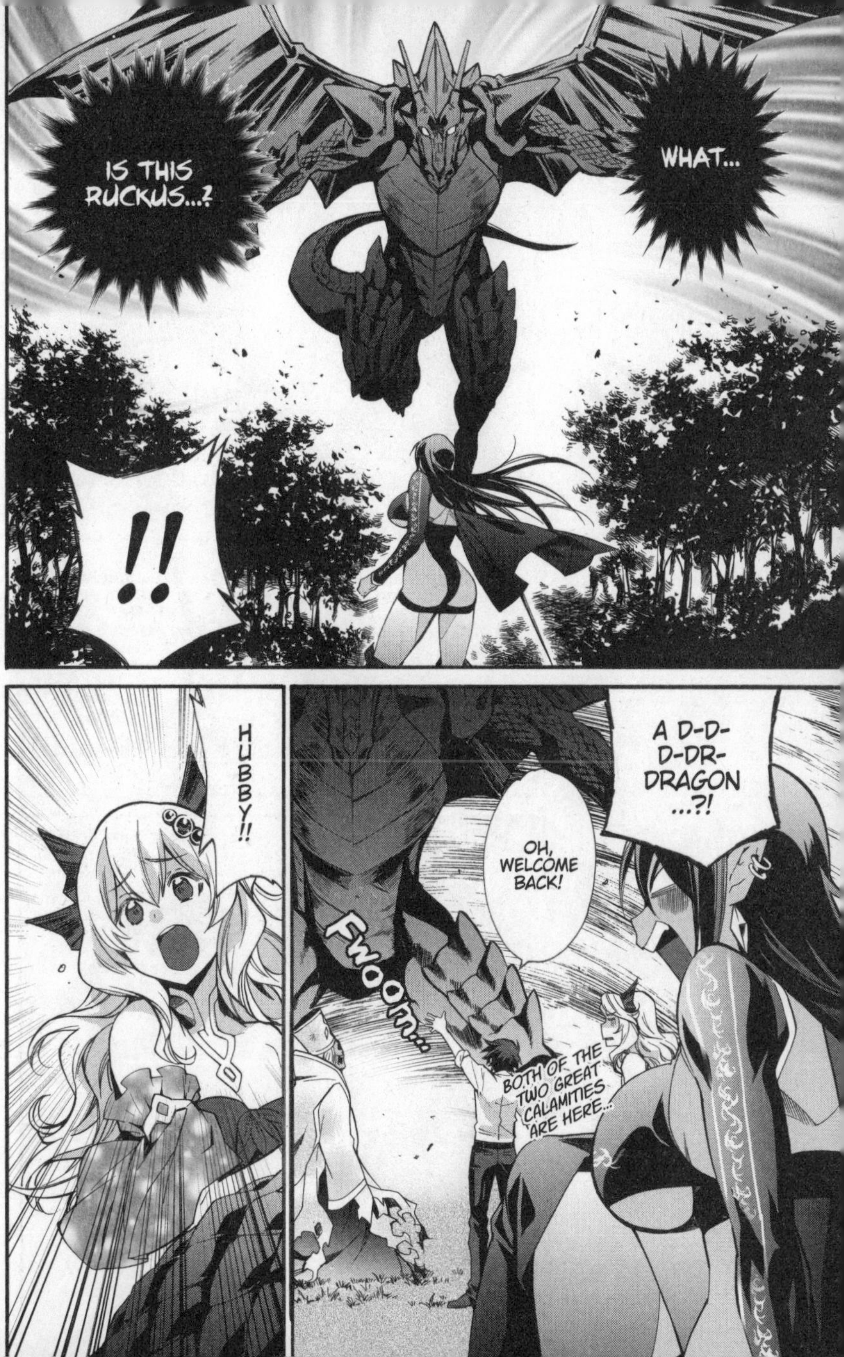
WHAT...
IS THIS RUCKUS...?
!!
A D-D-D-DR-DRAGON...?!
OH, WELCOME BACK!
FWOOM...
BOTH OF THE TWO GREAT CALAMITIES ARE HERE...
HUBBY!!

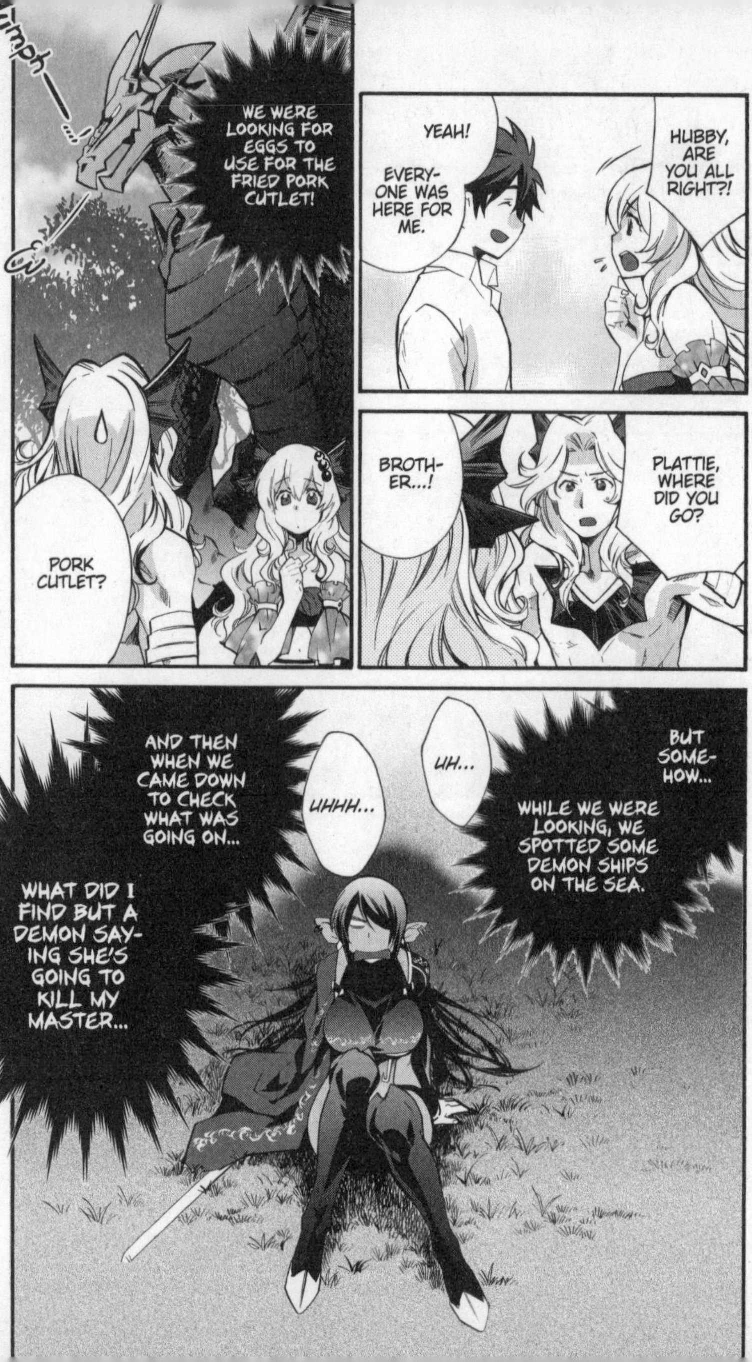
HUBBY, ARE YOU ALL RIGHT?!
YEAH!
EVERY-ONE WAS HERE FOR ME.
PLATTIE, WHERE DID YOU GO?
BROTH-ER...!
WE WERE LOOKING FOR EGGS TO USE FOR THE FRIED PORK CUTLET!
umph—...!
PORK CUTLET?
BUT SOME-HOW...
WHILE WE WERE LOOKING, WE SPOTTED SOME DEMON SHIPS ON THE SEA.
UH...
UHHH...
AND THEN WHEN WE CAME DOWN TO CHECK WHAT WAS GOING ON...
WHAT DID I FIND BUT A DEMON SAY-ING SHE'S GOING TO KILL MY MASTER...

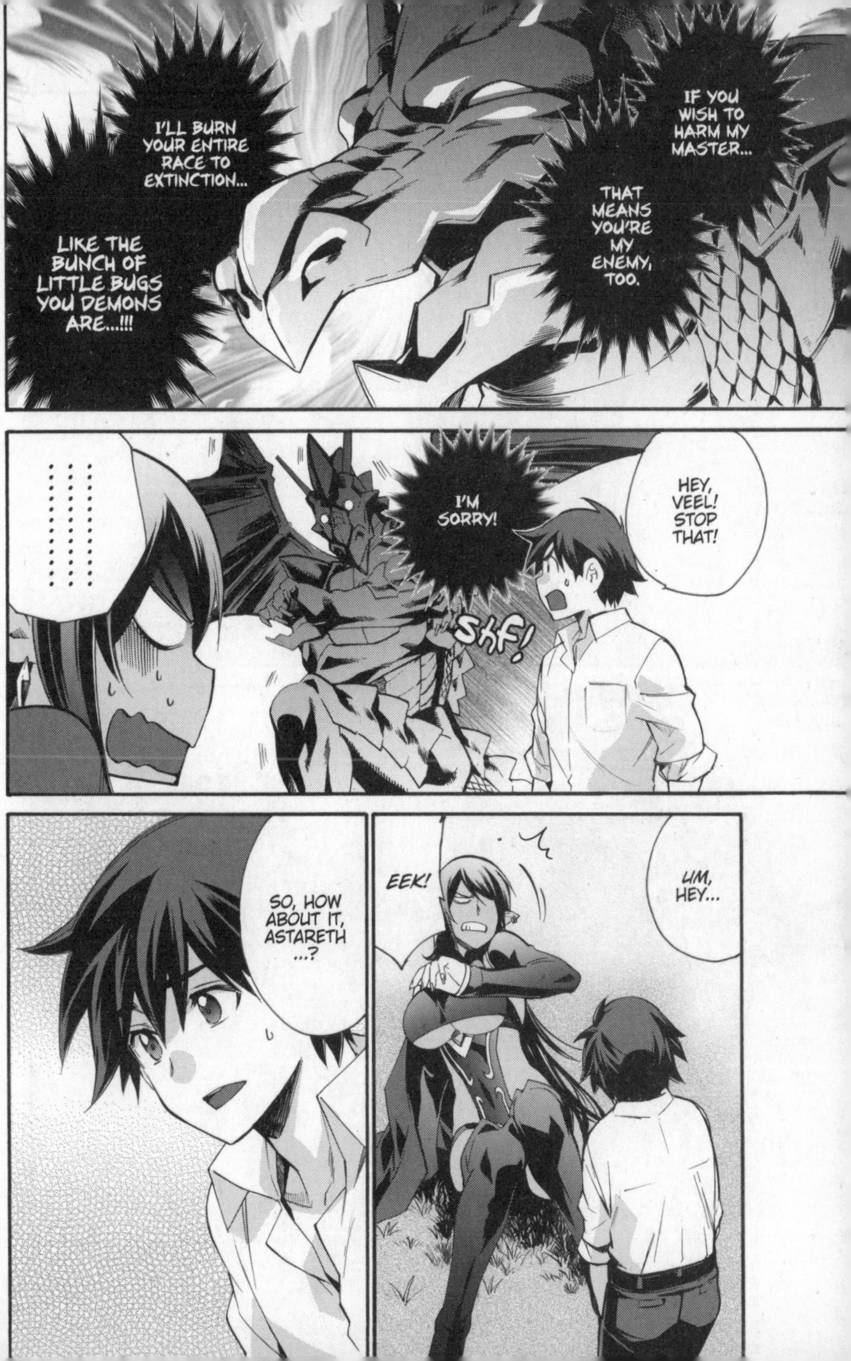
IF YOU WISH TO HARM MY MASTER...
THAT MEANS YOU'RE MY ENEMY, TOO.
I'LL BURN YOUR ENTIRE RACE TO EXTINCTION...
LIKE THE BUNCH OF LITTLE BUGS YOU DEMONS ARE...!!!
HEY, VEEL! STOP THAT!
I'M SORRY!
SHF!
......
UM, HEY...
EEK!
SO, HOW ABOUT IT, ASTARETH ...?

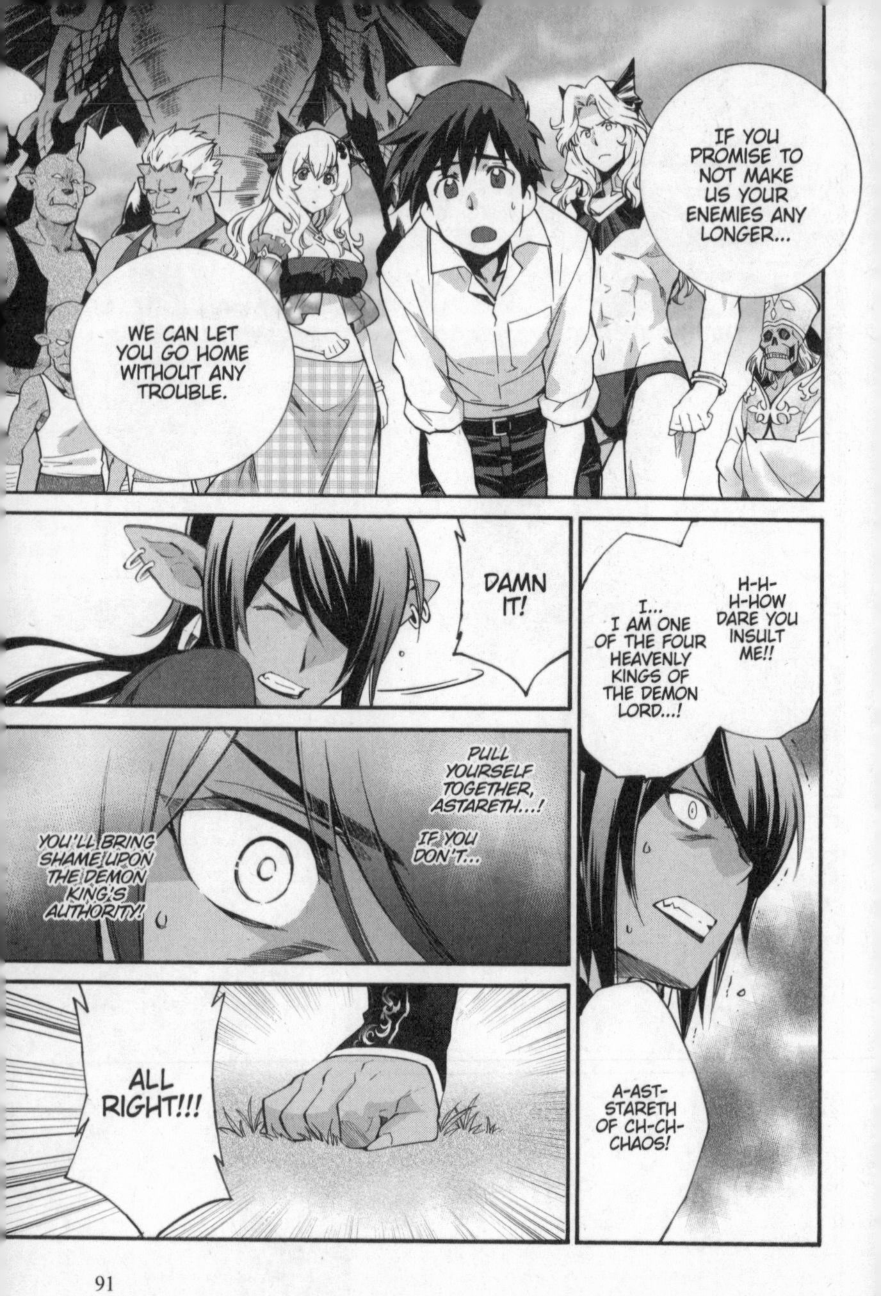
IF YOU PROMISE TO NOT MAKE US YOUR ENEMIES ANY LONGER...
WE CAN LET YOU GO HOME WITHOUT ANY TROUBLE.
H-H-H-HOW DARE YOU INSULT ME!!
I... I AM ONE OF THE FOUR HEAVENLY KINGS OF THE DEMON LORD...!
A-AST-STARETH OF CH-CH-CHAOS!
DAMN IT!
PULL YOURSELF TOGETHER, ASTARETH...!
IF YOU DON'T...
YOU'LL BRING SHAME UPON THE DEMON KING'S AUTHORITY!
ALL RIGHT!!!

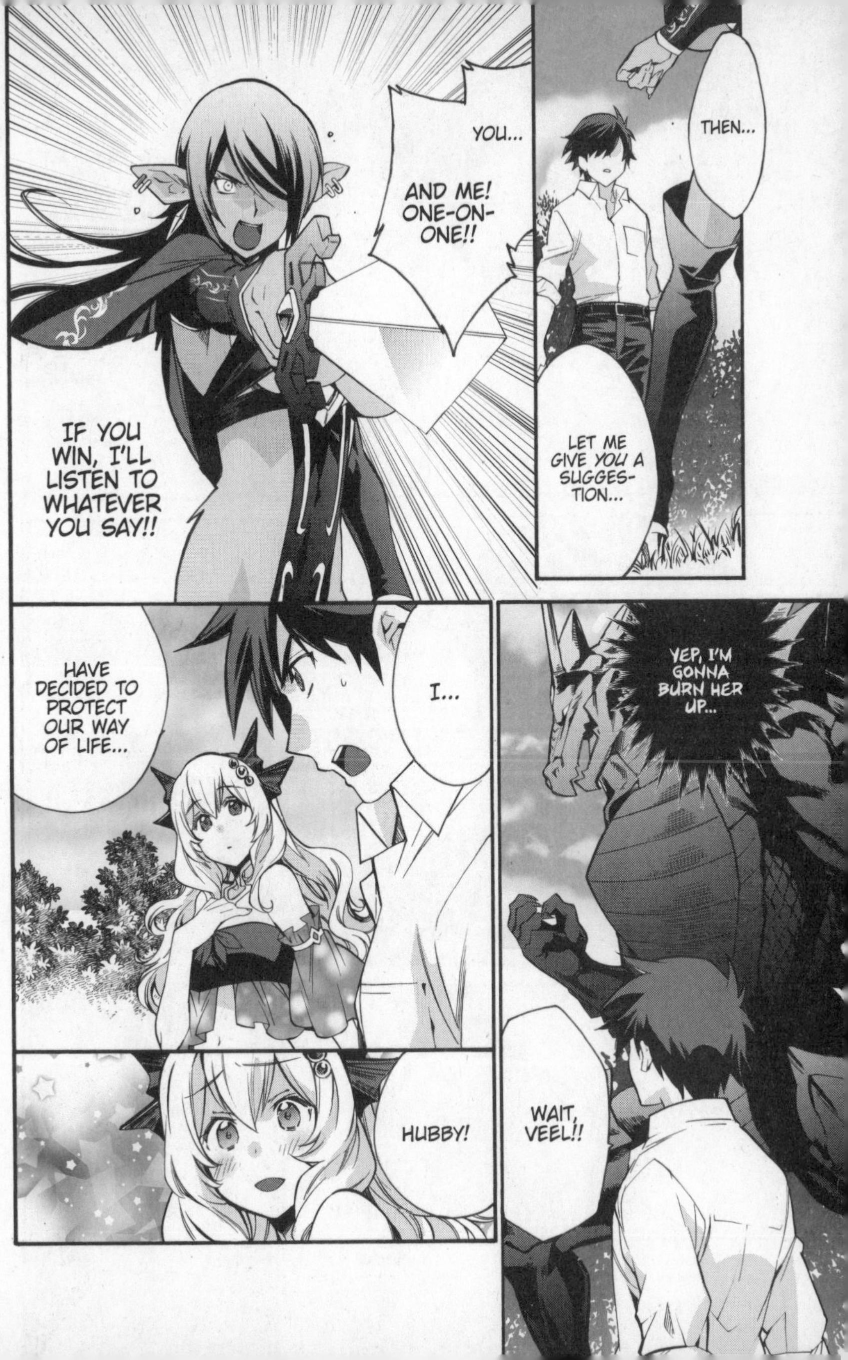
THEN...
LET ME GIVE YOU A SUGGES-TION...
YOU...
AND ME! ONE-ON-ONE!!
IF YOU WIN, I'LL LISTEN TO WHATEVER YOU SAY!!
YEP, I'M GONNA BURN HER UP...
WAIT, VEEL!!
I...
HAVE DECIDED TO PROTECT OUR WAY OF LIFE...
HUBBY!

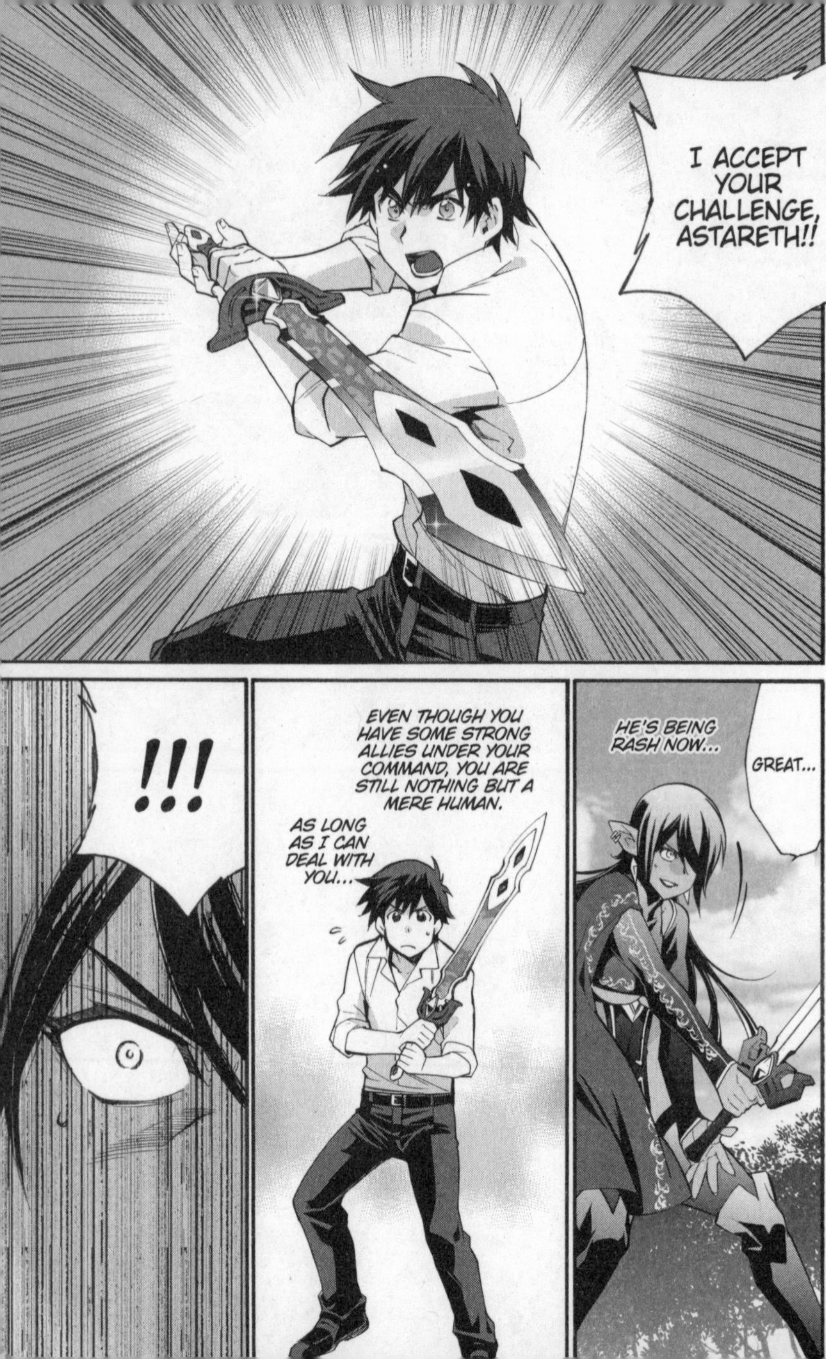
I ACCEPT YOUR CHALLENGE, ASTARETH!!
GREAT...
HE'S BEING RASH NOW...
EVEN THOUGH YOU HAVE SOME STRONG ALLIES UNDER YOUR COMMAND, YOU ARE STILL NOTHING BUT A MERE HUMAN.
AS LONG AS I CAN DEAL WITH YOU...
!!!

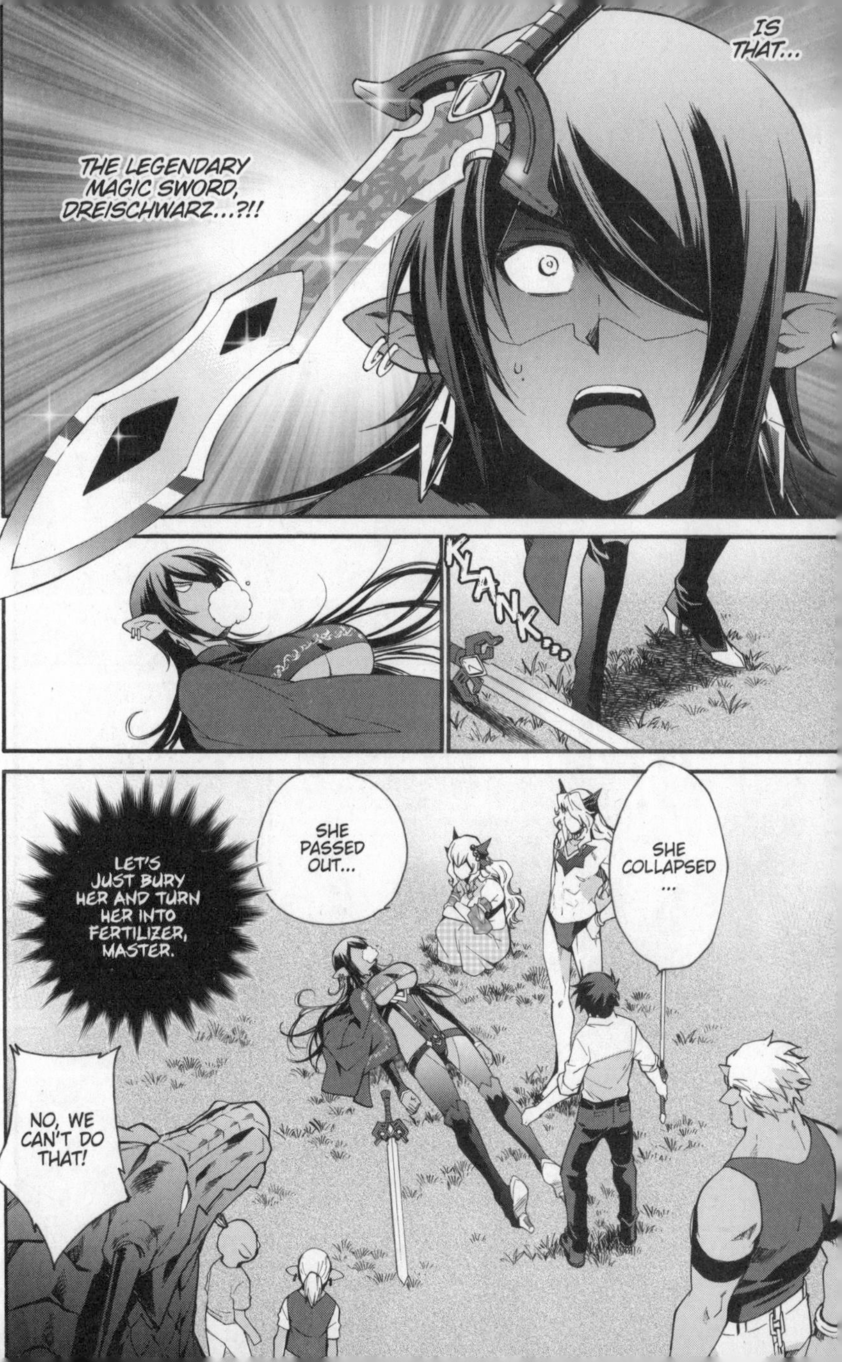
IS THAT...
THE LEGENDARY MAGIC SWORD, DREISCHWARZ...?!!
KLANK...
SHE COLLAPSED ...
SHE PASSED OUT...
LET'S JUST BURY HER AND TURN HER INTO FERTILIZER, MASTER.
NO, WE CAN'T DO THAT!

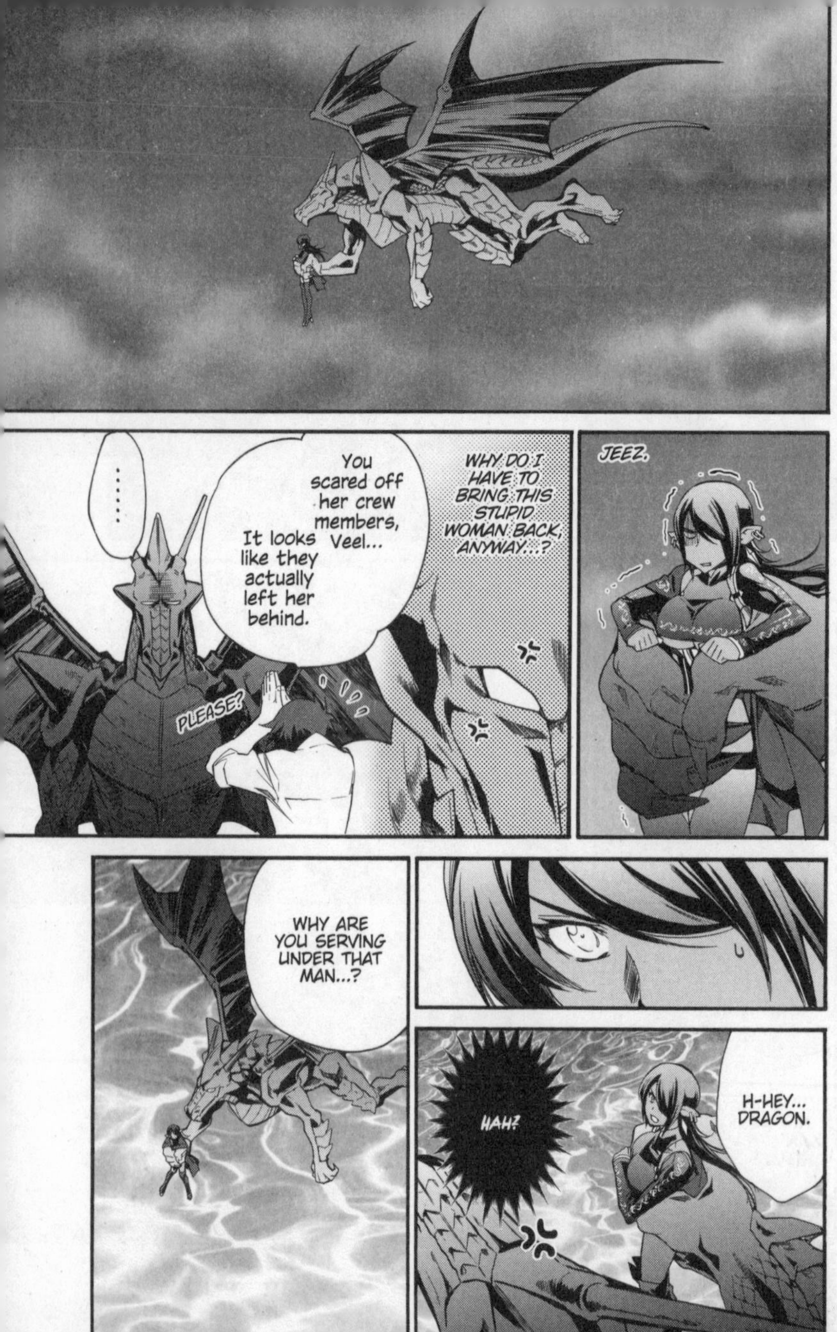
JEEZ.
WHY DO I HAVE TO BRING THIS STUPID WOMAN BACK, ANYWAY...?
You scared off her crew members, Veel...
It looks like they actually left her behind.
......
PLEASE?
H-HEY... DRAGON.
HAH?
WHY ARE YOU SERVING UNDER THAT MAN...?

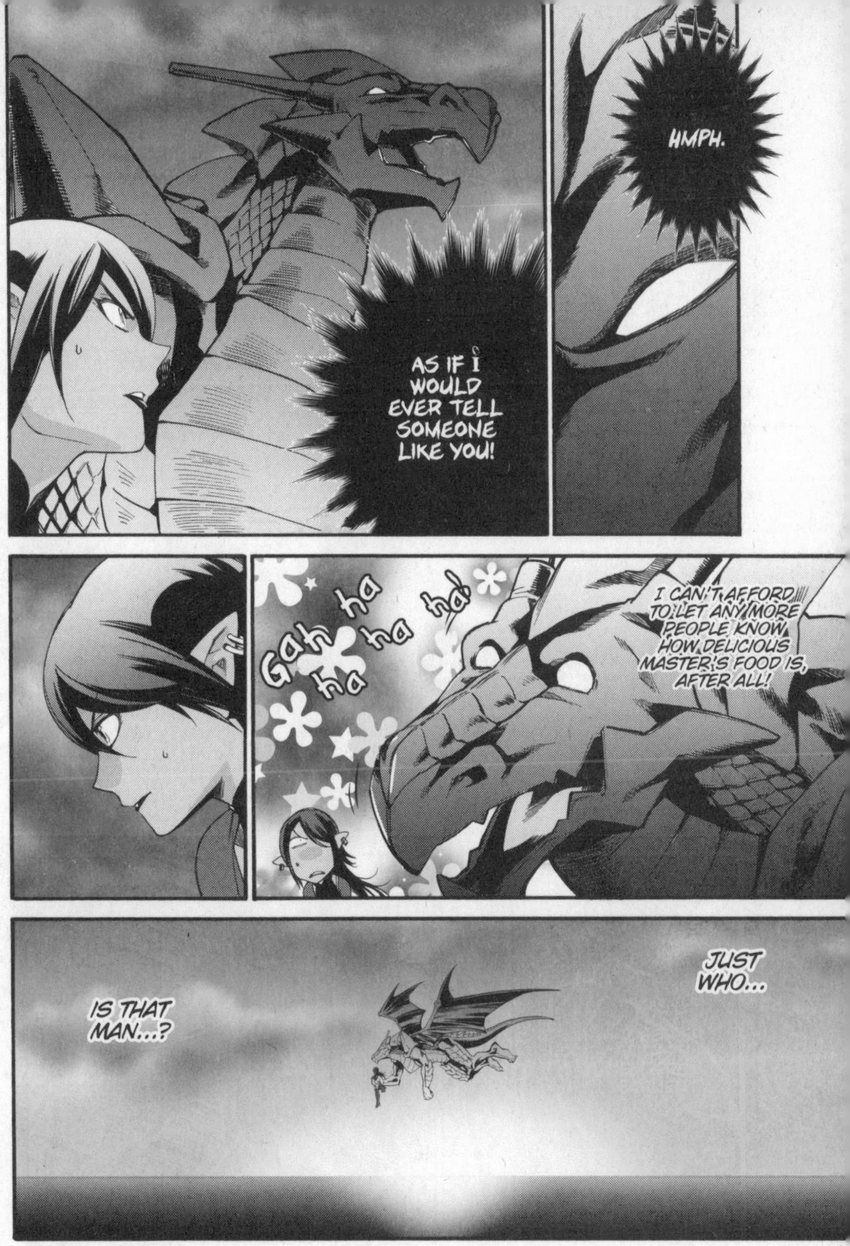
HMPH.
AS IF I WOULD EVER TELL SOMEONE LIKE YOU!
I CAN'T AFFORD TO LET ANY MORE PEOPLE KNOW HOW DELICIOUS MASTER'S FOOD IS, AFTER ALL!
Gah ha ha ha ha ha!
JUST WHO...
IS THAT MAN...?

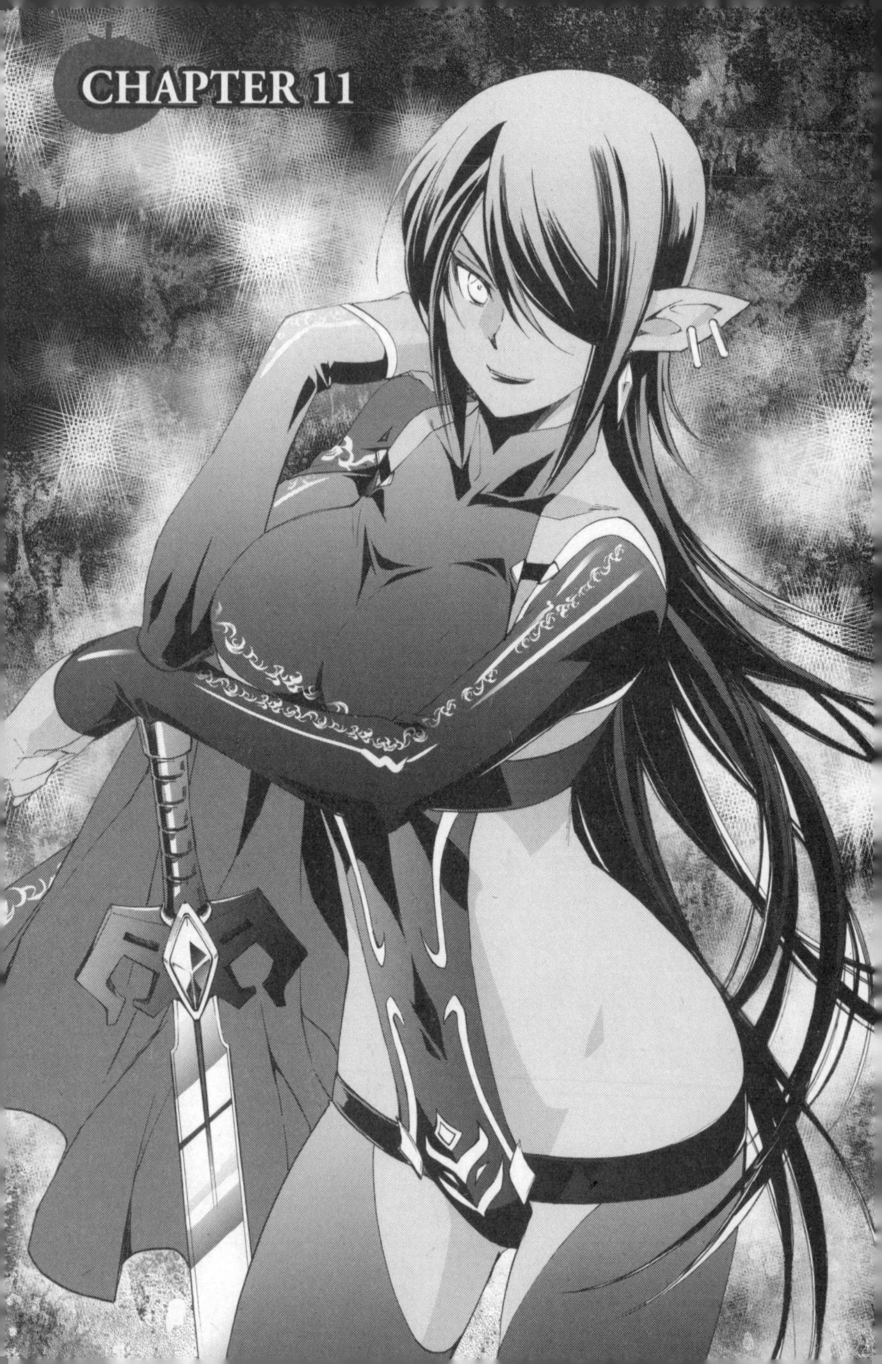
CHAPTER 11

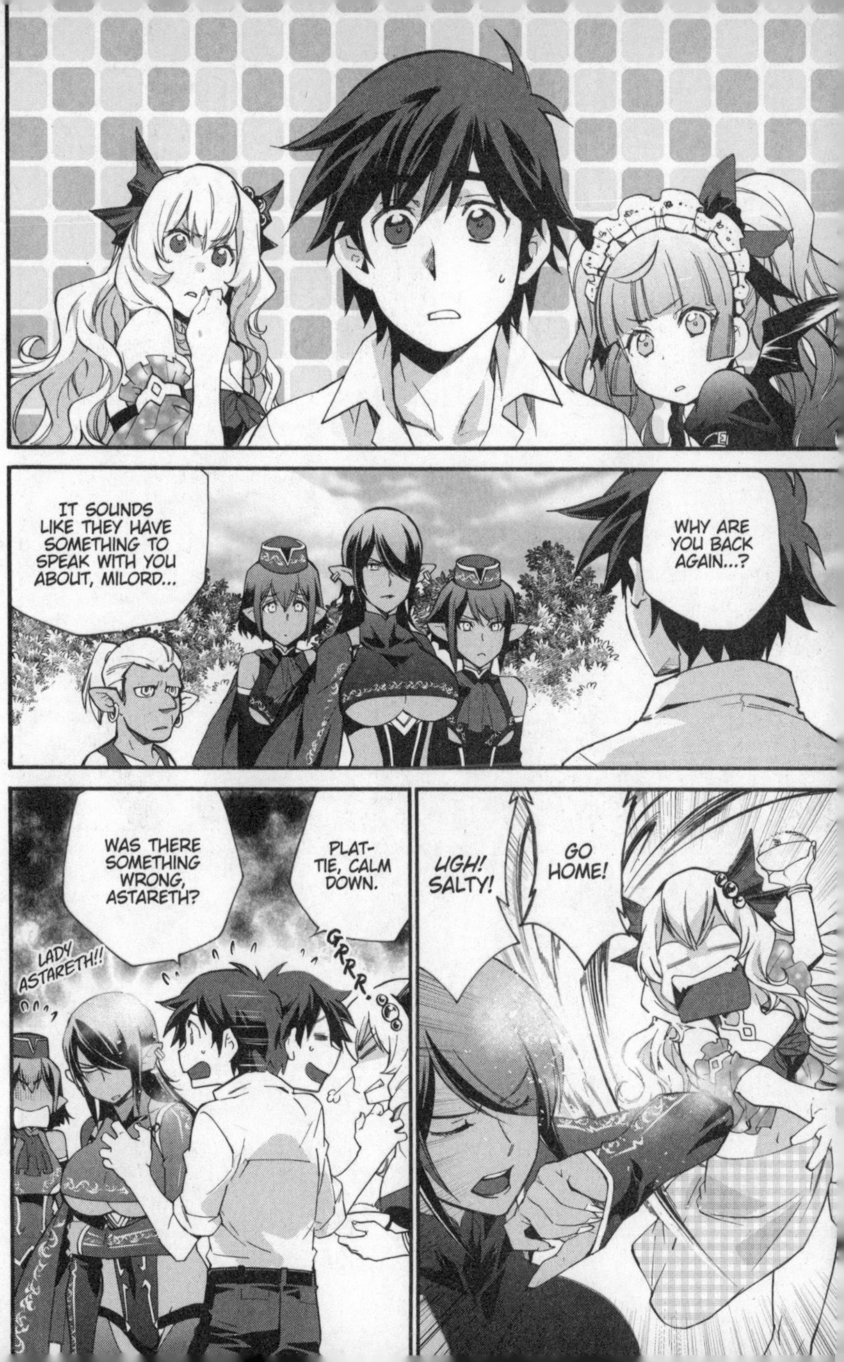
WHY ARE YOU BACK AGAIN...?
IT SOUNDS LIKE THEY HAVE SOMETHING TO SPEAK WITH YOU ABOUT, MILORD...
GO HOME!
UGH! SALTY!
PLAT-TIE, CALM DOWN.
GRRR.
WAS THERE SOMETHING WRONG, ASTARETH?
LADY ASTARETH!!

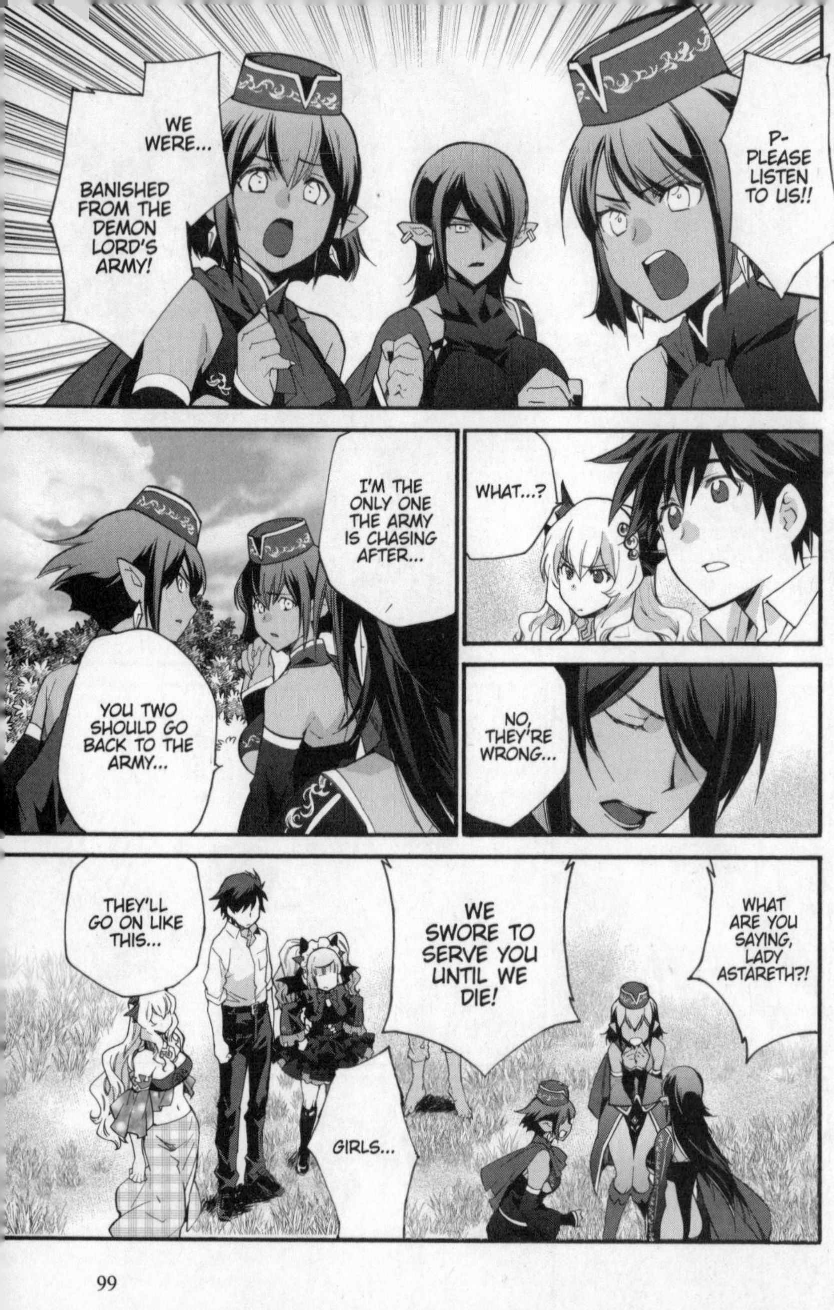
P-PLEASE LISTEN TO US!!
WE WERE...
BANISHED FROM THE DEMON LORD'S ARMY!
WHAT...?
NO, THEY'RE WRONG...
I'M THE ONLY ONE THE ARMY IS CHASING AFTER...
YOU TWO SHOULD GO BACK TO THE ARMY...
WHAT ARE YOU SAYING, LADY ASTARETH?!
WE SWORE TO SERVE YOU UNTIL WE DIE!
THEY'LL GO ON LIKE THIS...
GIRLS...

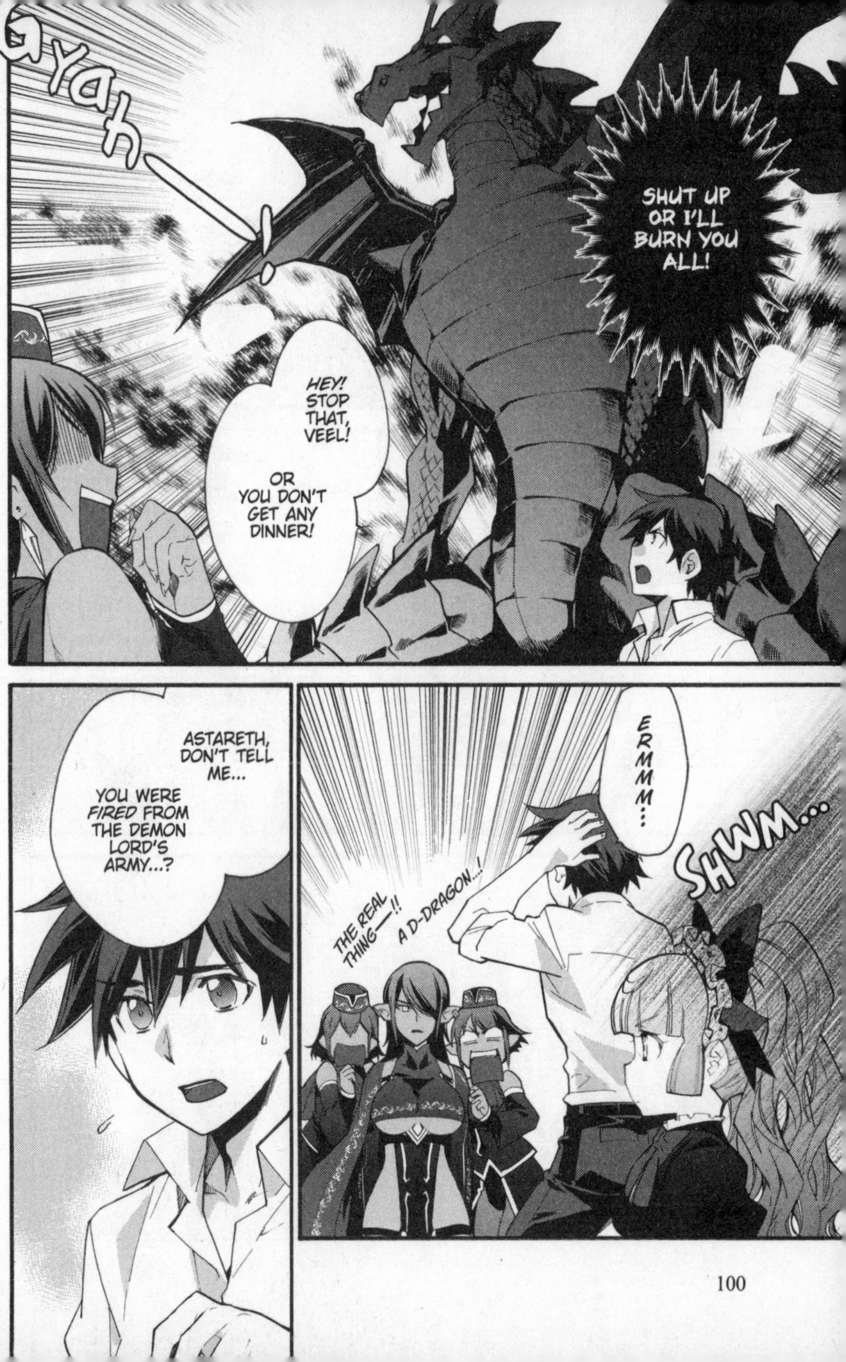
SHUT UP OR I'LL BURN YOU ALL!
GYAH—
HEY! STOP THAT, VEEL!
OR YOU DON'T GET ANY DINNER!
SHWM...
ERMMM...
A D-DRAGON...!
THE REAL THING—!!
ASTARETH, DON'T TELL ME...
YOU WERE *FIRED* FROM THE DEMON LORD'S ARMY...?

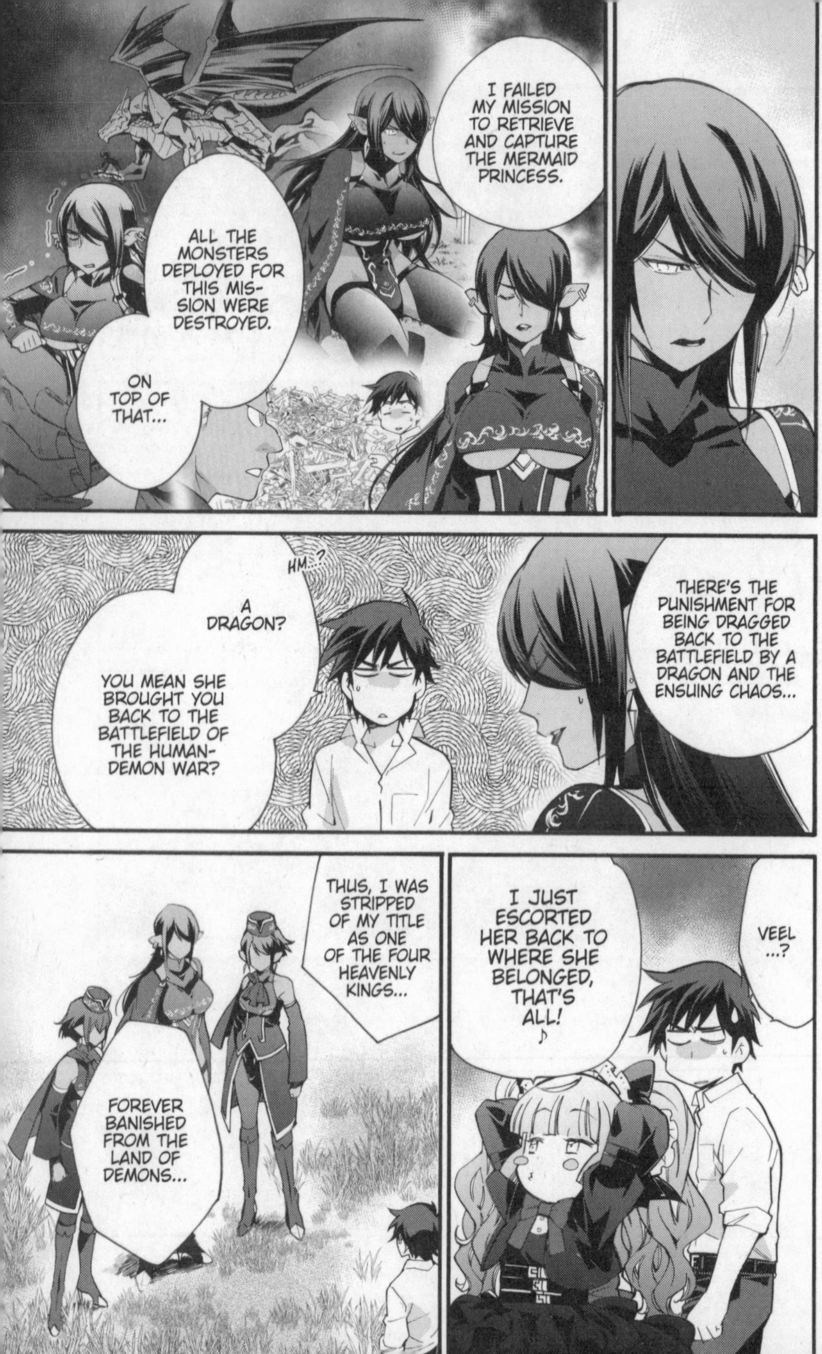
I FAILED MY MISSION TO RETRIEVE AND CAPTURE THE MERMAID PRINCESS.
ALL THE MONSTERS DEPLOYED FOR THIS MISSION WERE DESTROYED.
ON TOP OF THAT...
THERE'S THE PUNISHMENT FOR BEING DRAGGED BACK TO THE BATTLEFIELD BY A DRAGON AND THE ENSUING CHAOS...
HM...?
A DRAGON?
YOU MEAN SHE BROUGHT YOU BACK TO THE BATTLEFIELD OF THE HUMAN-DEMON WAR?
VEEL ...?
I JUST ESCORTED HER BACK TO WHERE SHE BELONGED, THAT'S ALL! ♪
THUS, I WAS STRIPPED OF MY TITLE AS ONE OF THE FOUR HEAVENLY KINGS...
FOREVER BANISHED FROM THE LAND OF DEMONS...

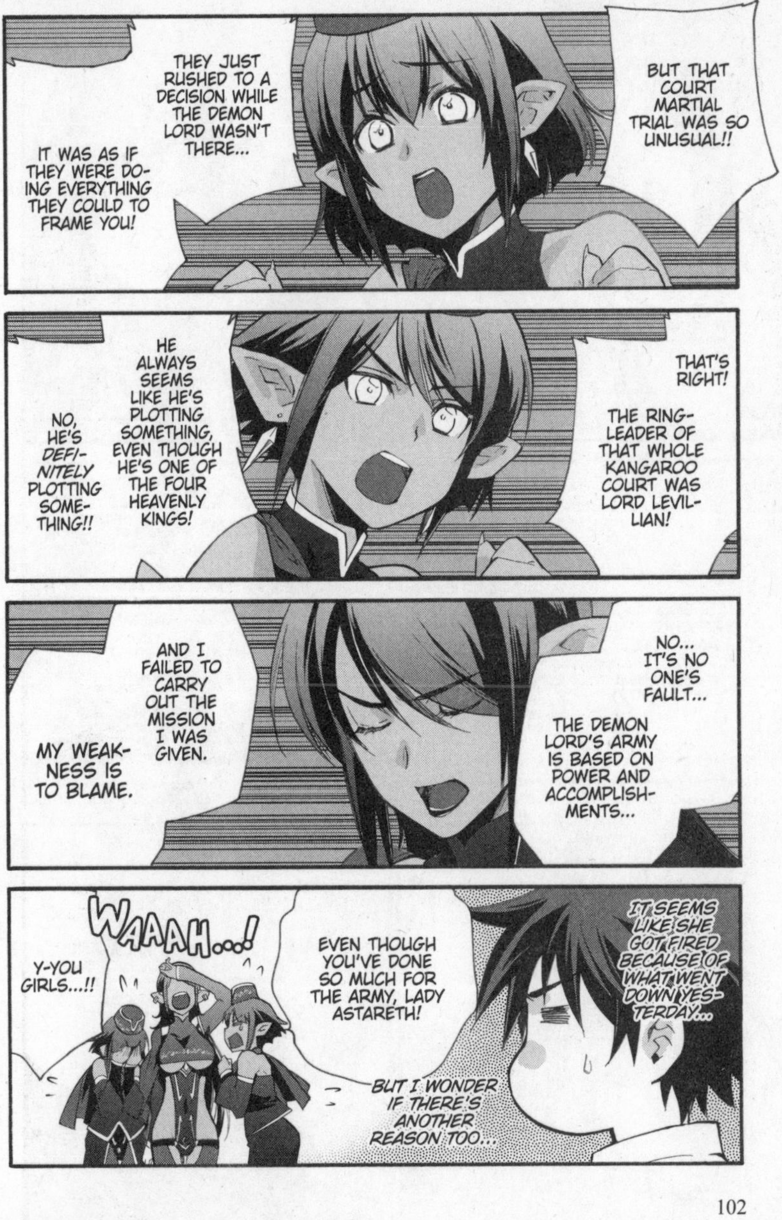
BUT THAT COURT MARTIAL TRIAL WAS SO UNUSUAL!!
THEY JUST RUSHED TO A DECISION WHILE THE DEMON LORD WASN'T THERE...
IT WAS AS IF THEY WERE DOING EVERYTHING THEY COULD TO FRAME YOU!
THAT'S RIGHT!
THE RINGLEADER OF THAT WHOLE KANGAROO COURT WAS LORD LEVILLIAN!
HE ALWAYS SEEMS LIKE HE'S PLOTTING SOMETHING, EVEN THOUGH HE'S ONE OF THE FOUR HEAVENLY KINGS!
NO, HE'S *DEFINITELY* PLOTTING SOMETHING!!
NO... IT'S NO ONE'S FAULT...
THE DEMON LORD'S ARMY IS BASED ON POWER AND ACCOMPLISHMENTS...
AND I FAILED TO CARRY OUT THE MISSION I WAS GIVEN.
MY WEAKNESS IS TO BLAME.
IT SEEMS LIKE SHE GOT FIRED BECAUSE OF WHAT WENT DOWN YESTERDAY...
BUT I WONDER IF THERE'S ANOTHER REASON TOO...
EVEN THOUGH YOU'VE DONE SO MUCH FOR THE ARMY, LADY ASTARETH!
WAAAH...!
Y-YOU GIRLS...!!

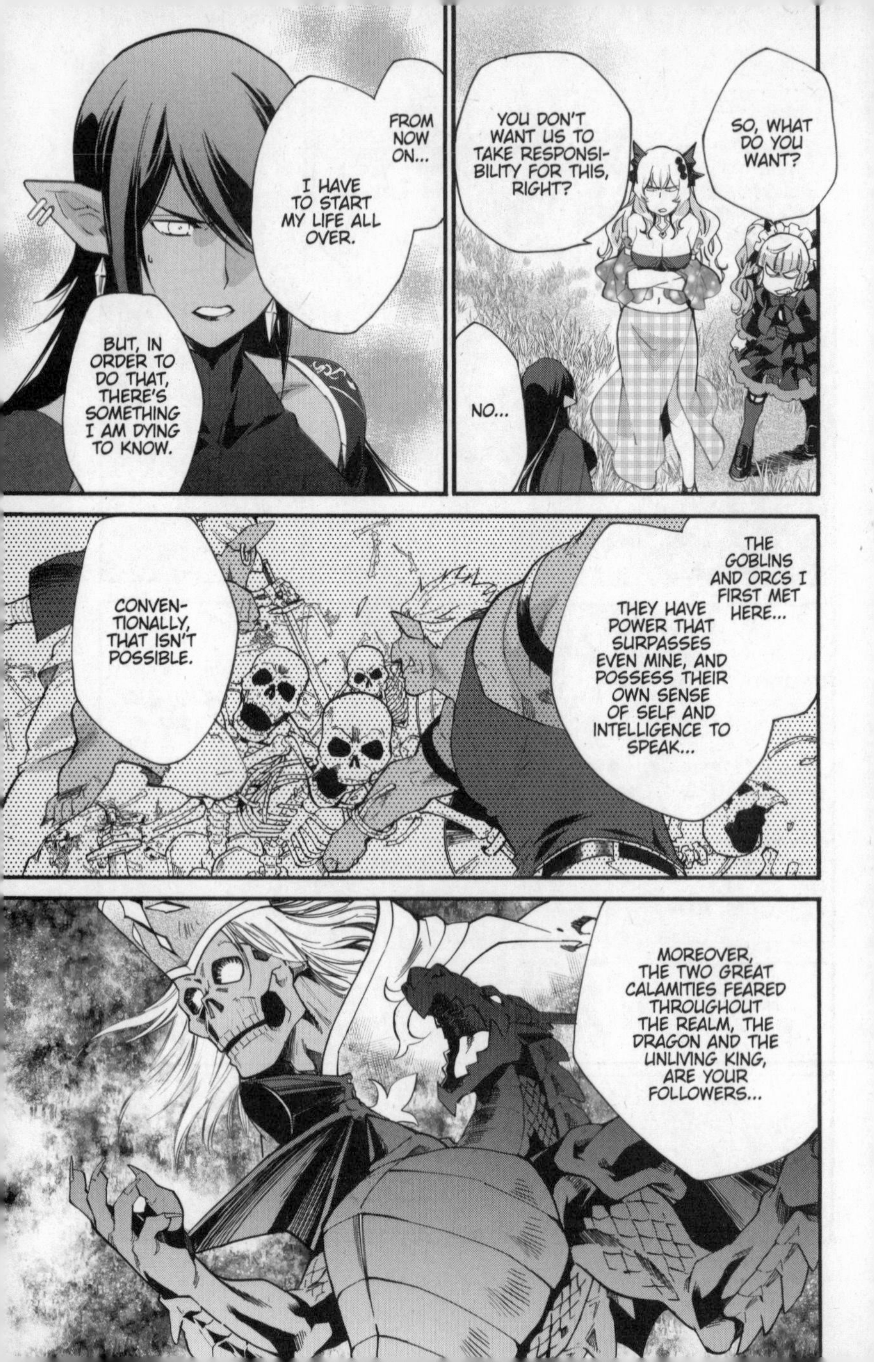
SO, WHAT DO YOU WANT?
YOU DON'T WANT US TO TAKE RESPONSIBILITY FOR THIS, RIGHT?
NO...
FROM NOW ON...
I HAVE TO START MY LIFE ALL OVER.
BUT, IN ORDER TO DO THAT, THERE'S SOMETHING I AM DYING TO KNOW.
THE GOBLINS AND ORCS I FIRST MET HERE...
THEY HAVE POWER THAT SURPASSES EVEN MINE, AND POSSESS THEIR OWN SENSE OF SELF AND INTELLIGENCE TO SPEAK...
CONVENTIONALLY, THAT ISN'T POSSIBLE.
MOREOVER, THE TWO GREAT CALAMITIES FEARED THROUGHOUT THE REALM, THE DRAGON AND THE UNLIVING KING, ARE YOUR FOLLOWERS...

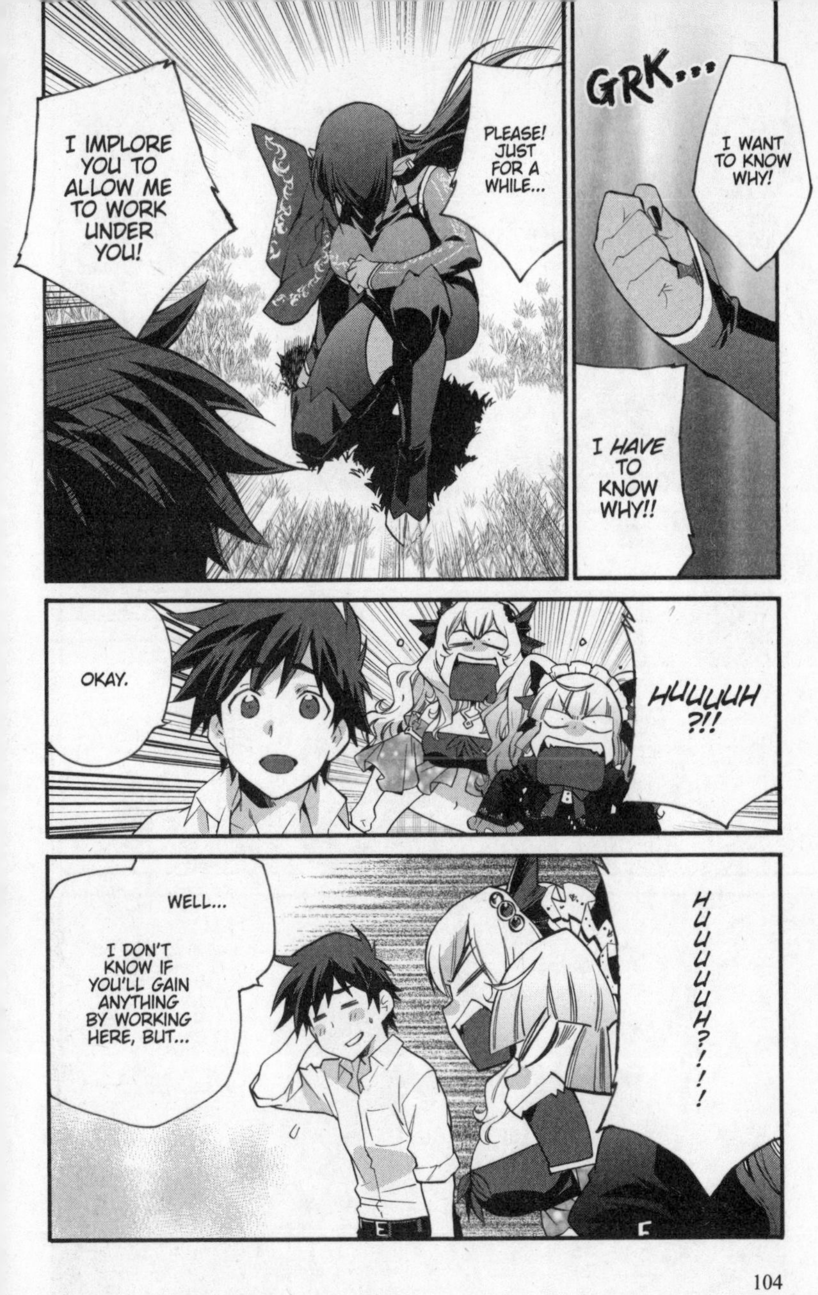
GRK...
I WANT TO KNOW WHY!
I HAVE TO KNOW WHY!!
PLEASE! JUST FOR A WHILE...
I IMPLORE YOU TO ALLOW ME TO WORK UNDER YOU!
HUUUUH ?!!
OKAY.
HUUUUUH?!!!
WELL...
I DON'T KNOW IF YOU'LL GAIN ANYTHING BY WORKING HERE, BUT...

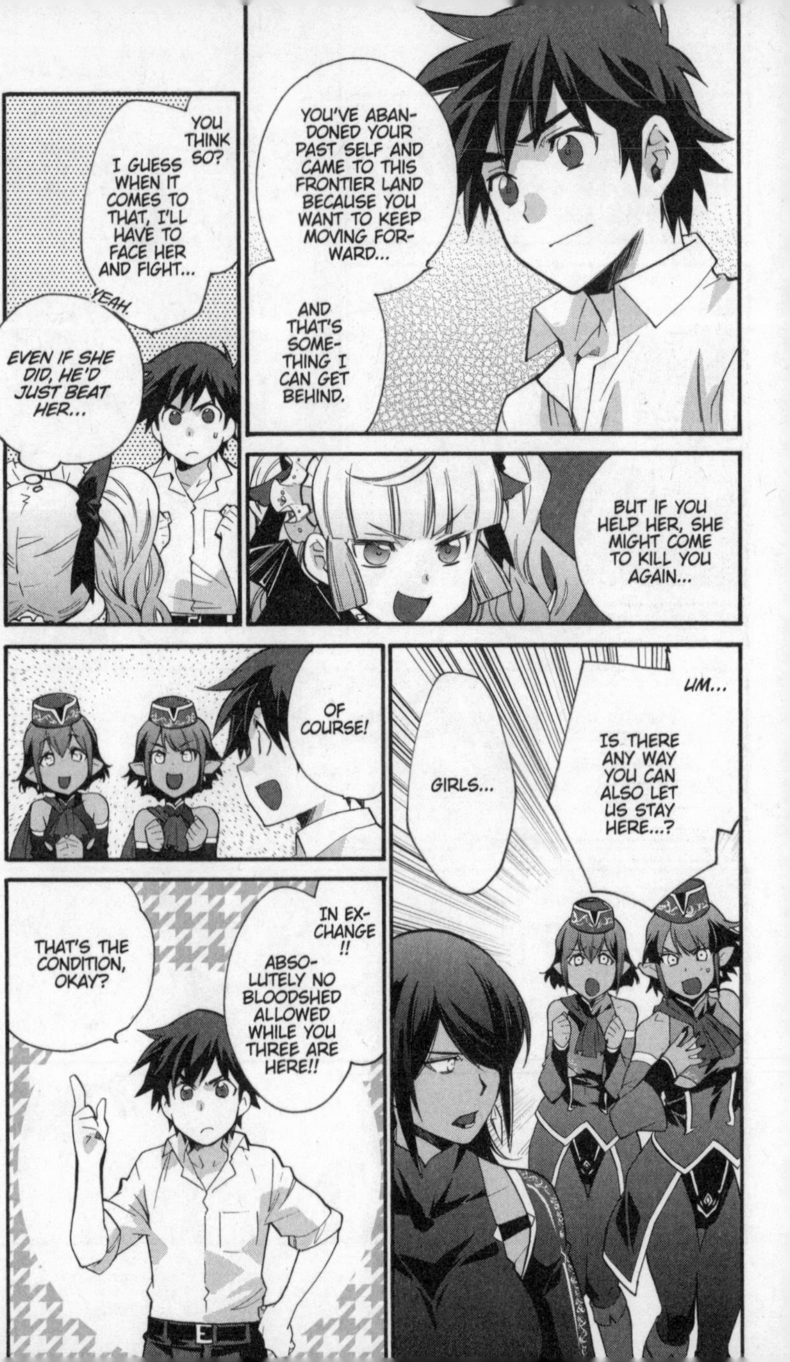
YOU'VE ABANDONED YOUR PAST SELF AND CAME TO THIS FRONTIER LAND BECAUSE YOU WANT TO KEEP MOVING FORWARD...
AND THAT'S SOMETHING I CAN GET BEHIND.
BUT IF YOU HELP HER, SHE MIGHT COME TO KILL YOU AGAIN...
YOU THINK SO?
I GUESS WHEN IT COMES TO THAT, I'LL HAVE TO FACE HER AND FIGHT...
YEAH.
EVEN IF SHE DID, HE'D JUST BEAT HER...
UM...
GIRLS...
IS THERE ANY WAY YOU CAN ALSO LET US STAY HERE...?
OF COURSE!
IN EXCHANGE!!
ABSOLUTELY NO BLOODSHED ALLOWED WHILE YOU THREE ARE HERE!!
THAT'S THE CONDITION, OKAY?

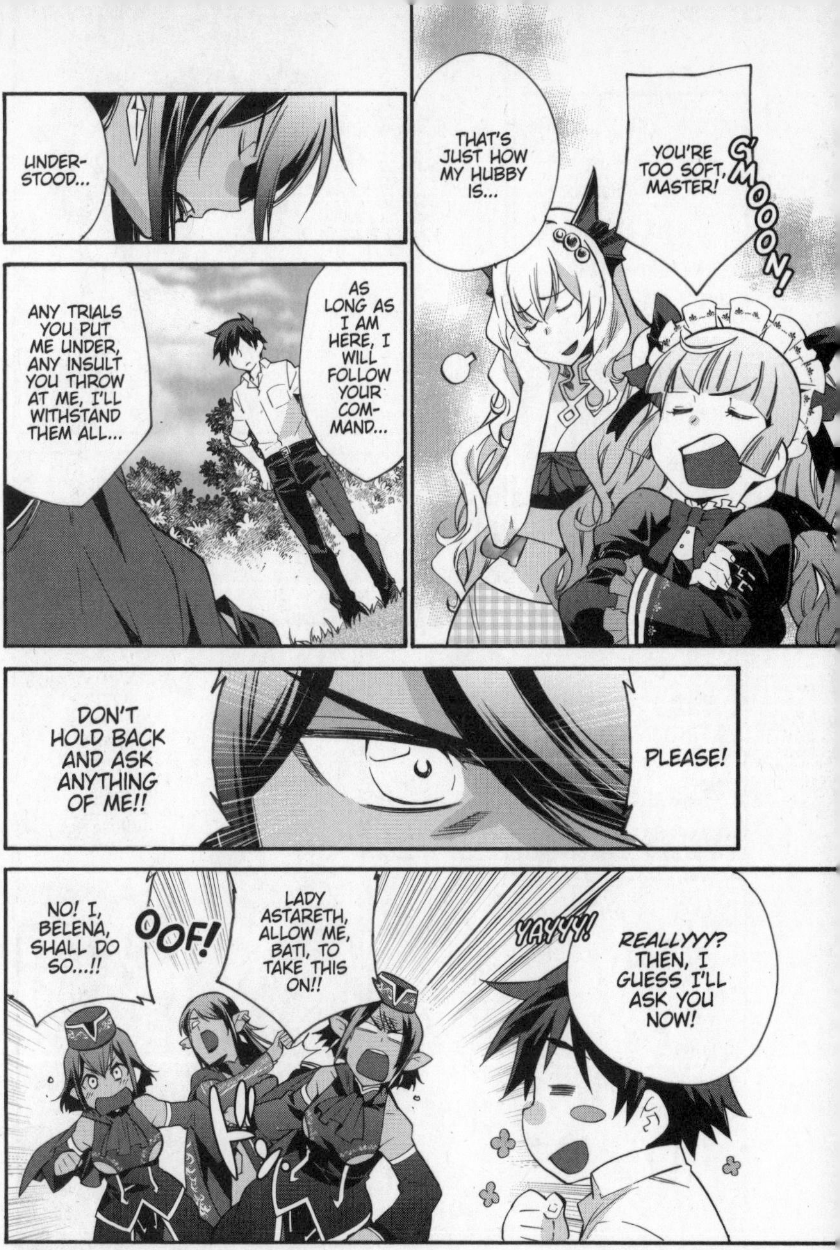
YOU'RE TOO SOFT, MASTER!
G'MOOON!
THAT'S JUST HOW MY HUBBY IS...
UNDERSTOOD...
AS LONG AS I AM HERE, I WILL FOLLOW YOUR COMMAND...
ANY TRIALS YOU PUT ME UNDER, ANY INSULT YOU THROW AT ME, I'LL WITHSTAND THEM ALL...
PLEASE!
DON'T HOLD BACK AND ASK ANYTHING OF ME!!
REALLYYY? THEN, I GUESS I'LL ASK YOU NOW!
YAYYY!
LADY ASTARETH, ALLOW ME, BATI, TO TAKE THIS ON!!
OOF!
NO! I, BELENA, SHALL DO SO...!!

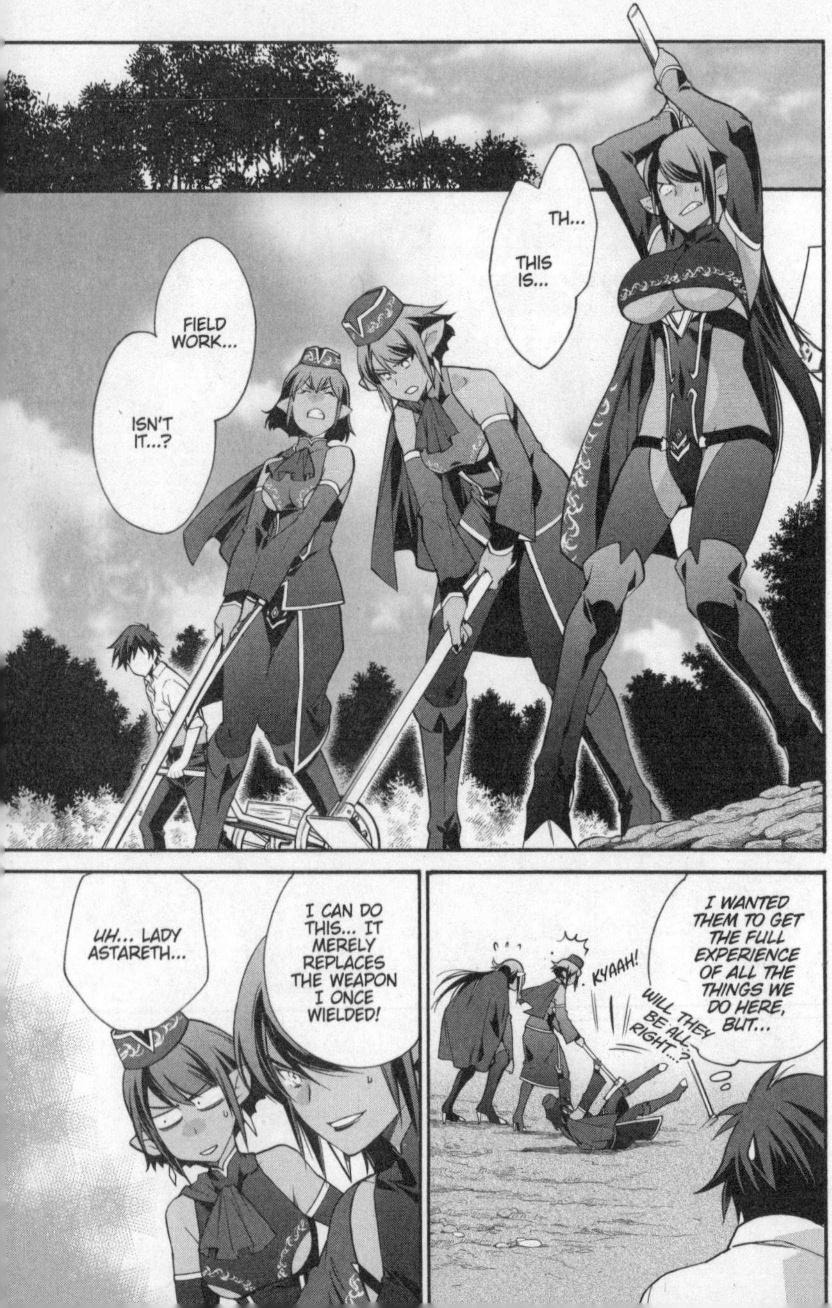
TH... THIS IS...
FIELD WORK... ISN'T IT...?
I WANTED THEM TO GET THE FULL EXPERIENCE OF ALL THE THINGS WE DO HERE, BUT...
WILL THEY BE ALL RIGHT...?
KYAAH!
I CAN DO THIS... IT MERELY REPLACES THE WEAPON I ONCE WIELDED!
UH... LADY ASTARETH...

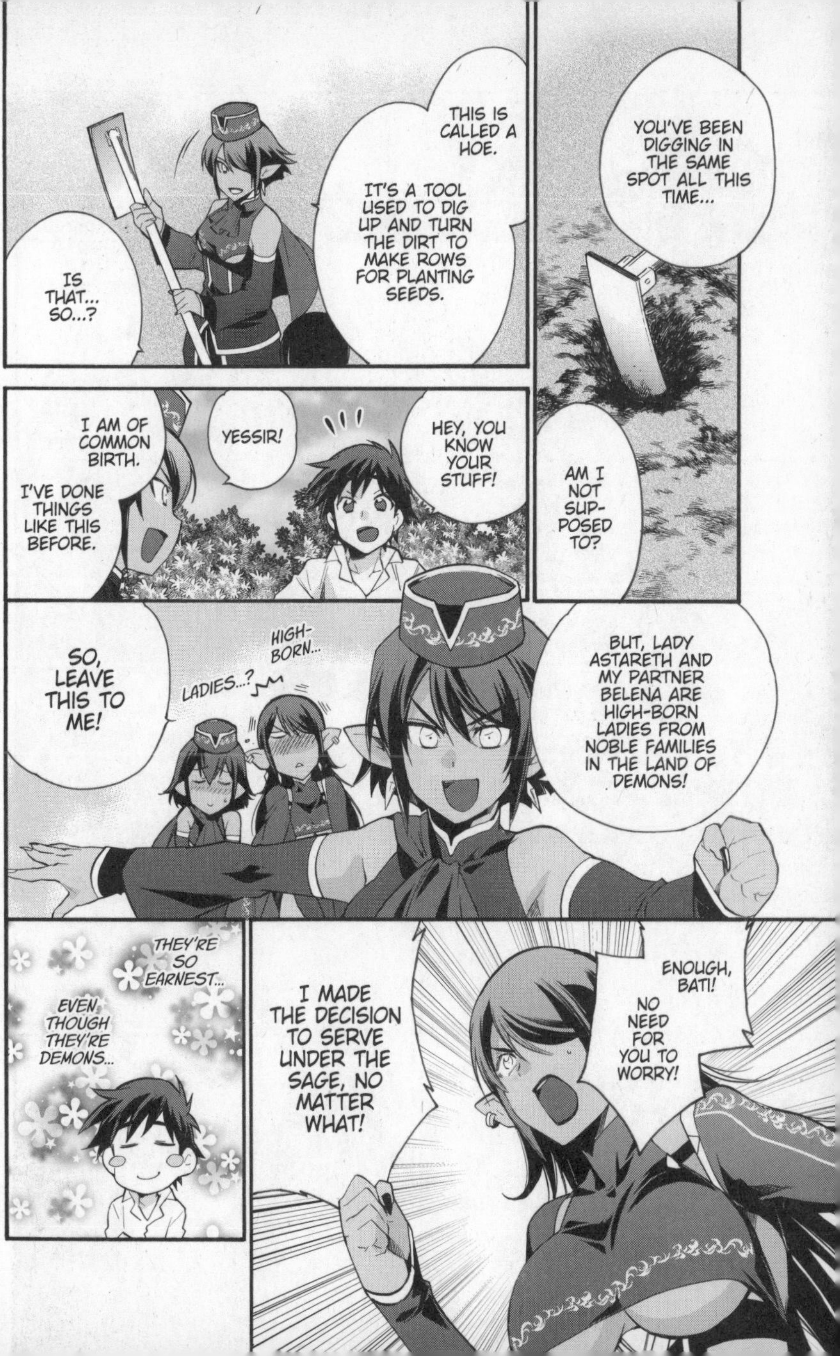
YOU'VE BEEN DIGGING IN THE SAME SPOT ALL THIS TIME...
AM I NOT SUP-POSED TO?
THIS IS CALLED A HOE.
IT'S A TOOL USED TO DIG UP AND TURN THE DIRT TO MAKE ROWS FOR PLANTING SEEDS.
IS THAT... SO...?
HEY, YOU KNOW YOUR STUFF!
YESSIR!
I AM OF COMMON BIRTH.
I'VE DONE THINGS LIKE THIS BEFORE.
BUT, LADY ASTARETH AND MY PARTNER BELENA ARE HIGH-BORN LADIES FROM NOBLE FAMILIES IN THE LAND OF DEMONS!
HIGH-BORN...
LADIES...?
SO, LEAVE THIS TO ME!
ENOUGH, BATI!
NO NEED FOR YOU TO WORRY!
I MADE THE DECISION TO SERVE UNDER THE SAGE, NO MATTER WHAT!
THEY'RE SO EARNEST...
EVEN THOUGH THEY'RE DEMONS...

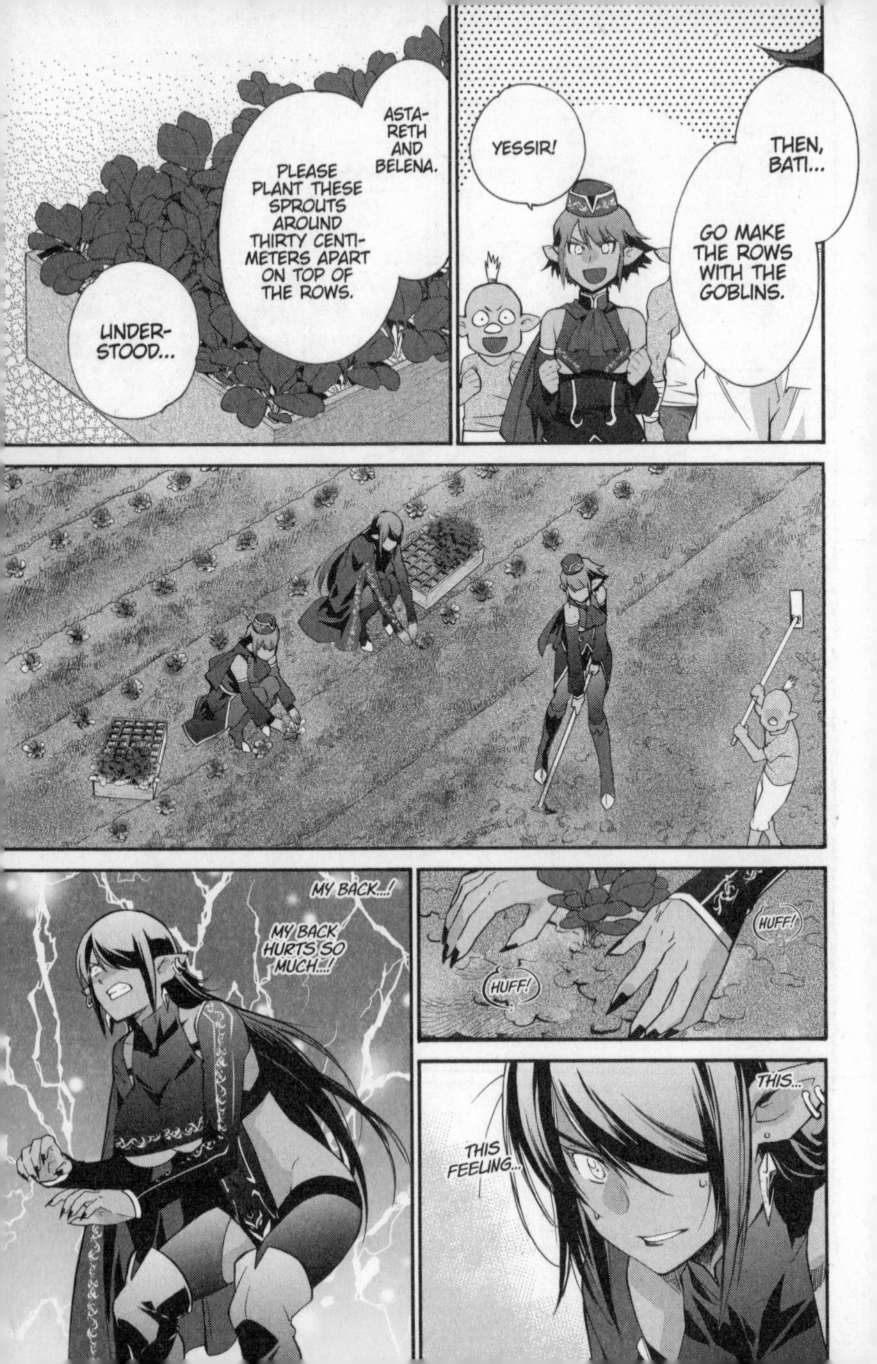
THEN, BATI...
GO MAKE THE ROWS WITH THE GOBLINS.
YESSIR!
ASTARETH AND BELENA.
PLEASE PLANT THESE SPROUTS AROUND THIRTY CENTIMETERS APART ON TOP OF THE ROWS.
UNDERSTOOD...
HUFF!
HUFF!
THIS...
THIS FEELING...
MY BACK...!
MY BACK HURTS SO MUCH...!

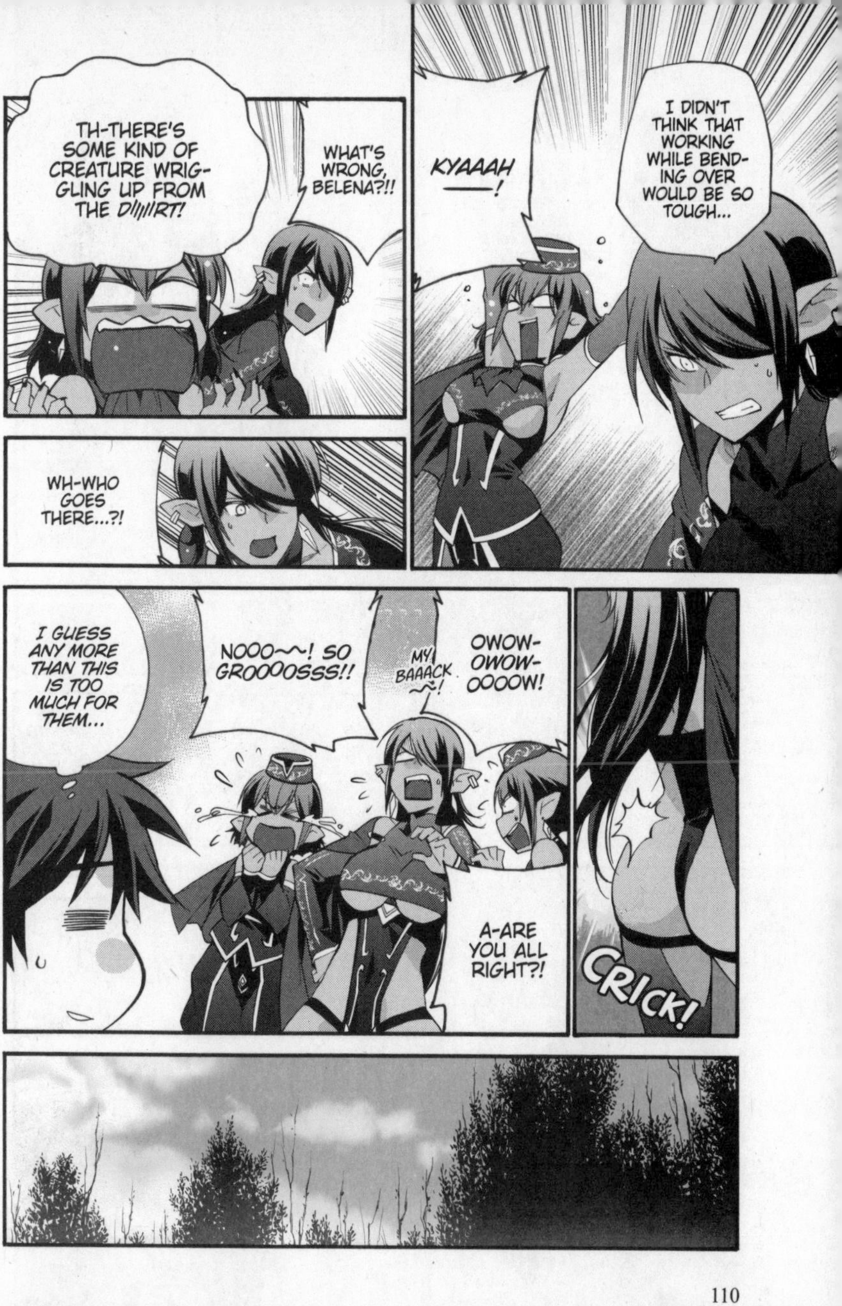
I DIDN'T THINK THAT WORKING WHILE BEND-ING OVER WOULD BE SO TOUGH...
KYAAAH ——!
WHAT'S WRONG, BELENA?!!
TH-THERE'S SOME KIND OF CREATURE WRIG-GLING UP FROM THE D////RT!
WH-WHO GOES THERE...?!
CRICK!
OWOW-OWOW-OOOOW!
MY BAAACK ~!
NOOO~~! SO GROOOOSSS!!
A-ARE YOU ALL RIGHT?!
I GUESS ANY MORE THAN THIS IS TOO MUCH FOR THEM...

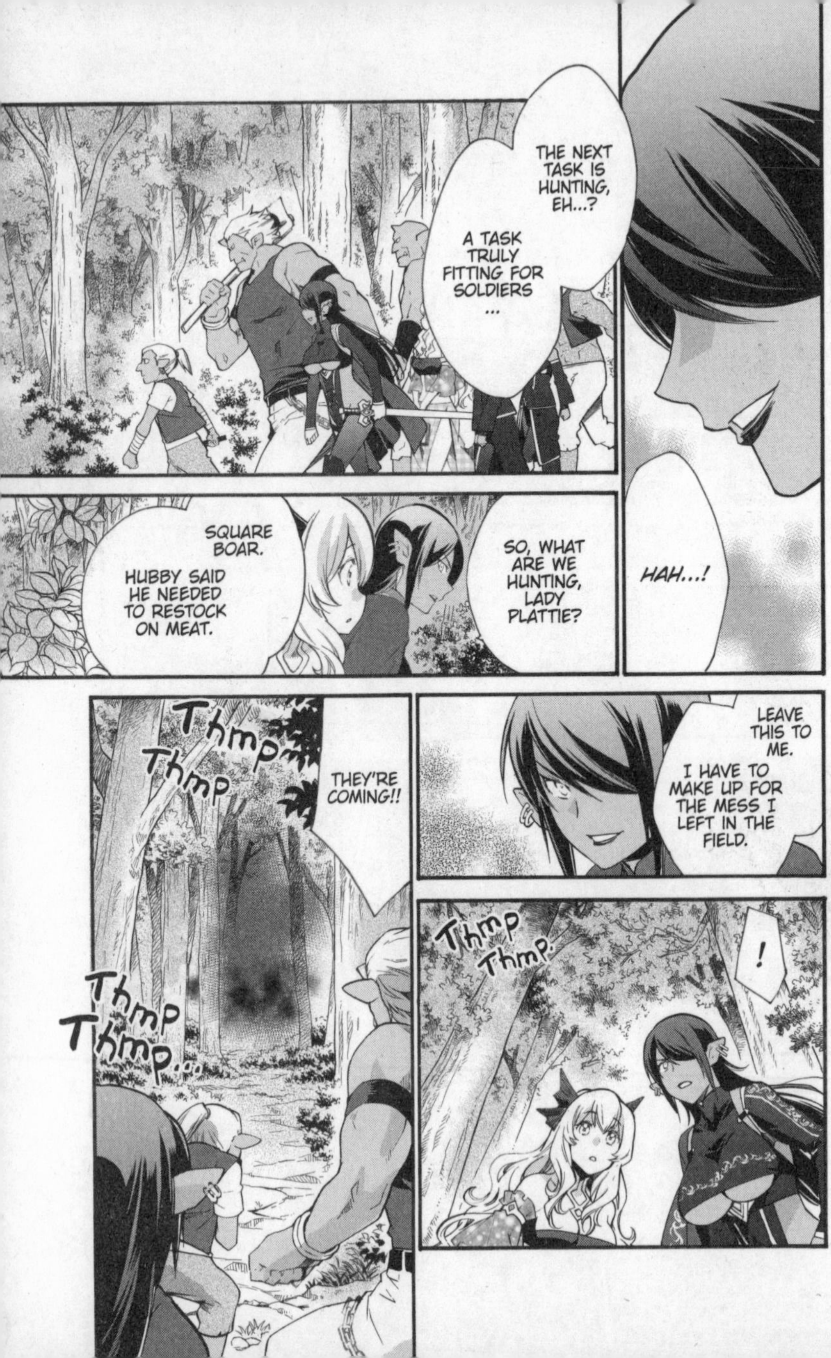
THE NEXT TASK IS HUNTING, EH...?
A TASK TRULY FITTING FOR SOLDIERS ...
HAH...!
SO, WHAT ARE WE HUNTING, LADY PLATTIE?
SQUARE BOAR.
HUBBY SAID HE NEEDED TO RESTOCK ON MEAT.
LEAVE THIS TO ME.
I HAVE TO MAKE UP FOR THE MESS I LEFT IN THE FIELD.
Thmp Thmp.
!
Thmp Thmp
THEY'RE COMING!!
Thmp Thmp...

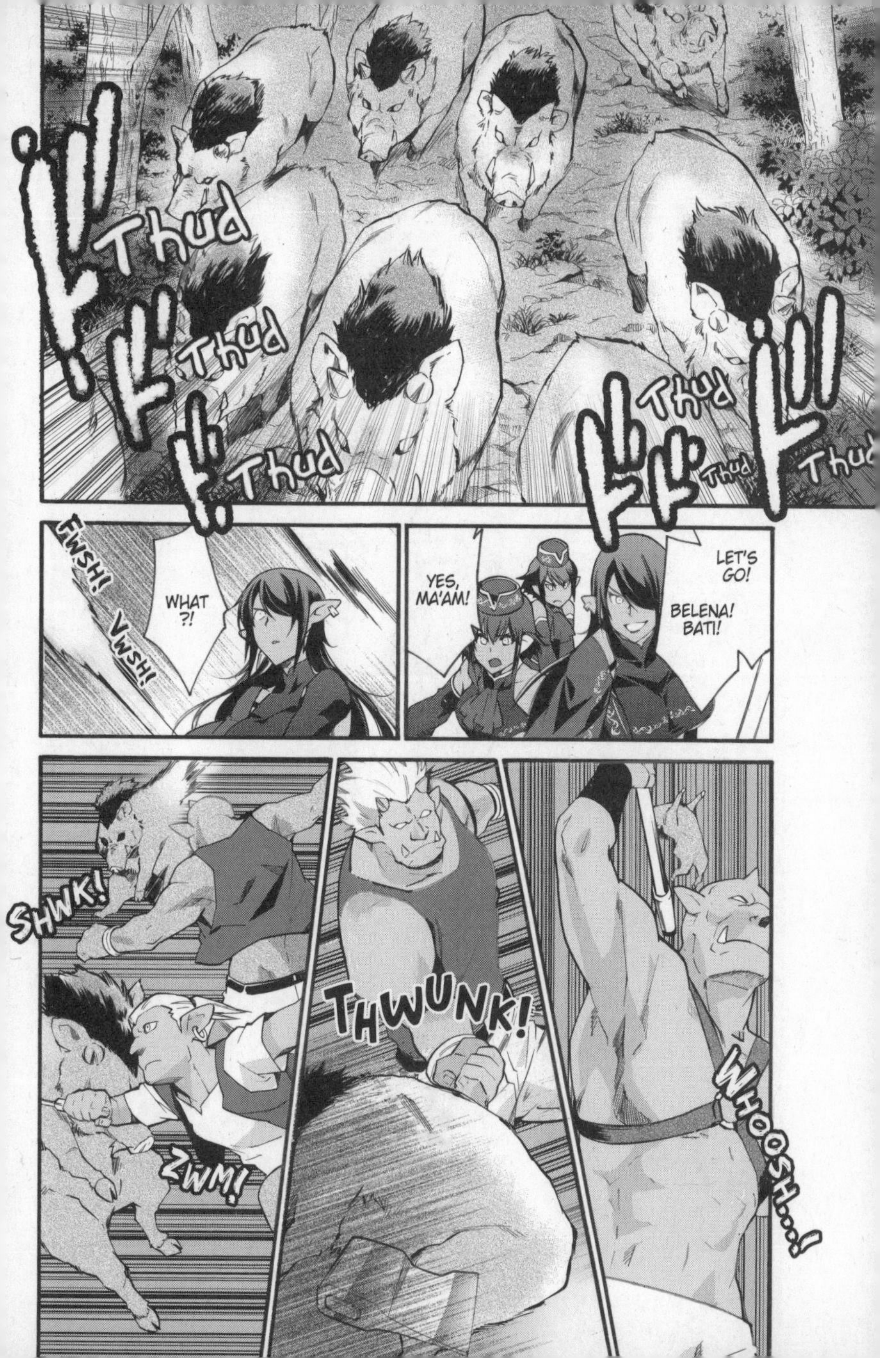
Thud
Thud
Thud
Thud
Thud
Thud
LET'S GO!
BELENA! BATI!
YES, MA'AM!
WHAT ?!
FWSH!
VWSH!
WHOOSH...!
THWUNK!
SHWK!
ZWM!

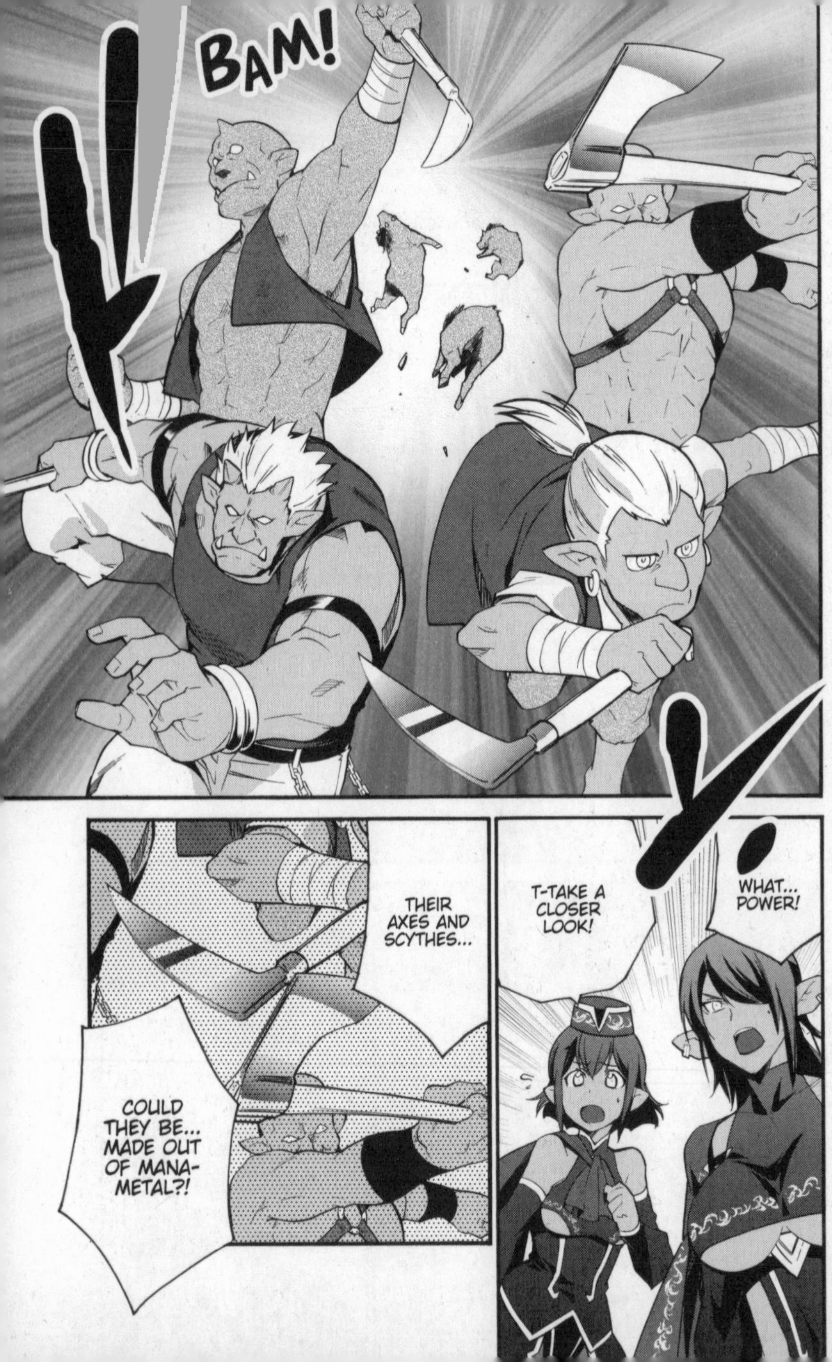
BAM!
WHAT... POWER!
T-TAKE A CLOSER LOOK!
THEIR AXES AND SCYTHES...
COULD THEY BE... MADE OUT OF MANA-METAL?!

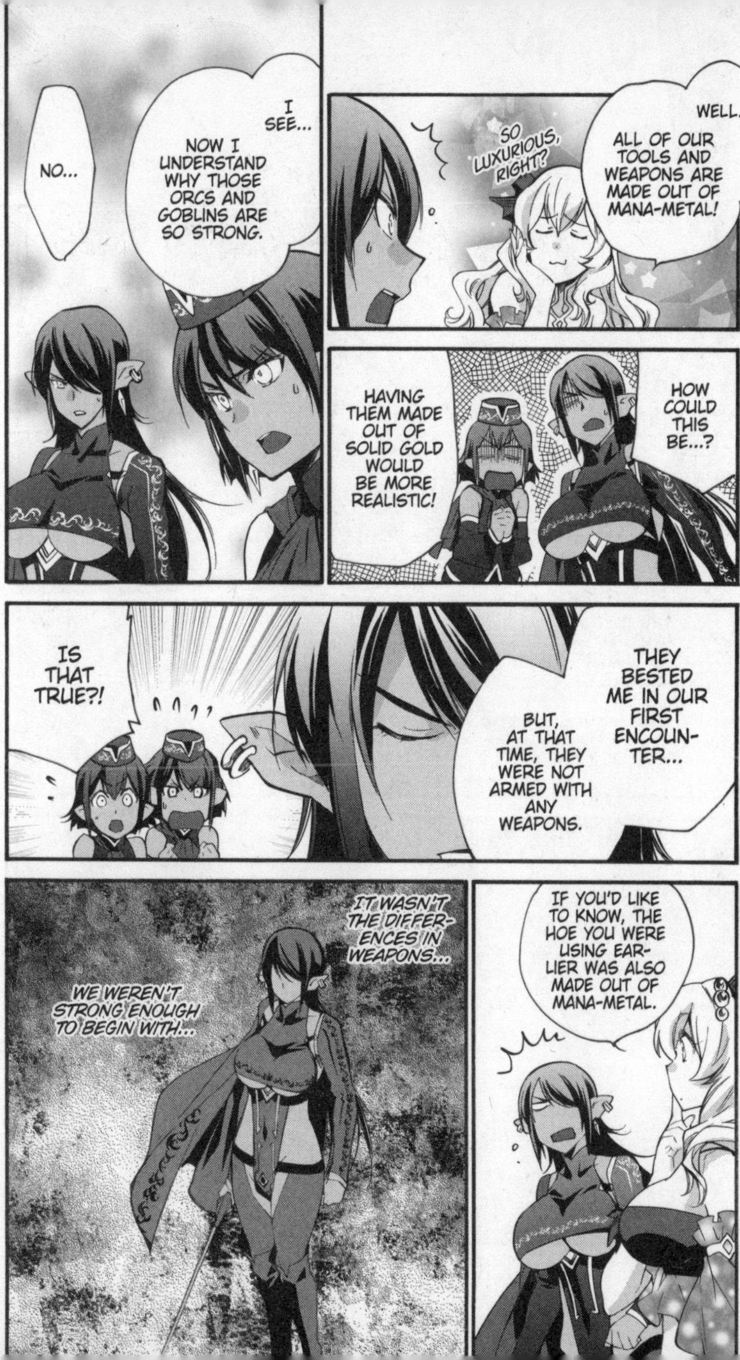
WELL...
ALL OF OUR TOOLS AND WEAPONS ARE MADE OUT OF MANA-METAL!
SO LUXURIOUS, RIGHT?
HOW COULD THIS BE...?
HAVING THEM MADE OUT OF SOLID GOLD WOULD BE MORE REALISTIC!
I SEE...
NOW I UNDERSTAND WHY THOSE ORCS AND GOBLINS ARE SO STRONG.
NO...
THEY BESTED ME IN OUR FIRST ENCOUNTER...
BUT, AT THAT TIME, THEY WERE NOT ARMED WITH ANY WEAPONS.
IS THAT TRUE?!
IF YOU'D LIKE TO KNOW, THE HOE YOU WERE USING EARLIER WAS ALSO MADE OUT OF MANA-METAL.
IT WASN'T THE DIFFERENCES IN WEAPONS...
WE WEREN'T STRONG ENOUGH TO BEGIN WITH...

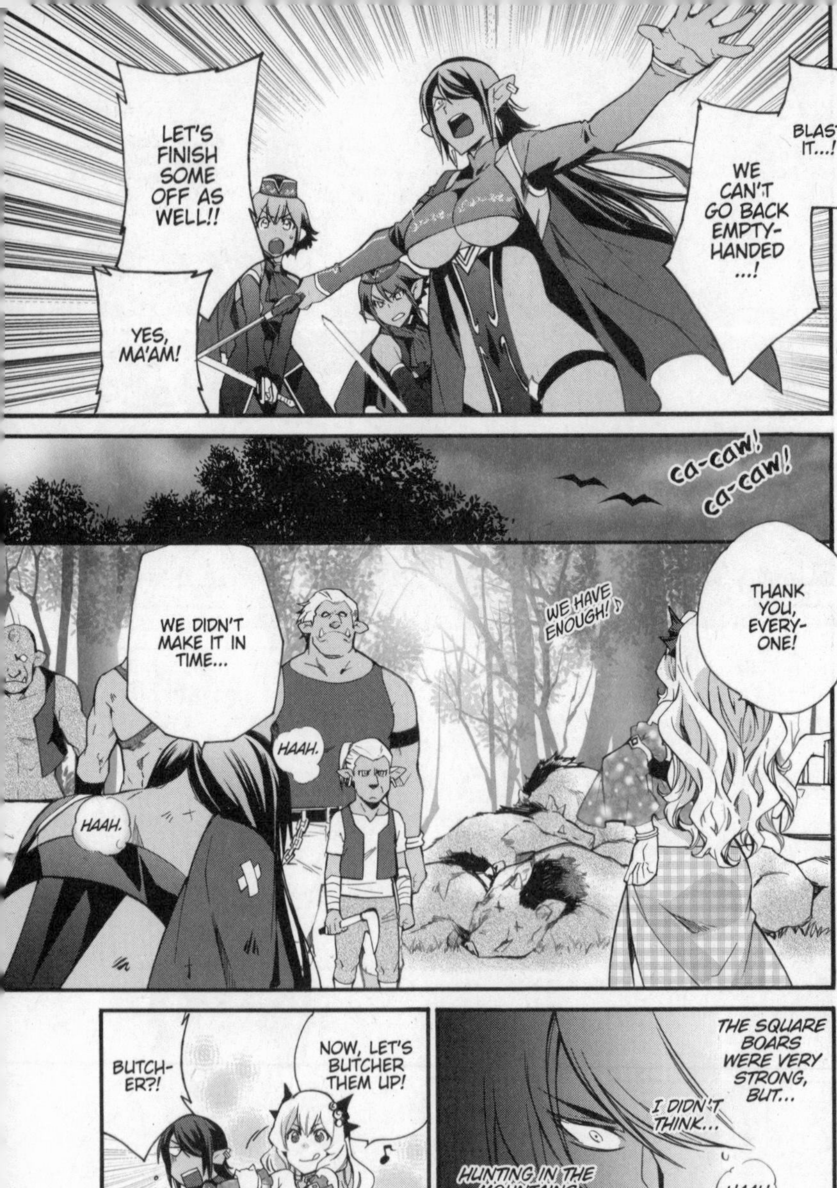
BLAST IT...!
WE CAN'T GO BACK EMPTY-HANDED...!
LET'S FINISH SOME OFF AS WELL!!
YES, MA'AM!
CA-CAW! CA-CAW!
THANK YOU, EVERYONE!
WE HAVE ENOUGH! ♪
WE DIDN'T MAKE IT IN TIME...
HAAH.
HAAH.
THE SQUARE BOARS WERE VERY STRONG, BUT...
I DIDN'T THINK...
HAAH.
HUNTING IN THE MOUNTAINS WOULD BE THIS DIFFICULT...
NOW, LET'S BUTCHER THEM UP!
BUTCHER?!

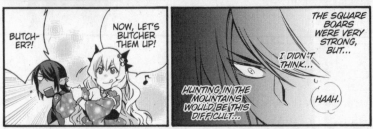

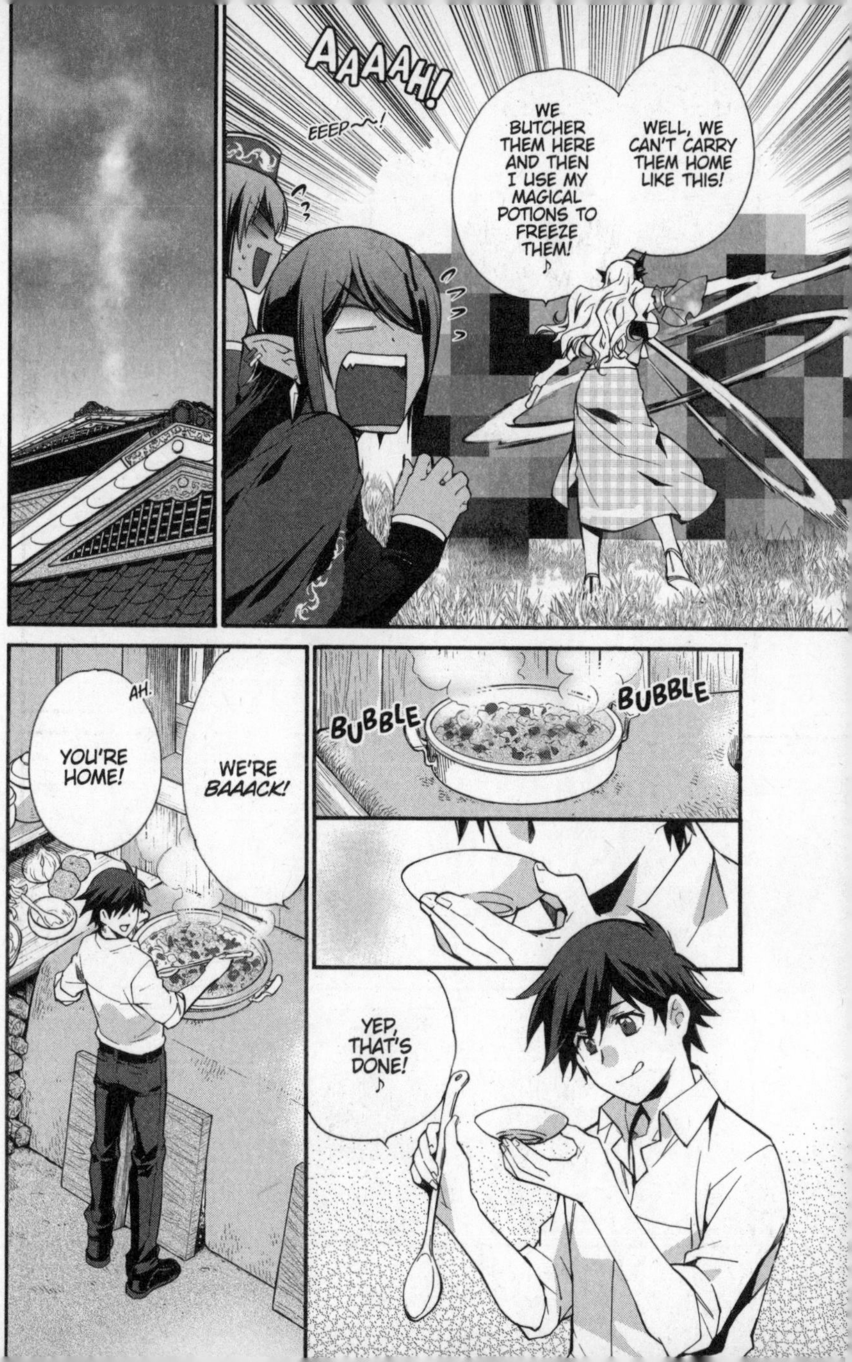
WELL, WE CAN'T CARRY THEM HOME LIKE THIS!
WE BUTCHER THEM HERE AND THEN I USE MY MAGICAL POTIONS TO FREEZE THEM! ♪
AAAAH!
EEEP~~!
BUBBLE
BUBBLE
YEP, THAT'S DONE! ♪
WE'RE BAAACK!
AH.
YOU'RE HOME!

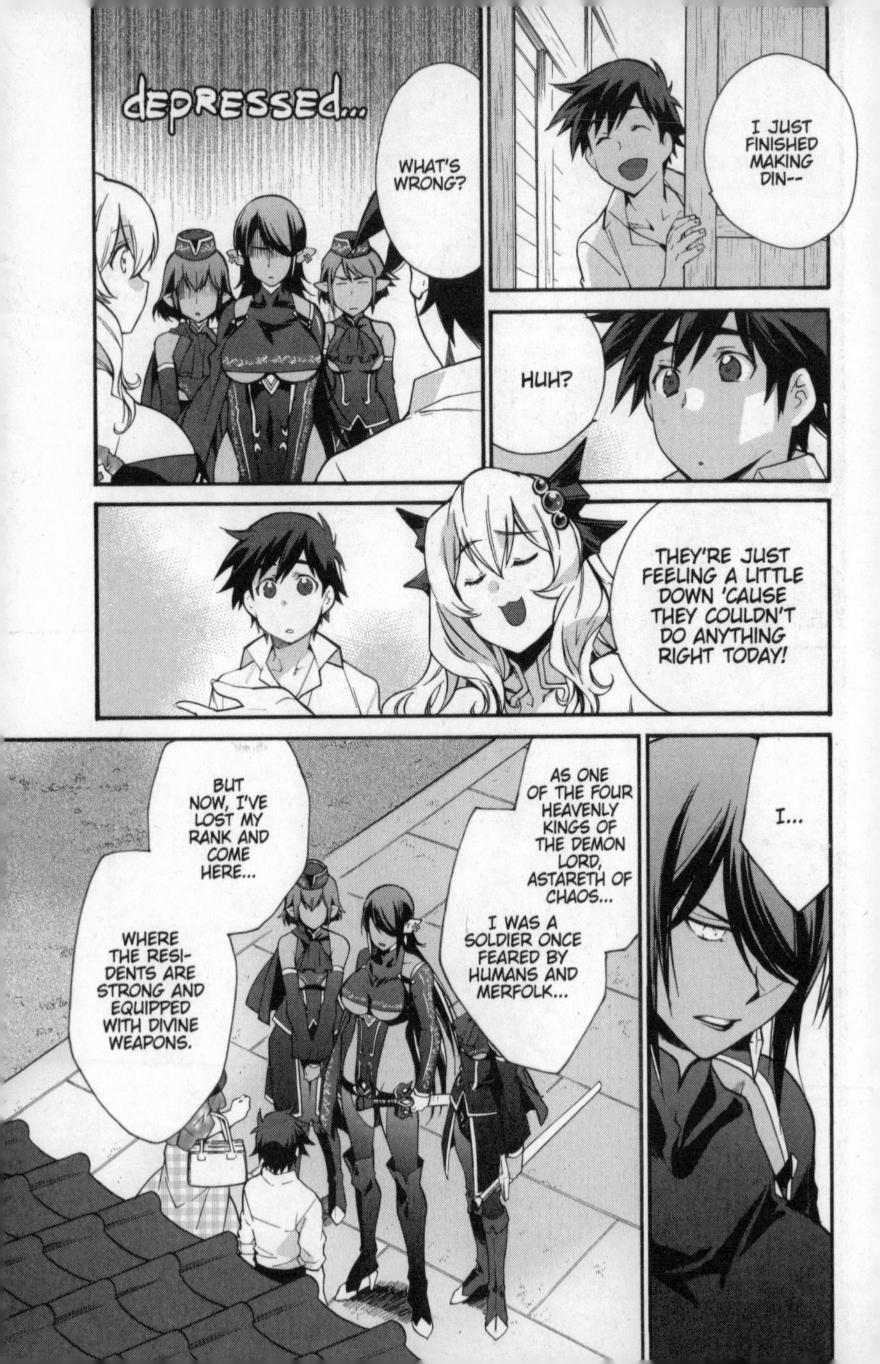
I JUST FINISHED MAKING DIN--
HUH?
depressed...
WHAT'S WRONG?
THEY'RE JUST FEELING A LITTLE DOWN 'CAUSE THEY COULDN'T DO ANYTHING RIGHT TODAY!
I...
AS ONE OF THE FOUR HEAVENLY KINGS OF THE DEMON LORD, ASTARETH OF CHAOS...
I WAS A SOLDIER ONCE FEARED BY HUMANS AND MERFOLK...
BUT NOW, I'VE LOST MY RANK AND COME HERE...
WHERE THE RESI-DENTS ARE STRONG AND EQUIPPED WITH DIVINE WEAPONS.

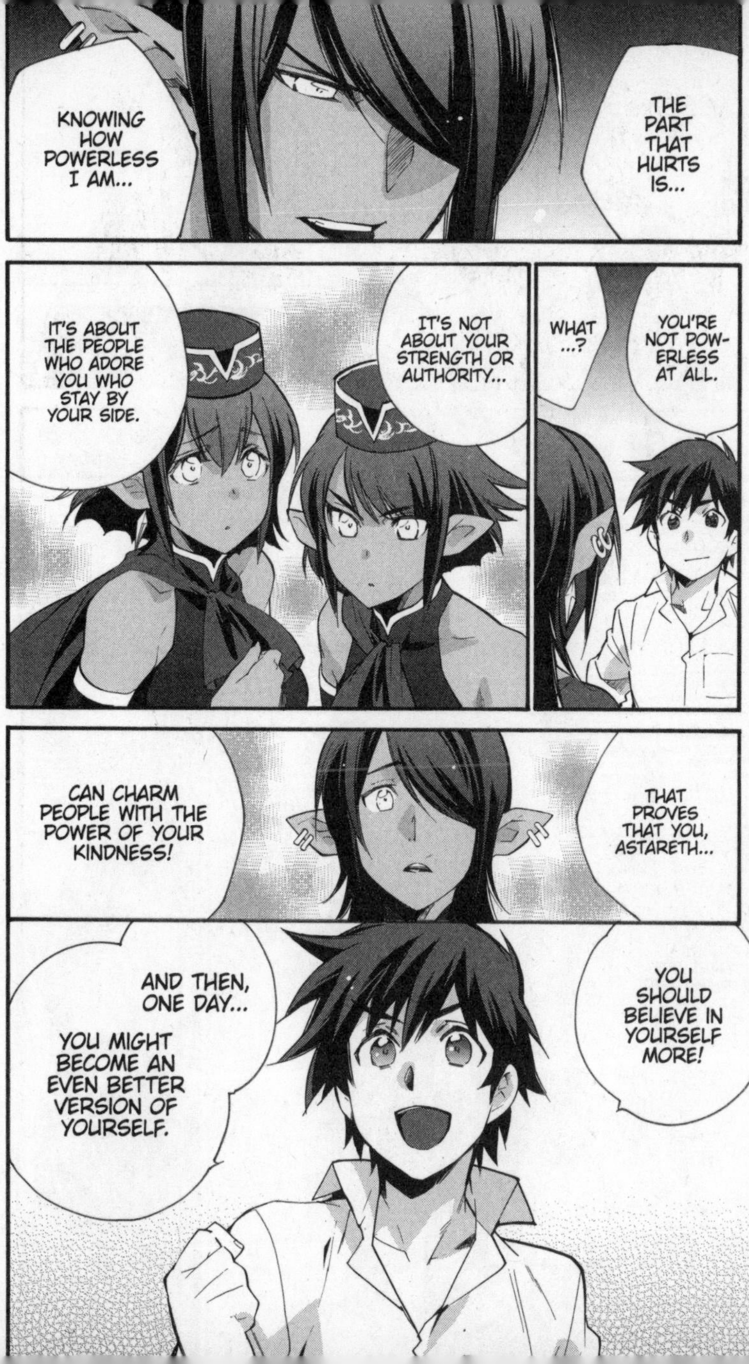
THE PART THAT HURTS IS...
KNOWING HOW POWERLESS I AM...
YOU'RE NOT POWERLESS AT ALL.
WHAT ...?
IT'S NOT ABOUT YOUR STRENGTH OR AUTHORITY...
IT'S ABOUT THE PEOPLE WHO ADORE YOU WHO STAY BY YOUR SIDE.
THAT PROVES THAT YOU, ASTARETH...
CAN CHARM PEOPLE WITH THE POWER OF YOUR KINDNESS!
YOU SHOULD BELIEVE IN YOURSELF MORE!
AND THEN, ONE DAY...
YOU MIGHT BECOME AN EVEN BETTER VERSION OF YOURSELF.

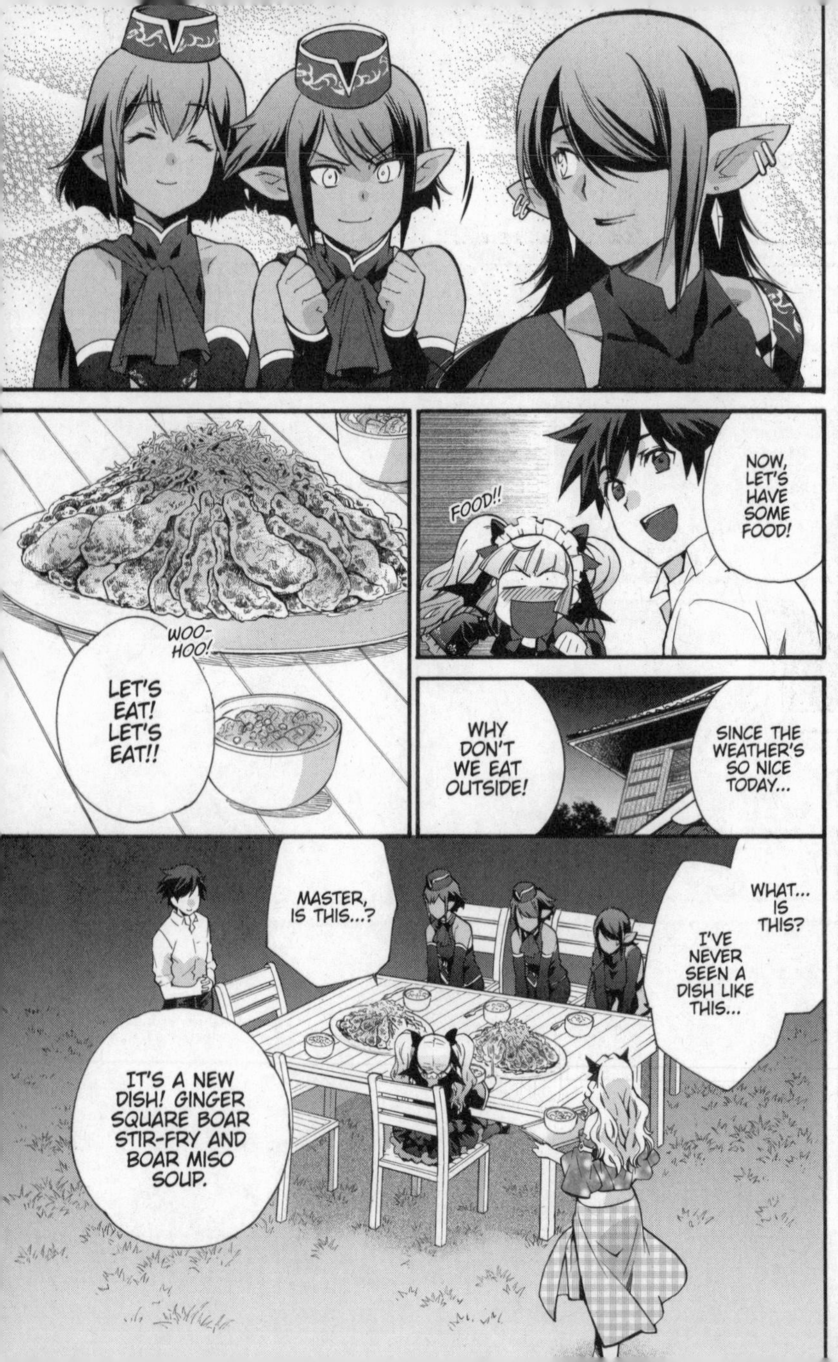
NOW, LET'S HAVE SOME FOOD!
FOOD!!
SINCE THE WEATHER'S SO NICE TODAY...
WHY DON'T WE EAT OUTSIDE!
WOO-HOO!
LET'S EAT! LET'S EAT!!
WHAT... IS THIS?
I'VE NEVER SEEN A DISH LIKE THIS...
MASTER, IS THIS...?
IT'S A NEW DISH! GINGER SQUARE BOAR STIR-FRY AND BOAR MISO SOUP.

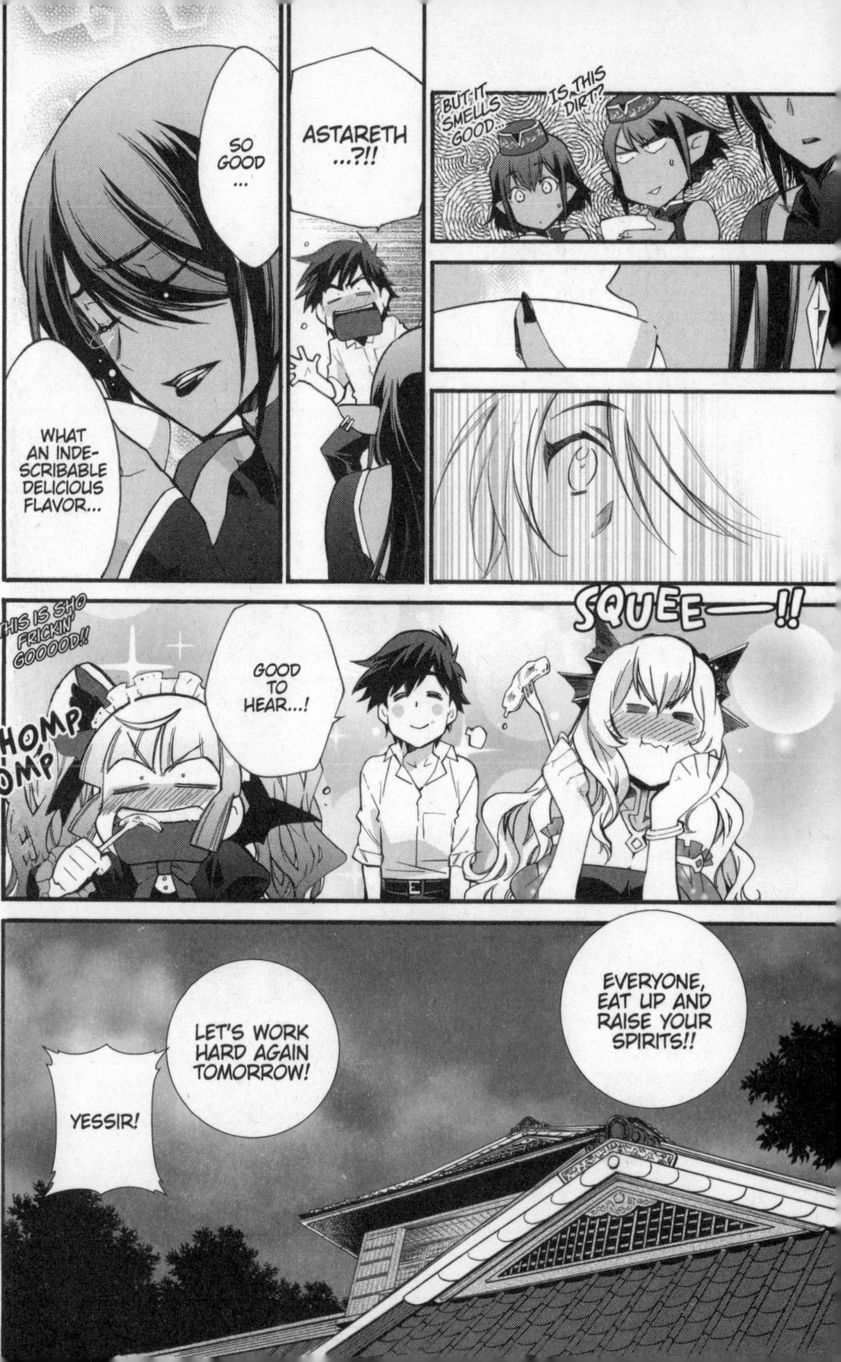
IS THIS DIRT?
BUT IT SMELLS GOOD...
ASTARETH ...?!!
SO GOOD ...
WHAT AN INDE-SCRIBABLE DELICIOUS FLAVOR...
SQUEE—!!
GOOD TO HEAR...!
THIS IS SHO FRICKIN' GOOOOD!!
CHOMP CHOMP
EVERYONE, EAT UP AND RAISE YOUR SPIRITS!!
LET'S WORK HARD AGAIN TOMORROW!
YESSIR!

CHAPTER 12

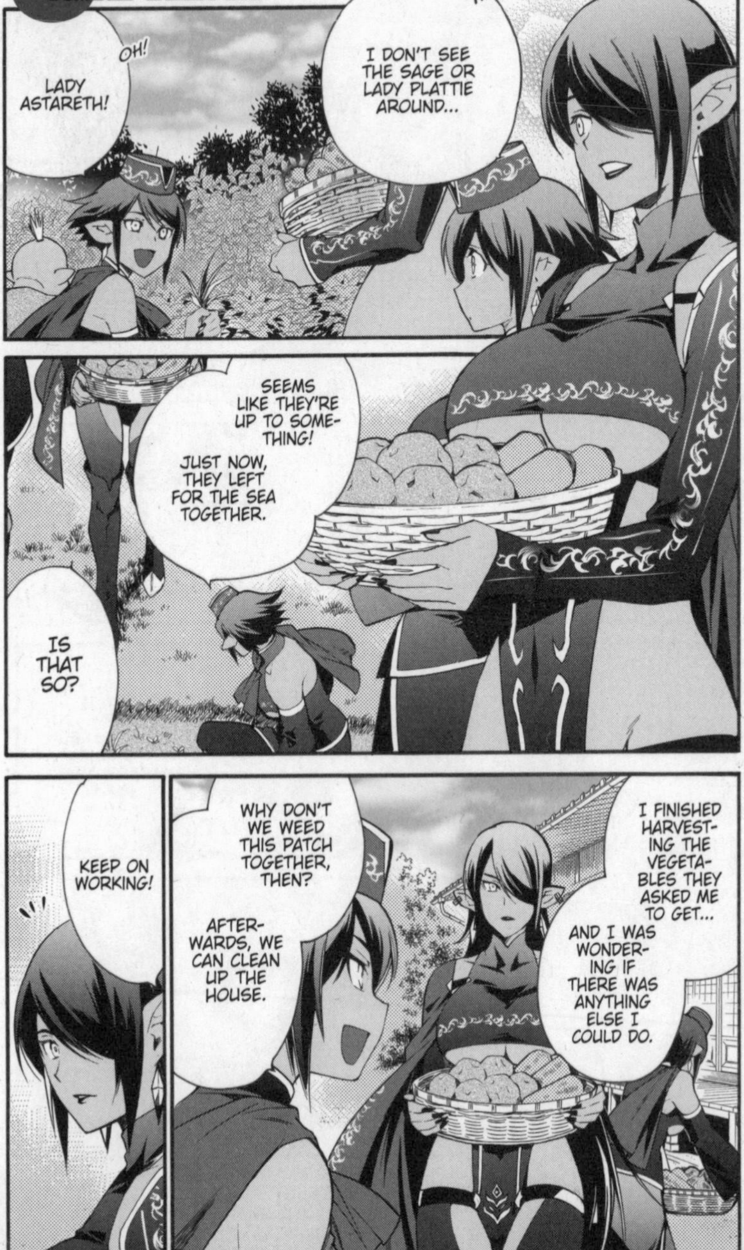
HMM...
I DON'T SEE THE SAGE OR LADY PLATTIE AROUND...
OH!
LADY ASTARETH!
SEEMS LIKE THEY'RE UP TO SOME-THING!
JUST NOW, THEY LEFT FOR THE SEA TOGETHER.
IS THAT SO?
I FINISHED HARVEST-ING THE VEGETA-BLES THEY ASKED ME TO GET...
AND I WAS WONDER-ING IF THERE WAS ANYTHING ELSE I COULD DO.
WHY DON'T WE WEED THIS PATCH TOGETHER, THEN?
AFTER-WARDS, WE CAN CLEAN UP THE HOUSE.
KEEP ON WORKING!

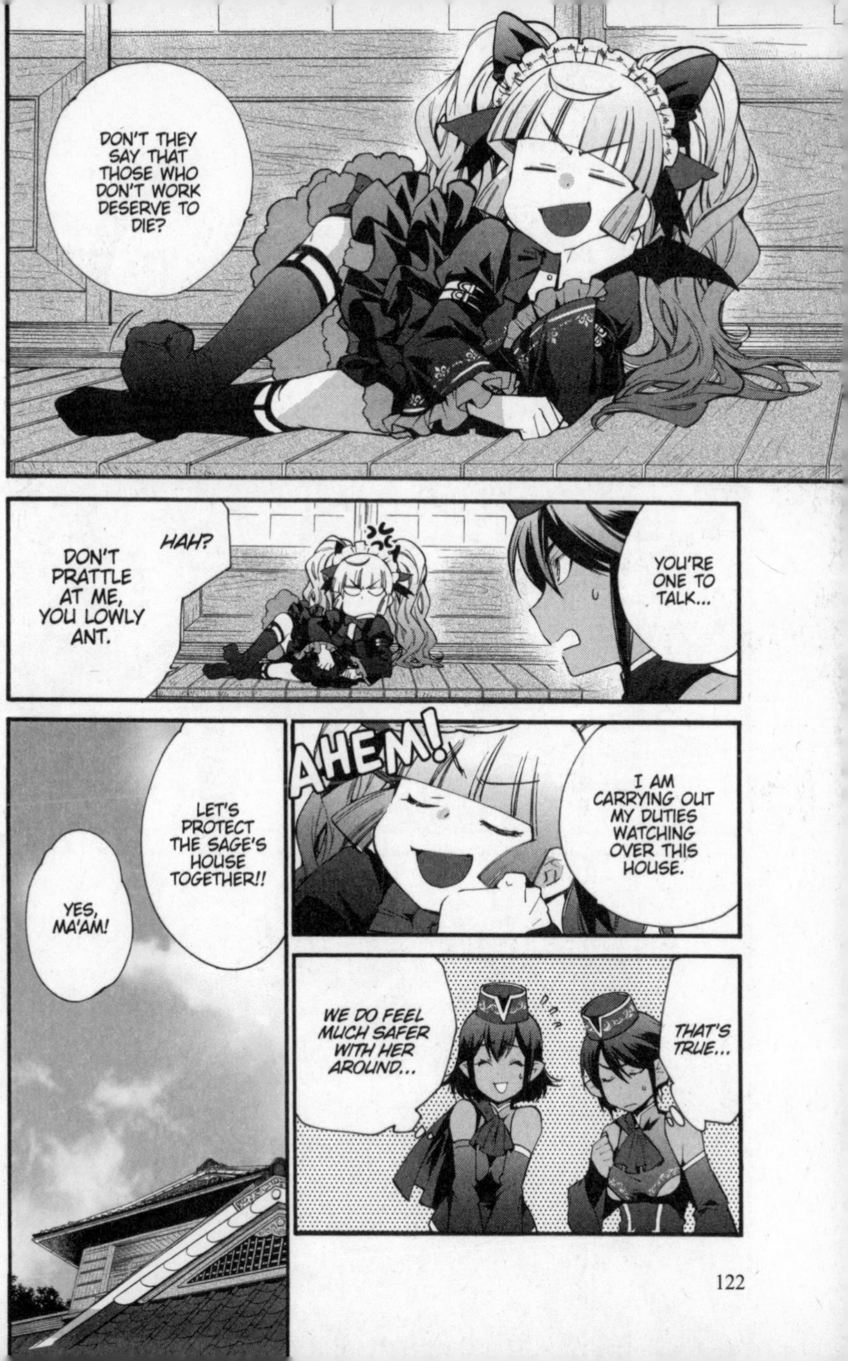
DON'T THEY SAY THAT THOSE WHO DON'T WORK DESERVE TO DIE?
YOU'RE ONE TO TALK...
HAH?
DON'T PRATTLE AT ME, YOU LOWLY ANT.
AHEM!
I AM CARRYING OUT MY DUTIES WATCHING OVER THIS HOUSE.
WE DO FEEL MUCH SAFER WITH HER AROUND...
THAT'S TRUE...
LET'S PROTECT THE SAGE'S HOUSE TOGETHER!!
YES, MA'AM!

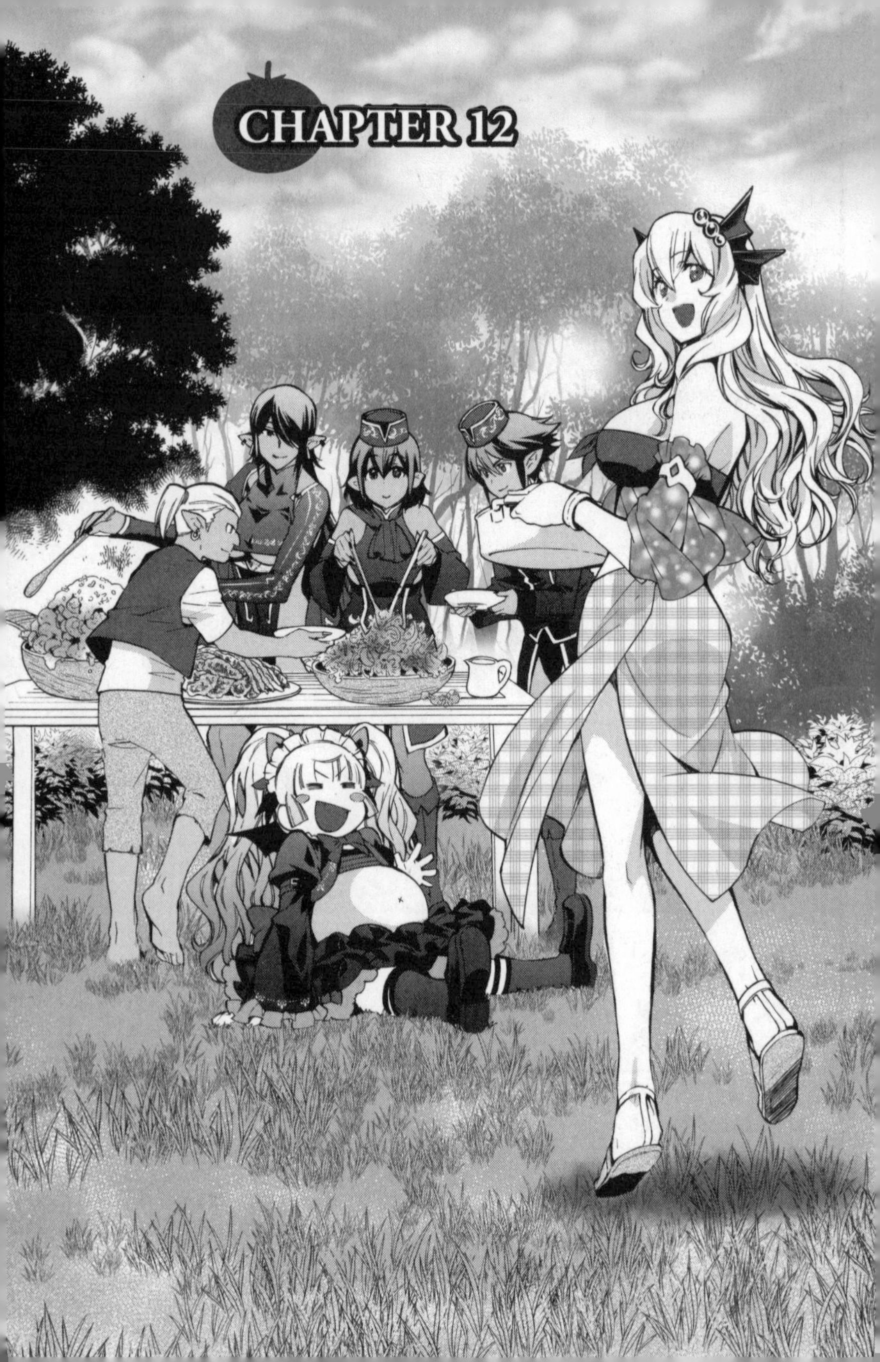
CHAPTER 12

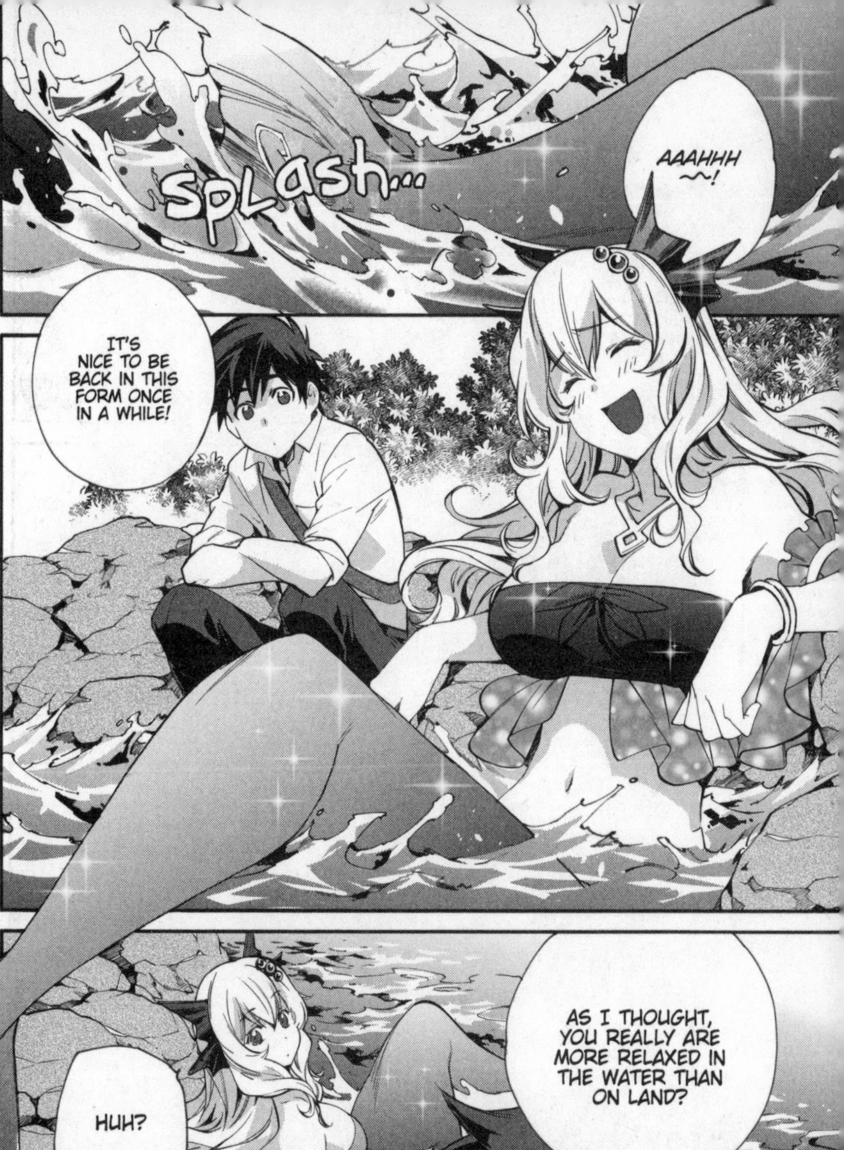
AAAHHH ~~!
SPLASH...
IT'S NICE TO BE BACK IN THIS FORM ONCE IN A WHILE!
AS I THOUGHT, YOU REALLY ARE MORE RELAXED IN THE WATER THAN ON LAND?
HUH?

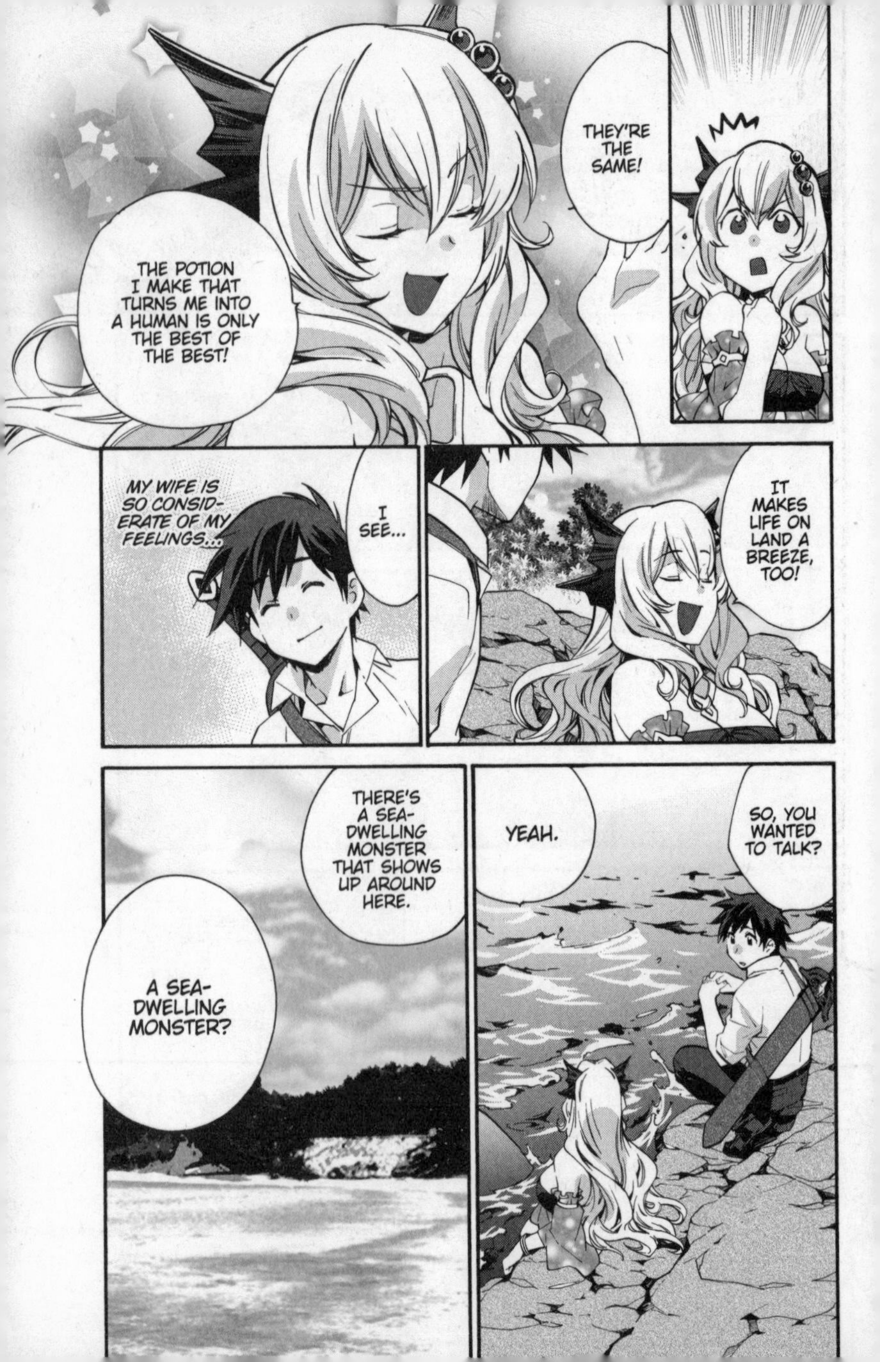
THEY'RE THE SAME!
THE POTION I MAKE THAT TURNS ME INTO A HUMAN IS ONLY THE BEST OF THE BEST!
IT MAKES LIFE ON LAND A BREEZE, TOO!
I SEE...
MY WIFE IS SO CONSIDERATE OF MY FEELINGS...
SO, YOU WANTED TO TALK?
YEAH.
THERE'S A SEA-DWELLING MONSTER THAT SHOWS UP AROUND HERE.
A SEA-DWELLING MONSTER?

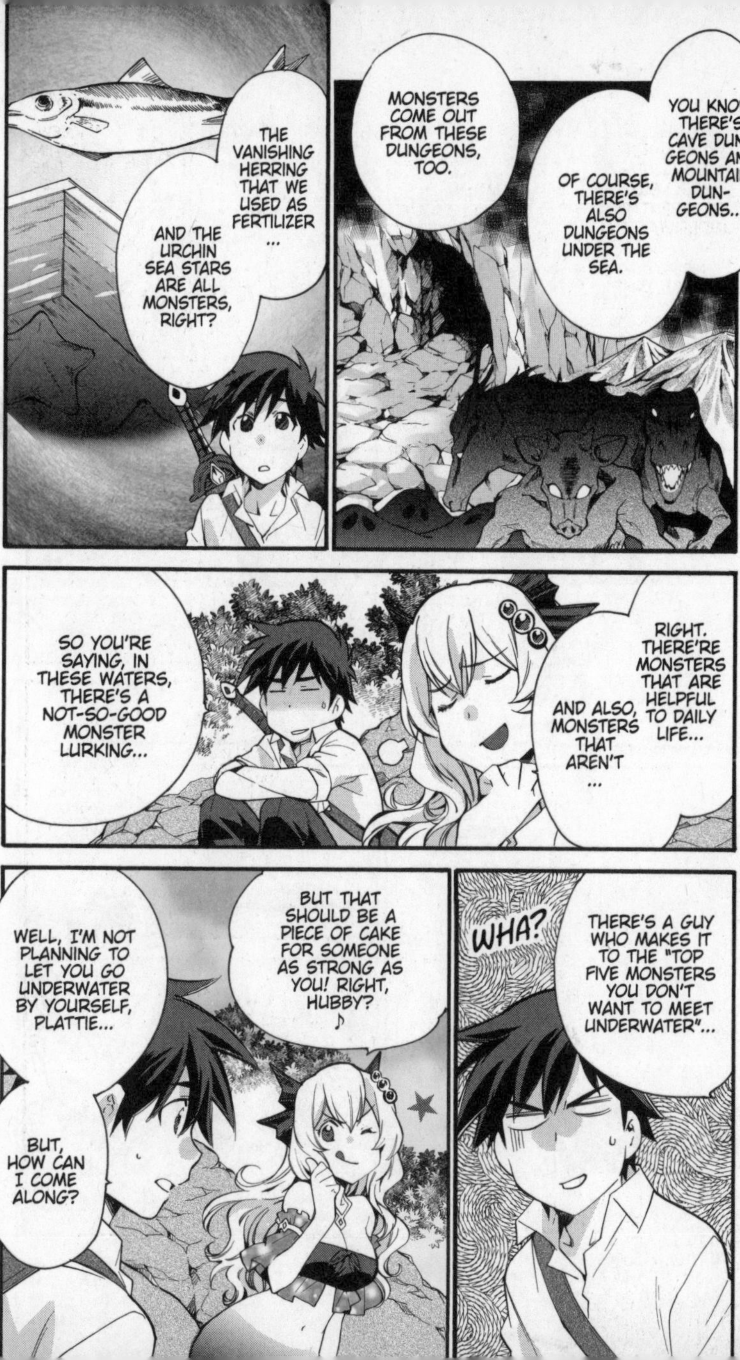
YOU KNOW THERE'S CAVE DUNGEONS AND MOUNTAIN DUNGEONS...
OF COURSE, THERE'S ALSO DUNGEONS UNDER THE SEA.
MONSTERS COME OUT FROM THESE DUNGEONS, TOO.
THE VANISHING HERRING THAT WE USED AS FERTILIZER ...
AND THE URCHIN SEA STARS ARE ALL MONSTERS, RIGHT?
RIGHT. THERE'RE MONSTERS THAT ARE HELPFUL TO DAILY LIFE...
AND ALSO, MONSTERS THAT AREN'T ...
SO YOU'RE SAYING, IN THESE WATERS, THERE'S A NOT-SO-GOOD MONSTER LURKING...
THERE'S A GUY WHO MAKES IT TO THE "TOP FIVE MONSTERS YOU DON'T WANT TO MEET UNDERWATER"...
WHA?
BUT THAT SHOULD BE A PIECE OF CAKE FOR SOMEONE AS STRONG AS YOU! RIGHT, HUBBY? ♪
WELL, I'M NOT PLANNING TO LET YOU GO UNDERWATER BY YOURSELF, PLATTIE...
BUT, HOW CAN I COME ALONG?

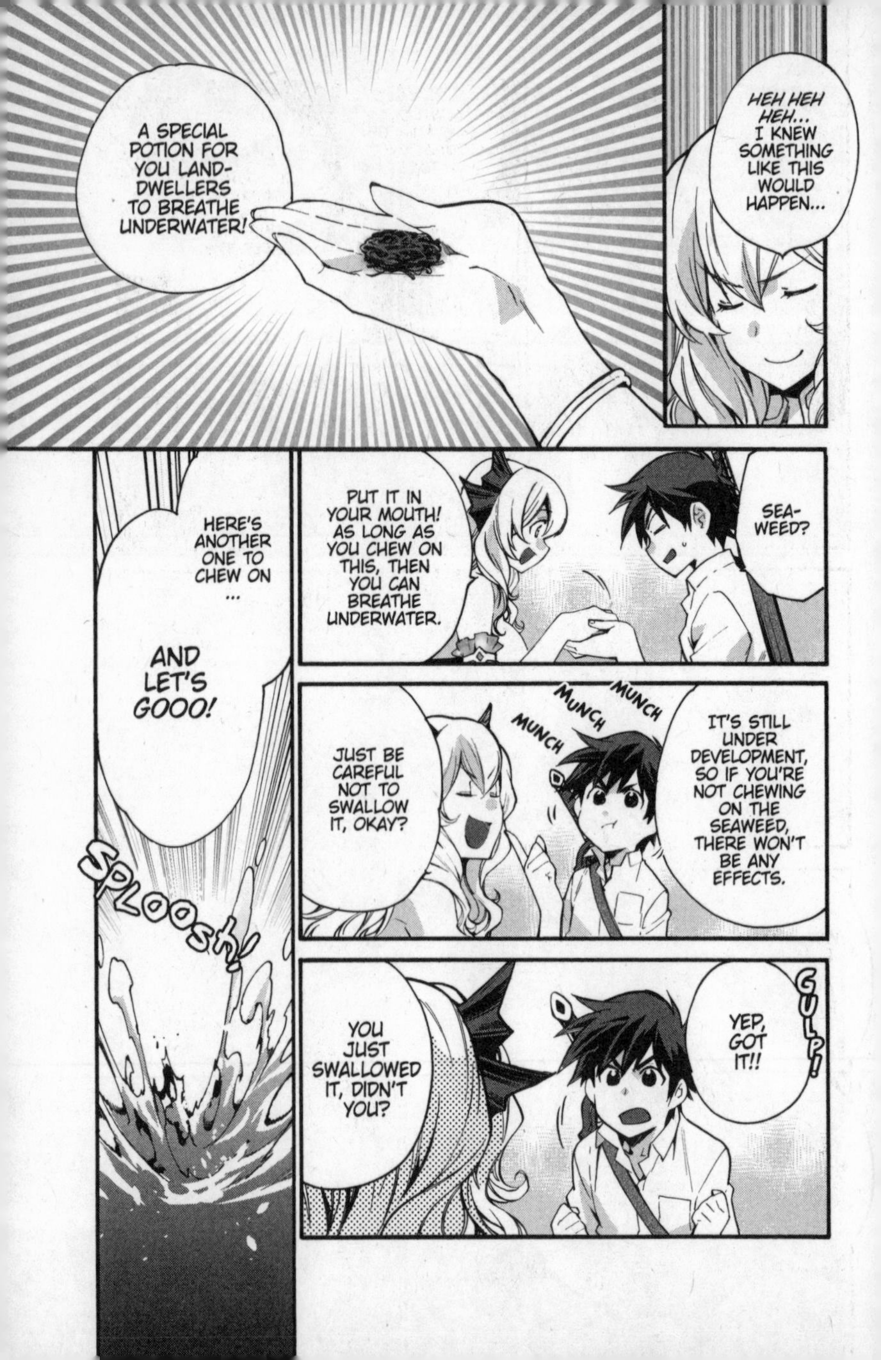
HEH HEH HEH... I KNEW SOMETHING LIKE THIS WOULD HAPPEN...
A SPECIAL POTION FOR YOU LAND-DWELLERS TO BREATHE UNDERWATER!
SEA-WEED?
PUT IT IN YOUR MOUTH! AS LONG AS YOU CHEW ON THIS, THEN YOU CAN BREATHE UNDERWATER.
IT'S STILL UNDER DEVELOPMENT, SO IF YOU'RE NOT CHEWING ON THE SEAWEED, THERE WON'T BE ANY EFFECTS.
MUNCH MUNCH MUNCH
JUST BE CAREFUL NOT TO SWALLOW IT, OKAY?
GULP!
YEP, GOT IT!!
YOU JUST SWALLOWED IT, DIDN'T YOU?
HERE'S ANOTHER ONE TO CHEW ON ...
AND LET'S GOOO!
SPLOOSH!

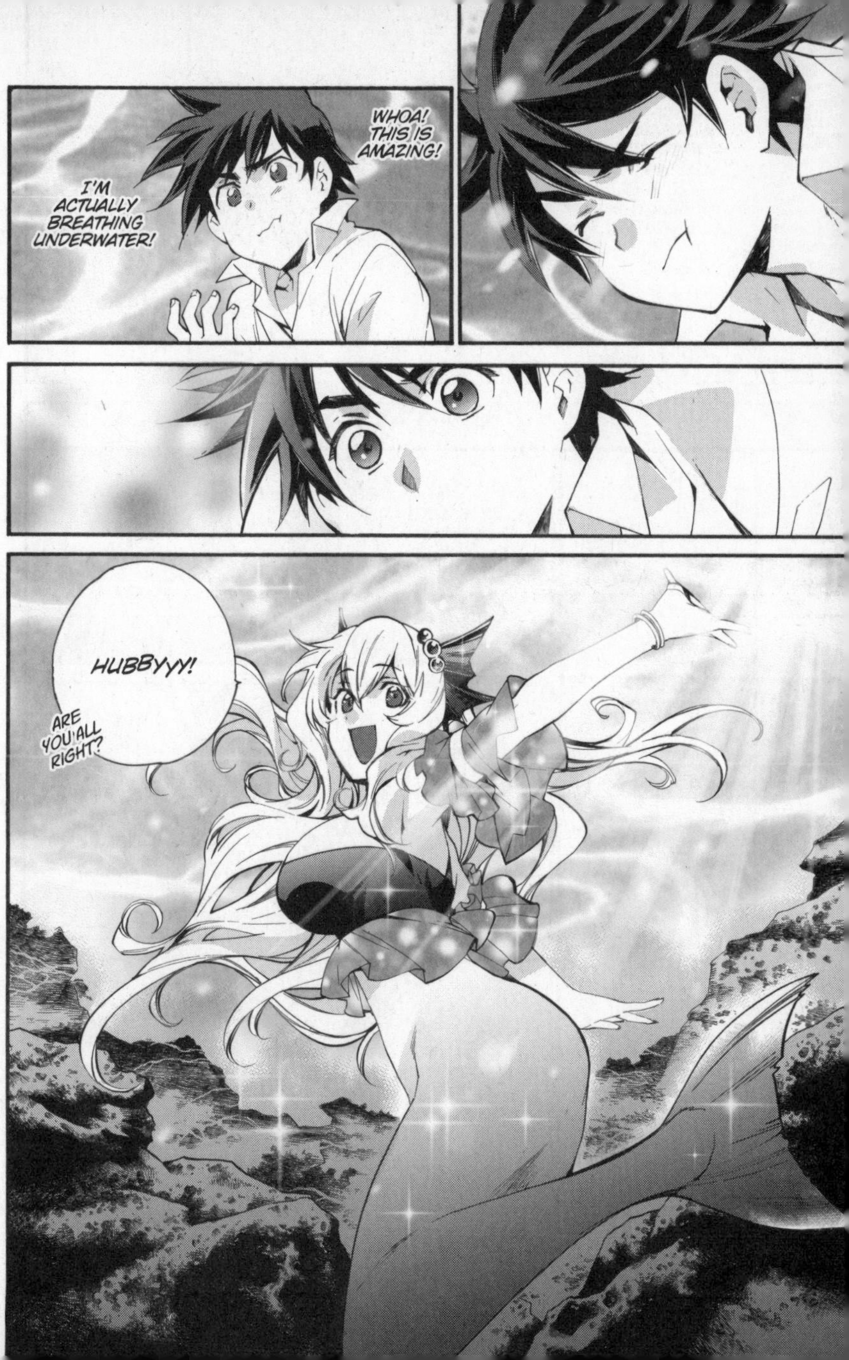
WHOA! THIS IS AMAZING!
I'M ACTUALLY BREATHING UNDERWATER!
HUBBYYY!
ARE YOU ALL RIGHT?

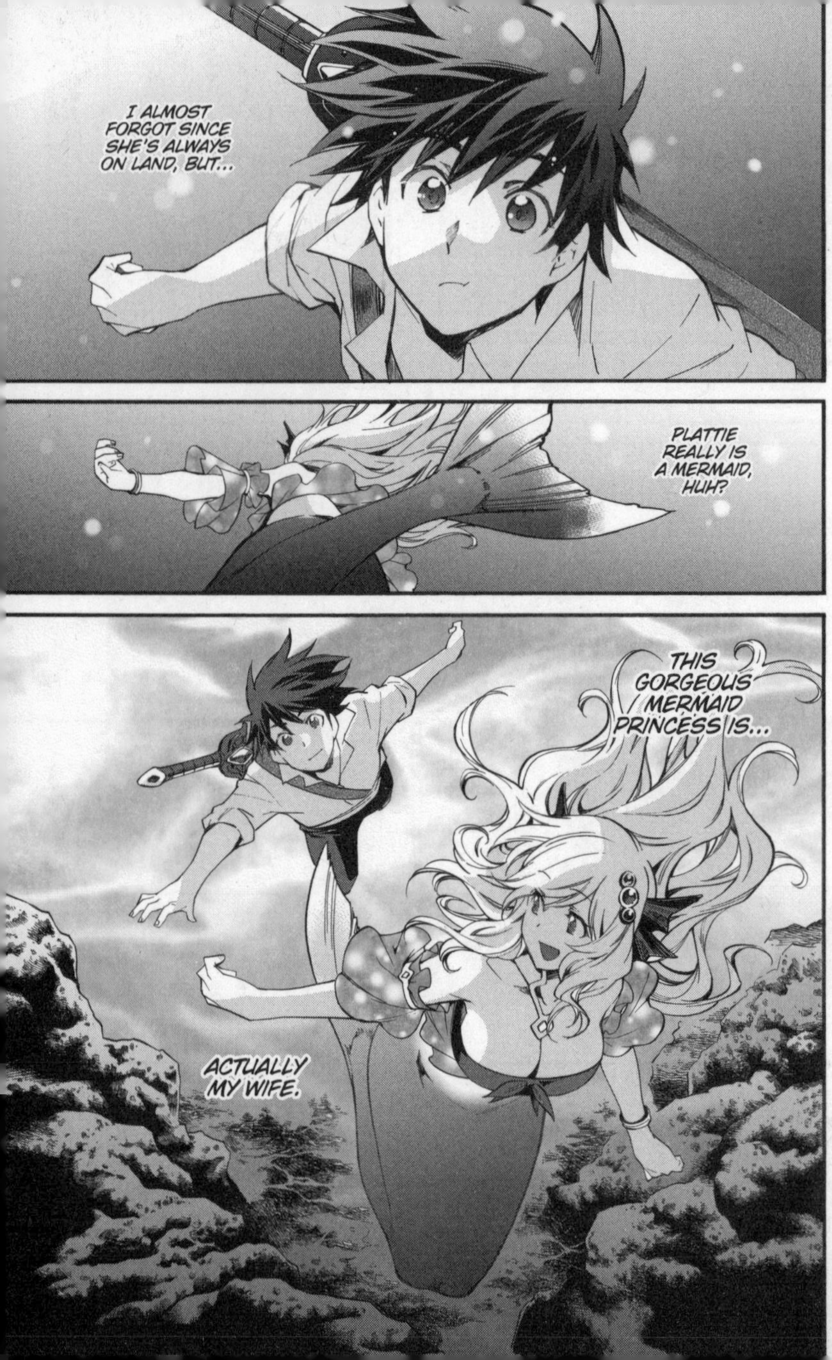
I ALMOST FORGOT SINCE SHE'S ALWAYS ON LAND, BUT...
PLATTIE REALLY IS A MERMAID, HUH?
THIS GORGEOUS MERMAID PRINCESS IS...
ACTUALLY MY WIFE.

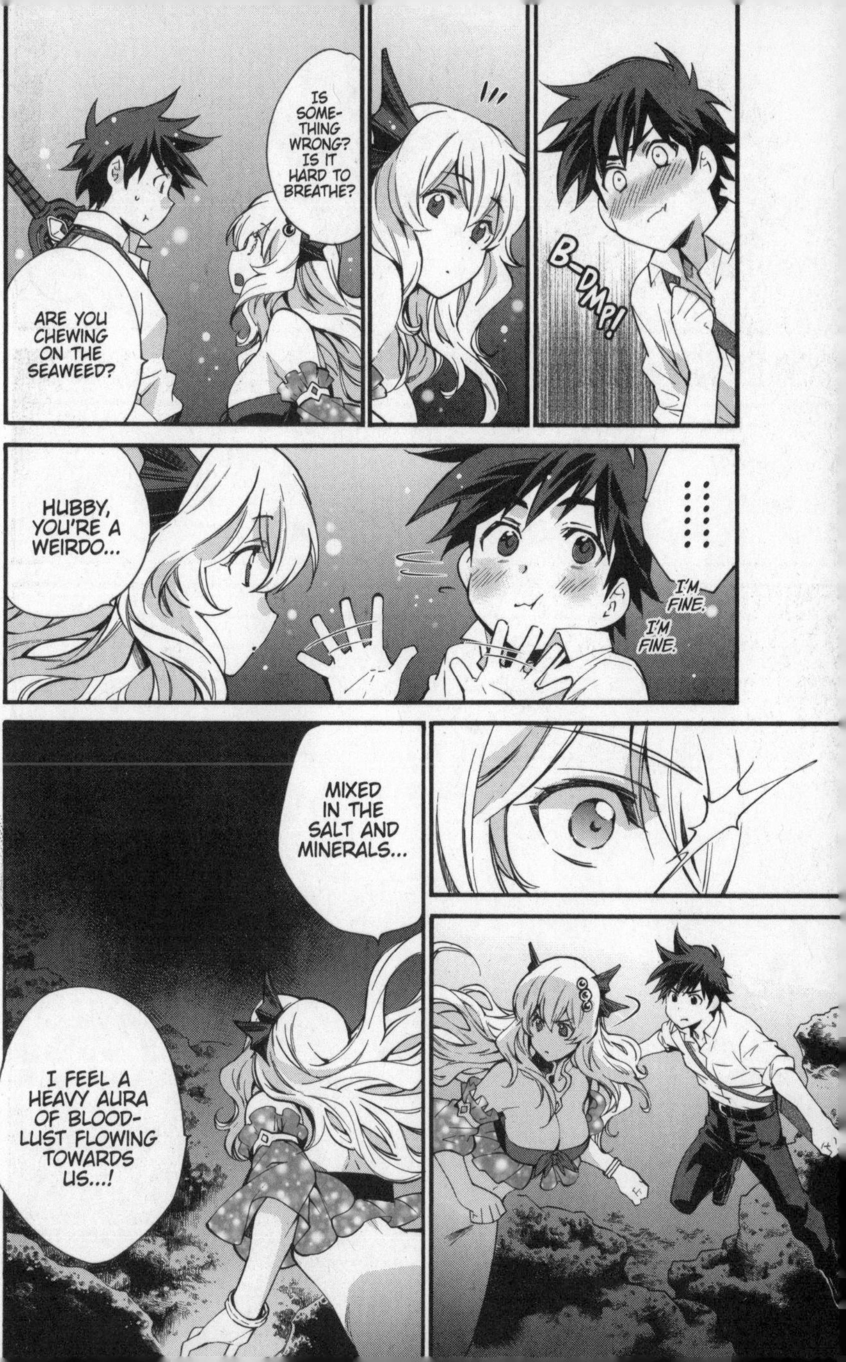
B-DMP!
IS SOMETHING WRONG? IS IT HARD TO BREATHE?
ARE YOU CHEWING ON THE SEAWEED?
......
I'M FINE.
I'M FINE.
HUBBY, YOU'RE A WEIRDO...
MIXED IN THE SALT AND MINERALS...
I FEEL A HEAVY AURA OF BLOOD-LUST FLOWING TOWARDS US...!

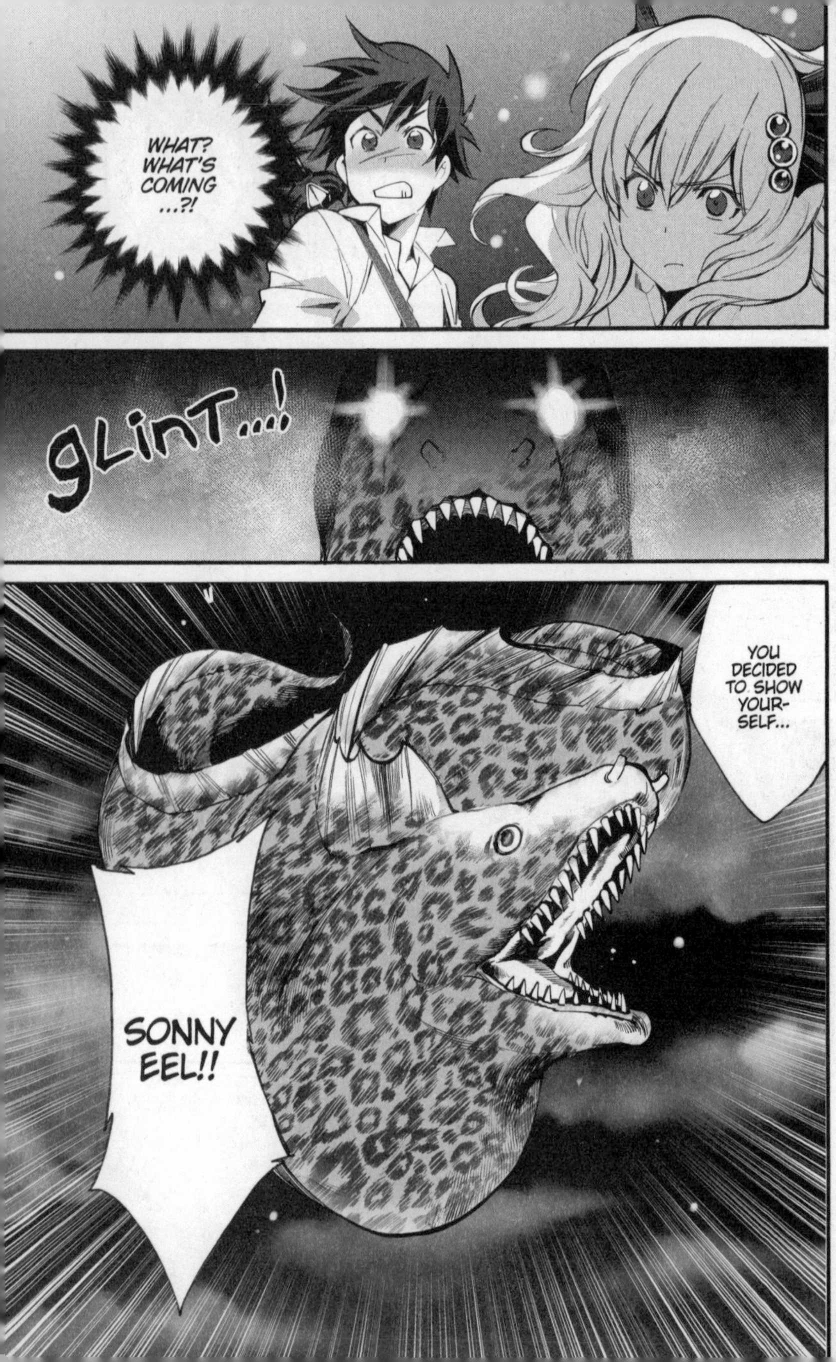
WHAT? WHAT'S COMING ...?!
gLinT...!
YOU DECIDED TO SHOW YOUR-SELF...
SONNY EEL!!

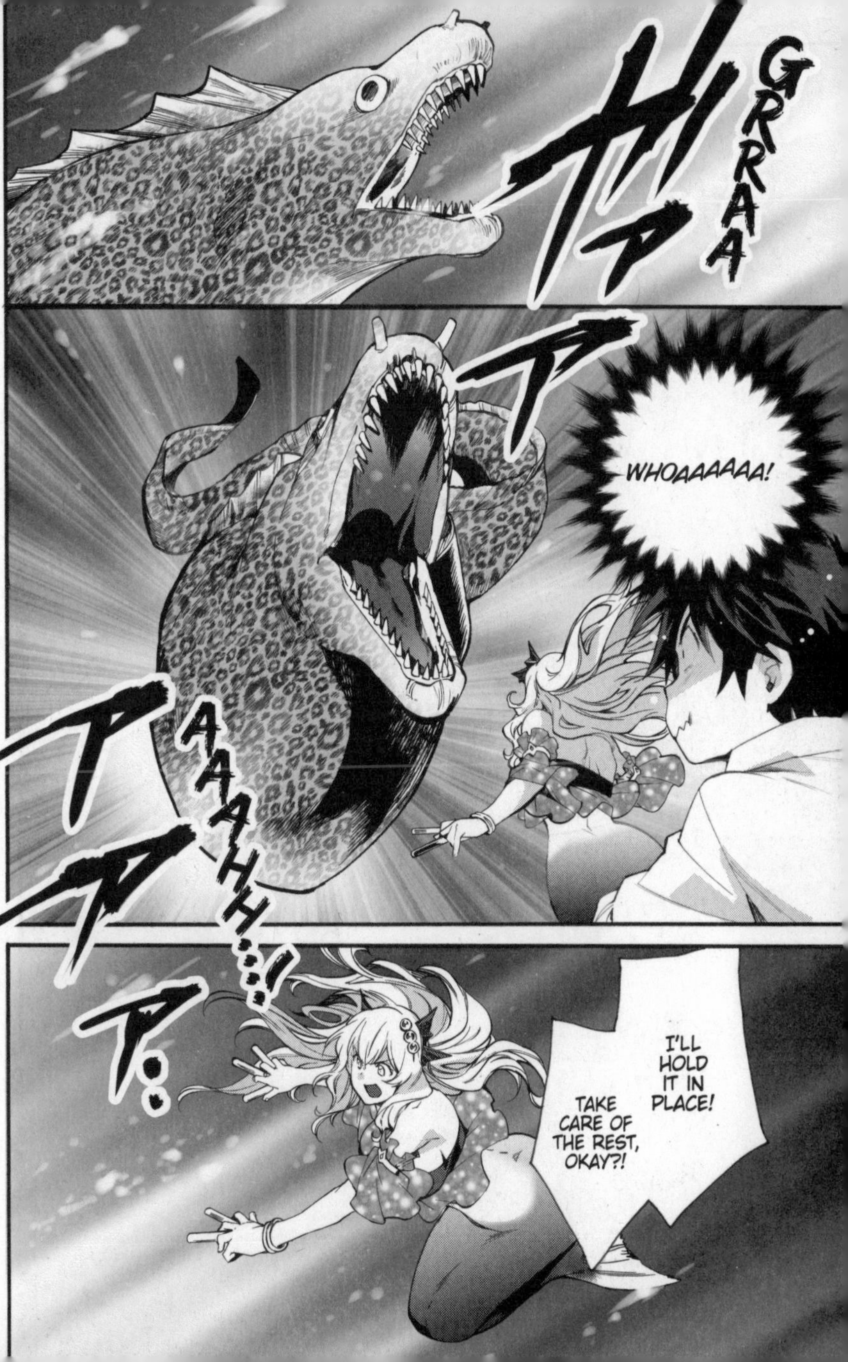
GRRAA
WHOAAAAAA!
AAAAHH...!
I'LL HOLD IT IN PLACE!
TAKE CARE OF THE REST, OKAY?!

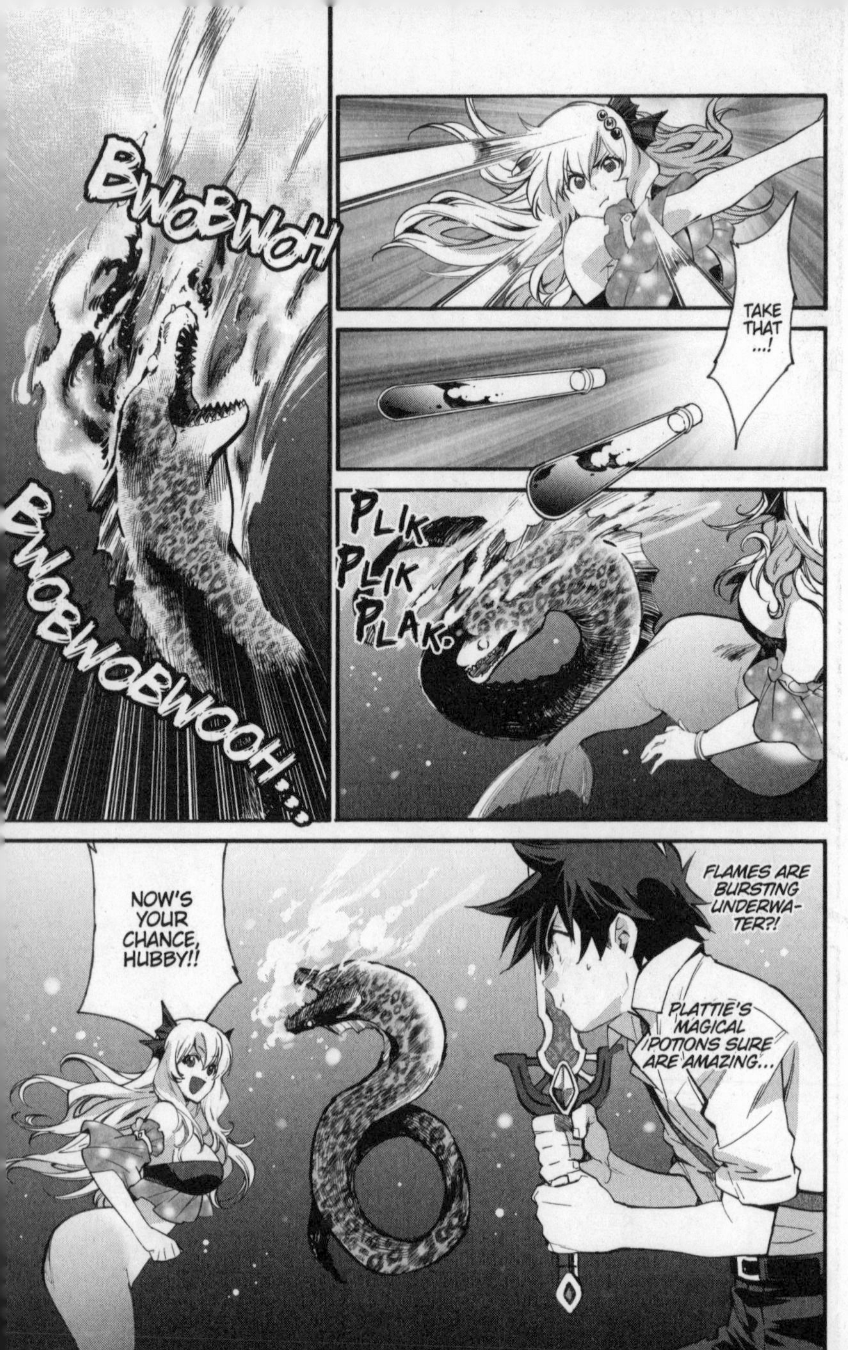
TAKE THAT ...!
PLIK PLIK PLAK.
BWOBWOH
BWOBWOBWOOH...
FLAMES ARE BURSTING UNDERWA-TER?!
PLATTIE'S MAGICAL POTIONS SURE ARE AMAZING...
NOW'S YOUR CHANCE, HUBBY!!

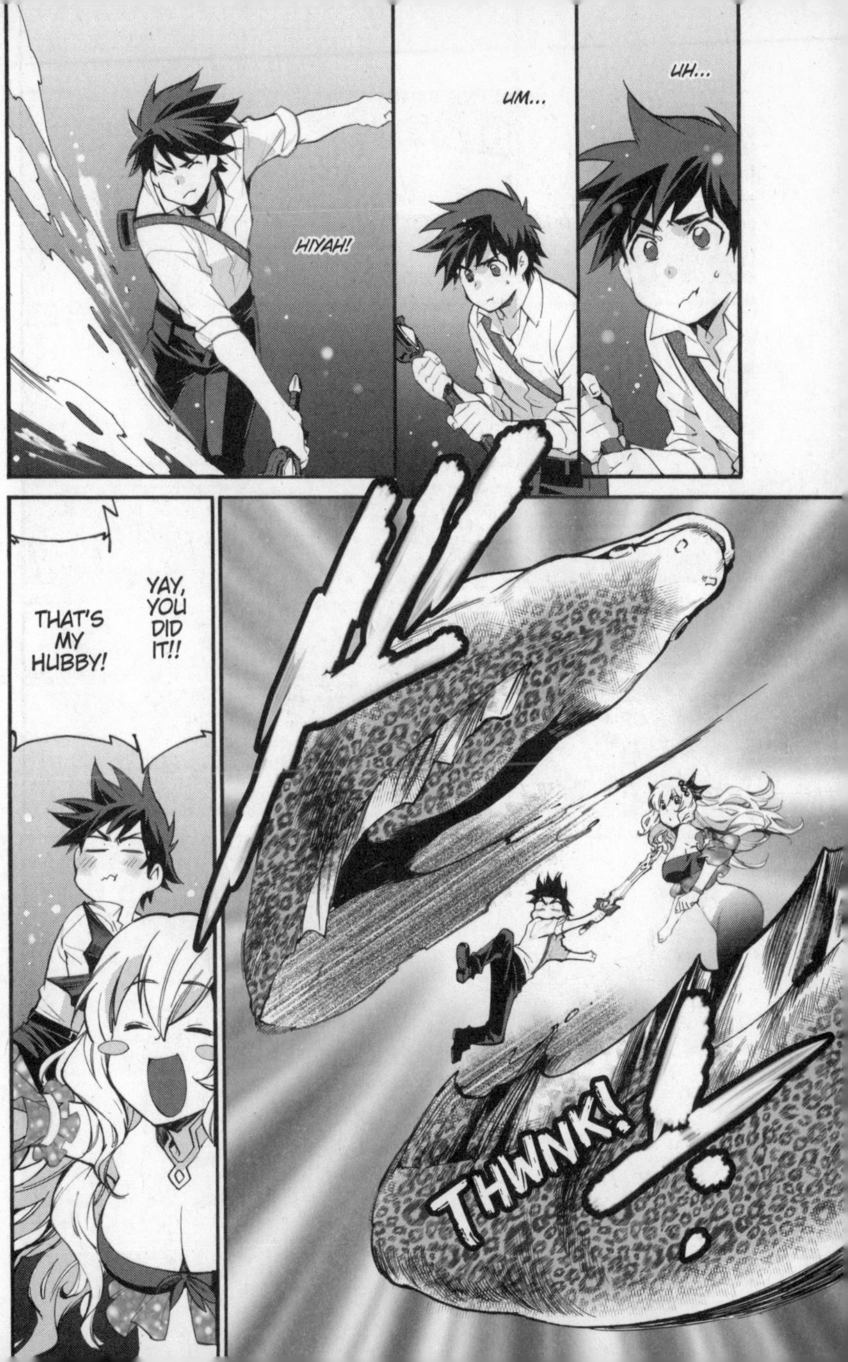
UH...
UM...
HIYAH!
THWNK!
YAY, YOU DID IT!!
THAT'S MY HUBBY!

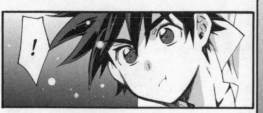

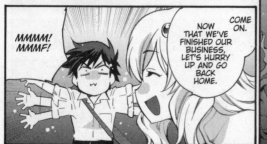

MMMM!
MMMF!

NOW THAT WE'VE FINISHED OUR BUSINESS, LET'S HURRY UP AND GO BACK HOME.

COME ON.

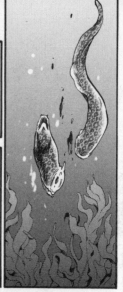

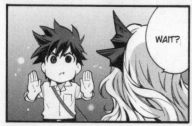

WAIT?

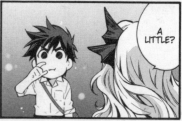

A LITTLE?

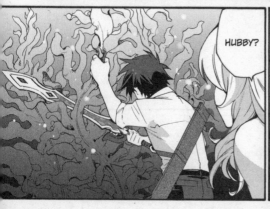

HUBBY?

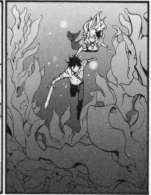

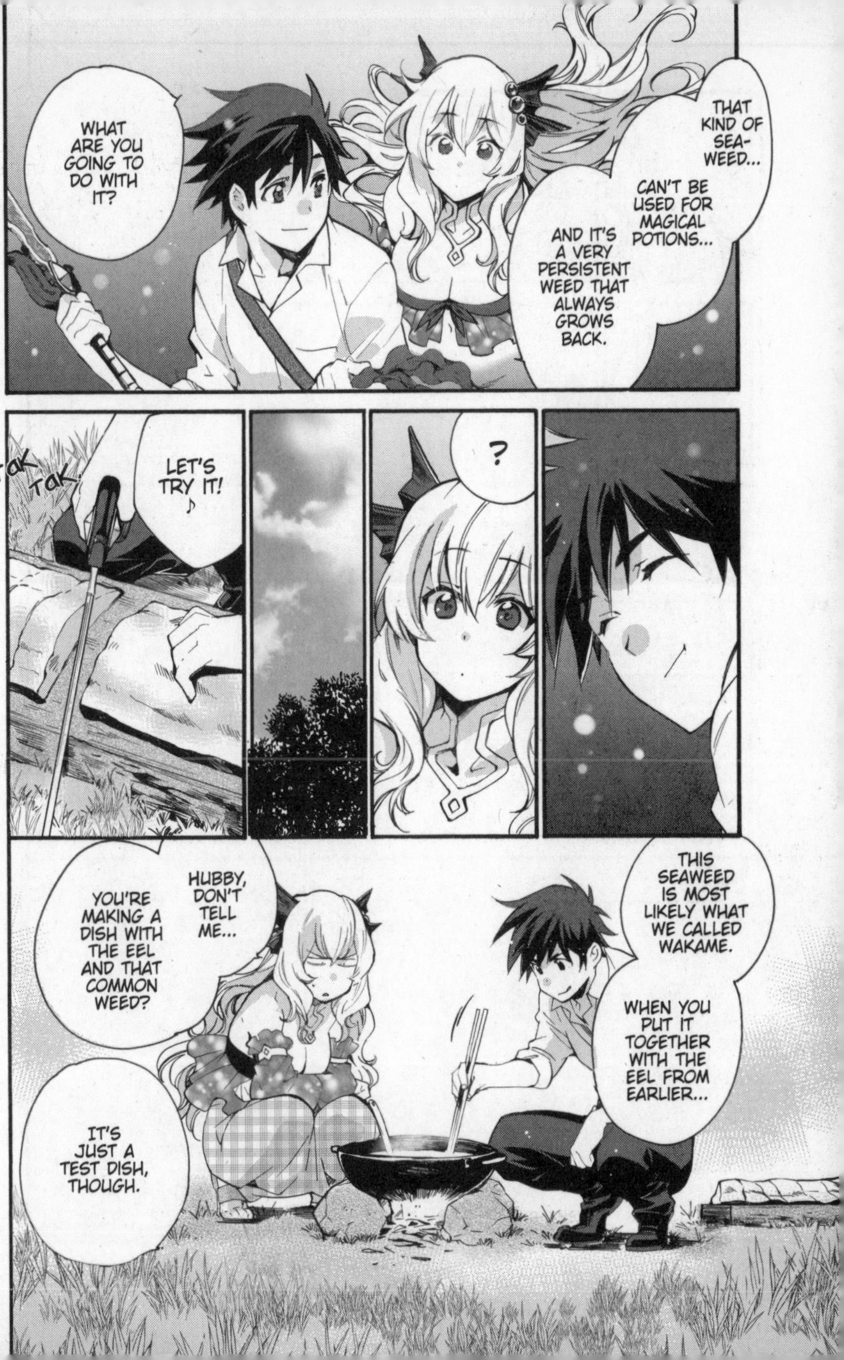
THAT KIND OF SEA-WEED...
CAN'T BE USED FOR MAGICAL POTIONS...
AND IT'S A VERY PERSISTENT WEED THAT ALWAYS GROWS BACK.
WHAT ARE YOU GOING TO DO WITH IT?
?
LET'S TRY IT! ♪
TAK TAK
THIS SEAWEED IS MOST LIKELY WHAT WE CALLED WAKAME.
WHEN YOU PUT IT TOGETHER WITH THE EEL FROM EARLIER...
HUBBY, DON'T TELL ME...
YOU'RE MAKING A DISH WITH THE EEL AND THAT COMMON WEED?
IT'S JUST A TEST DISH, THOUGH.

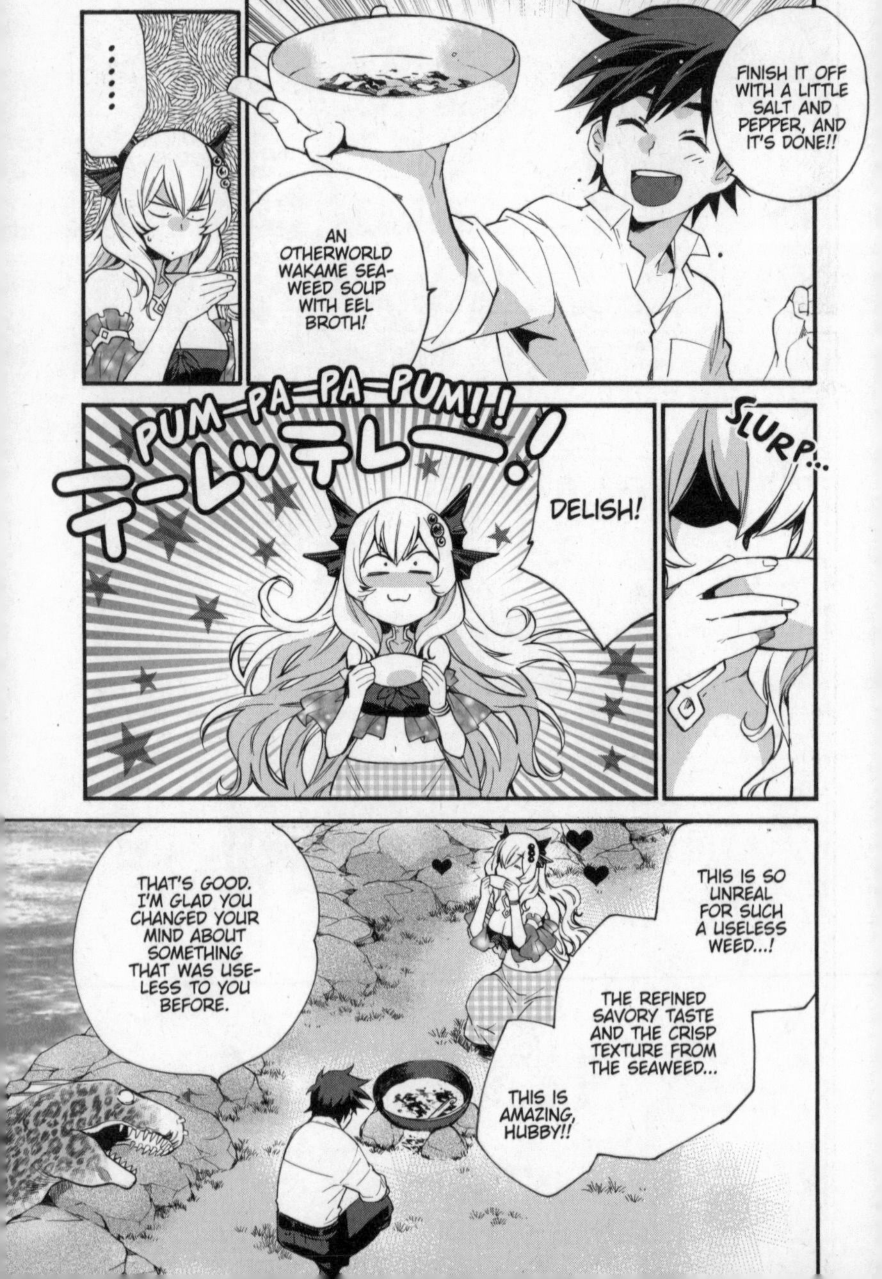
FINISH IT OFF WITH A LITTLE SALT AND PEPPER, AND IT'S DONE!!
AN OTHERWORLD WAKAME SEA-WEED SOUP WITH EEL BROTH!
......
SLURP...
PUM-PA-PA-PUM!!!
テーレッテレー!
DELISH!
THIS IS SO UNREAL FOR SUCH A USELESS WEED...!
THE REFINED SAVORY TASTE AND THE CRISP TEXTURE FROM THE SEAWEED...
THIS IS AMAZING, HUBBY!!
THAT'S GOOD. I'M GLAD YOU CHANGED YOUR MIND ABOUT SOMETHING THAT WAS USE-LESS TO YOU BEFORE.

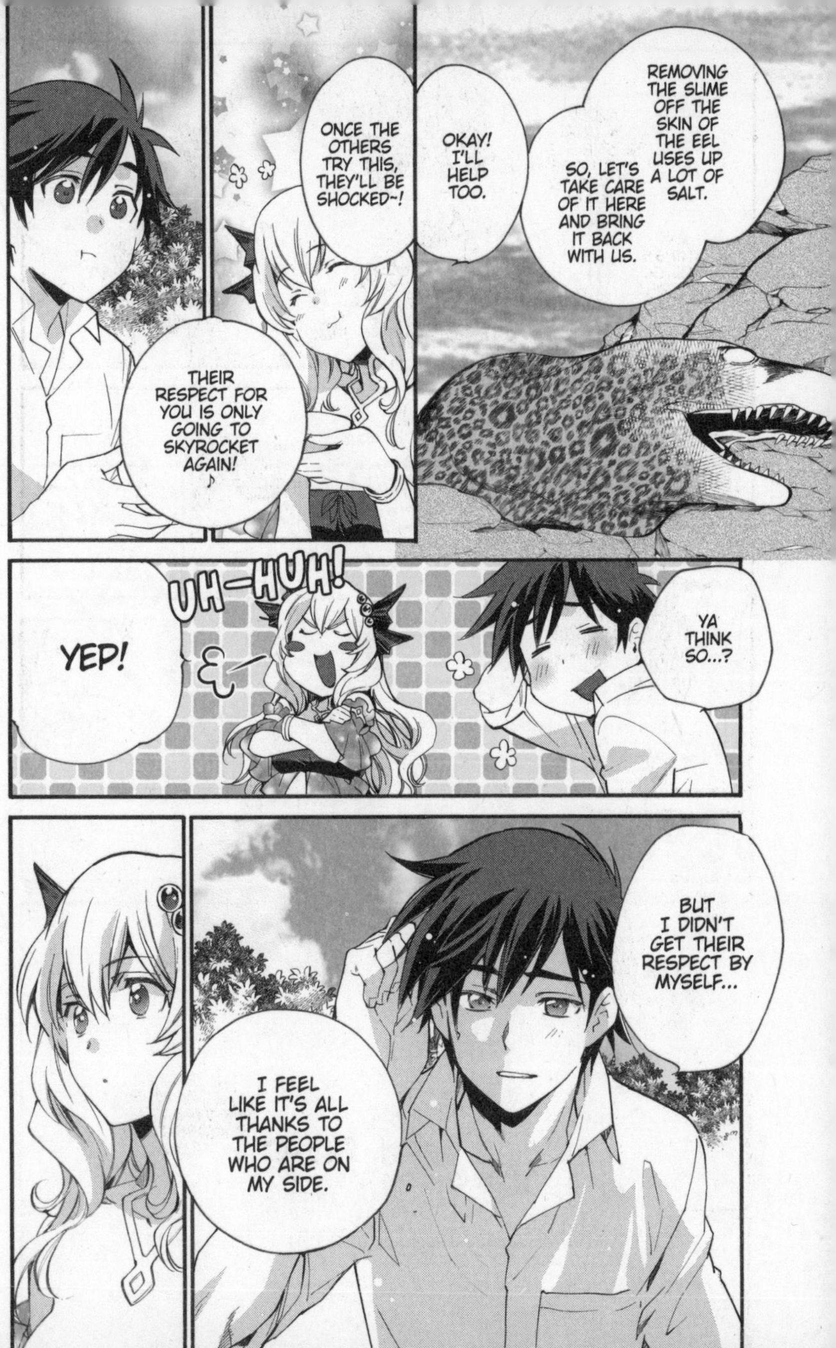
REMOVING THE SLIME OFF THE SKIN OF THE EEL USES UP A LOT OF SALT.
SO, LET'S TAKE CARE OF IT HERE AND BRING IT BACK WITH US.
OKAY! I'LL HELP TOO.
ONCE THE OTHERS TRY THIS, THEY'LL BE SHOCKED~!
THEIR RESPECT FOR YOU IS ONLY GOING TO SKYROCKET AGAIN! ♪
YA THINK SO...?
UH-HUH!
YEP!
BUT I DIDN'T GET THEIR RESPECT BY MYSELF...
I FEEL LIKE IT'S ALL THANKS TO THE PEOPLE WHO ARE ON MY SIDE.

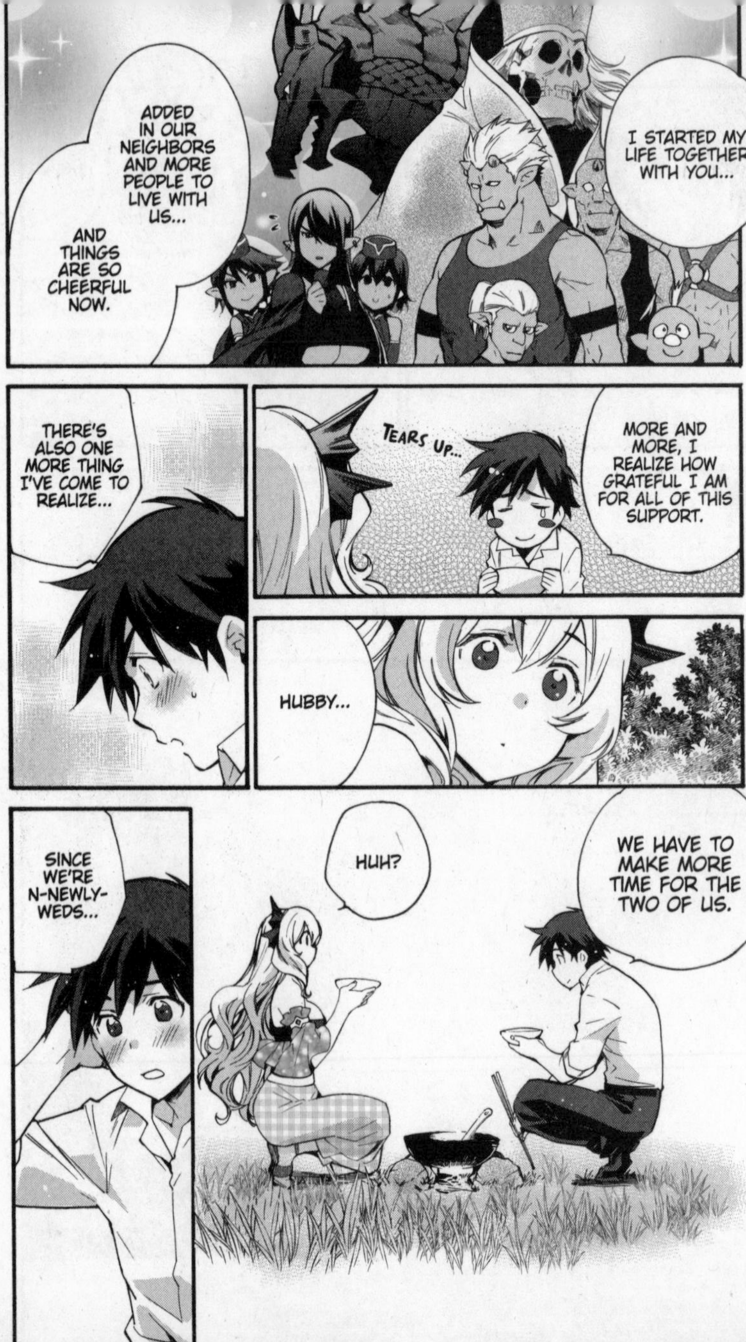
I STARTED MY LIFE TOGETHER WITH YOU...
ADDED IN OUR NEIGHBORS AND MORE PEOPLE TO LIVE WITH US...
AND THINGS ARE SO CHEERFUL NOW.
MORE AND MORE, I REALIZE HOW GRATEFUL I AM FOR ALL OF THIS SUPPORT.
TEARS UP...
HUBBY...
THERE'S ALSO ONE MORE THING I'VE COME TO REALIZE...
WE HAVE TO MAKE MORE TIME FOR THE TWO OF US.
HUH?
SINCE WE'RE N-NEWLY-WEDS...

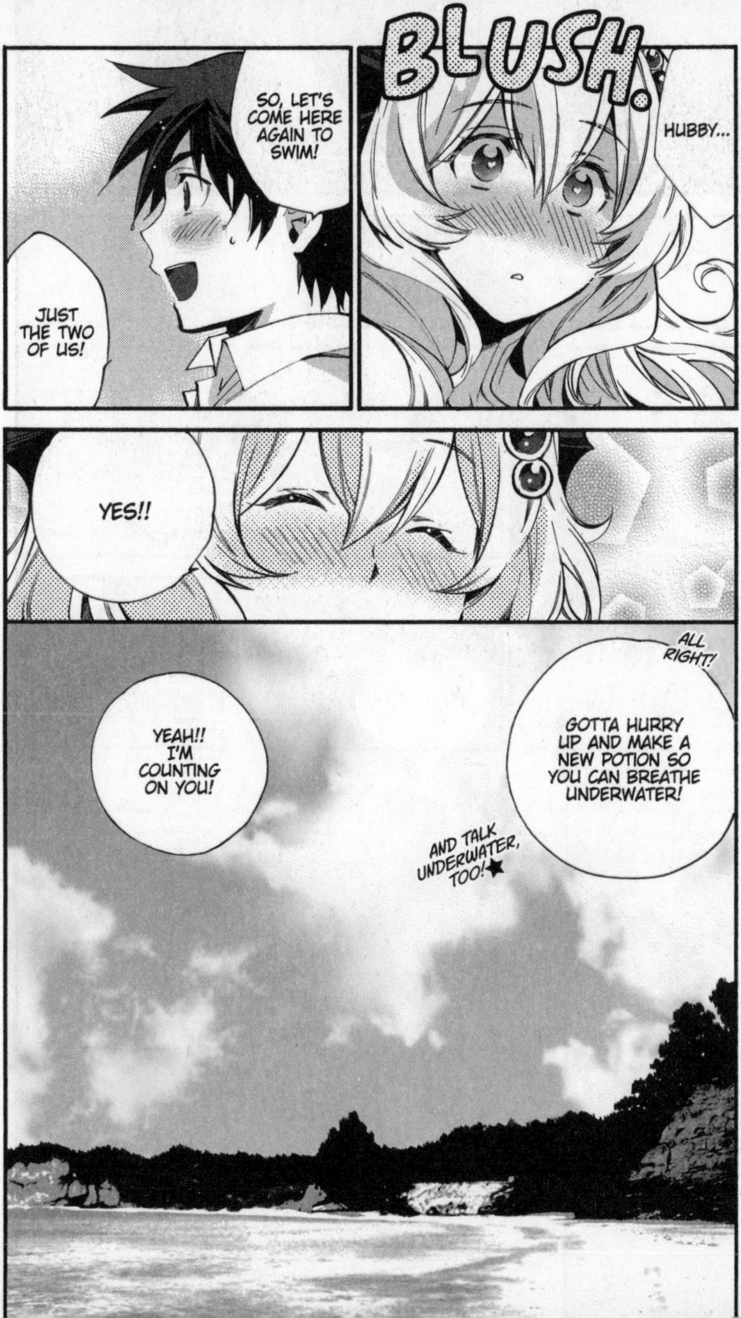
BLUSH.
HUBBY...
SO, LET'S COME HERE AGAIN TO SWIM!
JUST THE TWO OF US!
YES!!
ALL RIGHT!
GOTTA HURRY UP AND MAKE A NEW POTION SO YOU CAN BREATHE UNDERWATER!
AND TALK UNDERWATER, TOO!★
YEAH!! I'M COUNTING ON YOU!

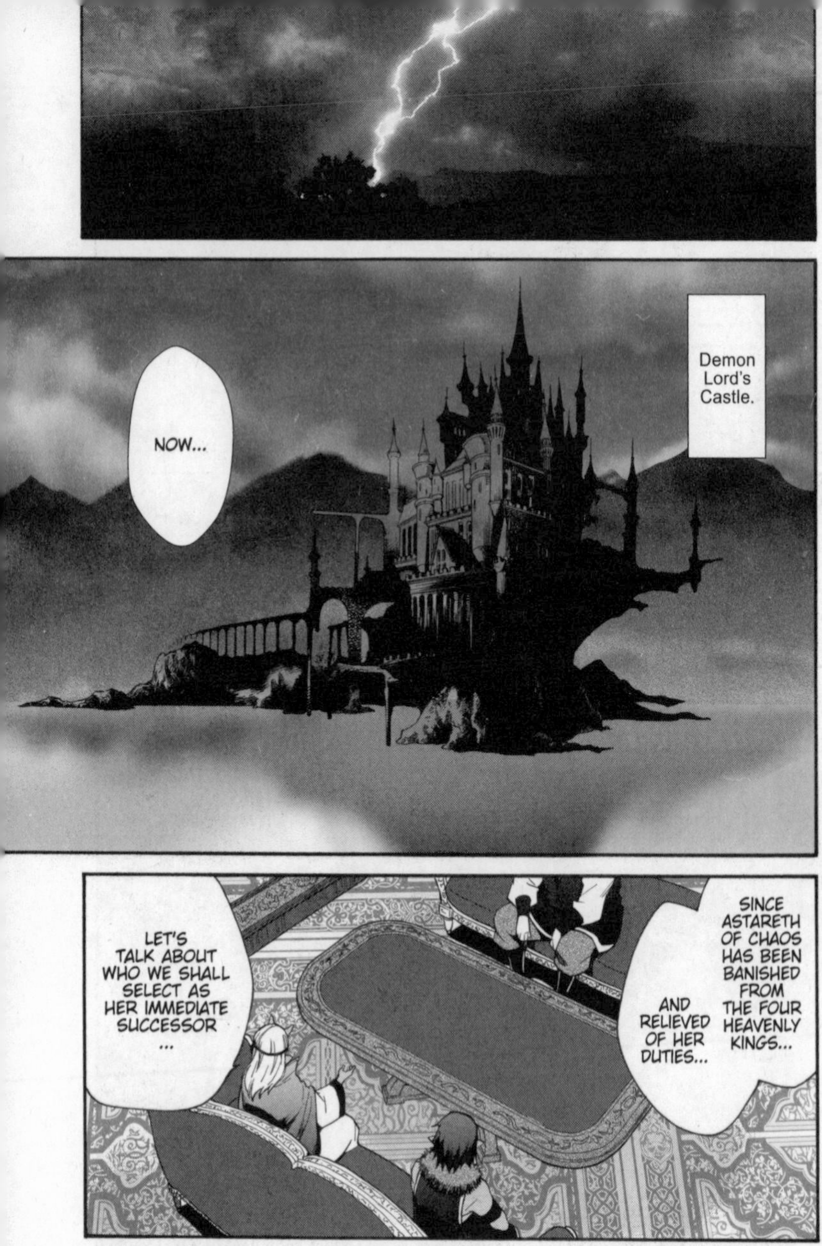
Demon Lord's Castle.
NOW...
SINCE ASTARETH OF CHAOS HAS BEEN BANISHED FROM THE FOUR HEAVENLY KINGS...
AND RELIEVED OF HER DUTIES...
LET'S TALK ABOUT WHO WE SHALL SELECT AS HER IMMEDIATE SUCCESSOR ...

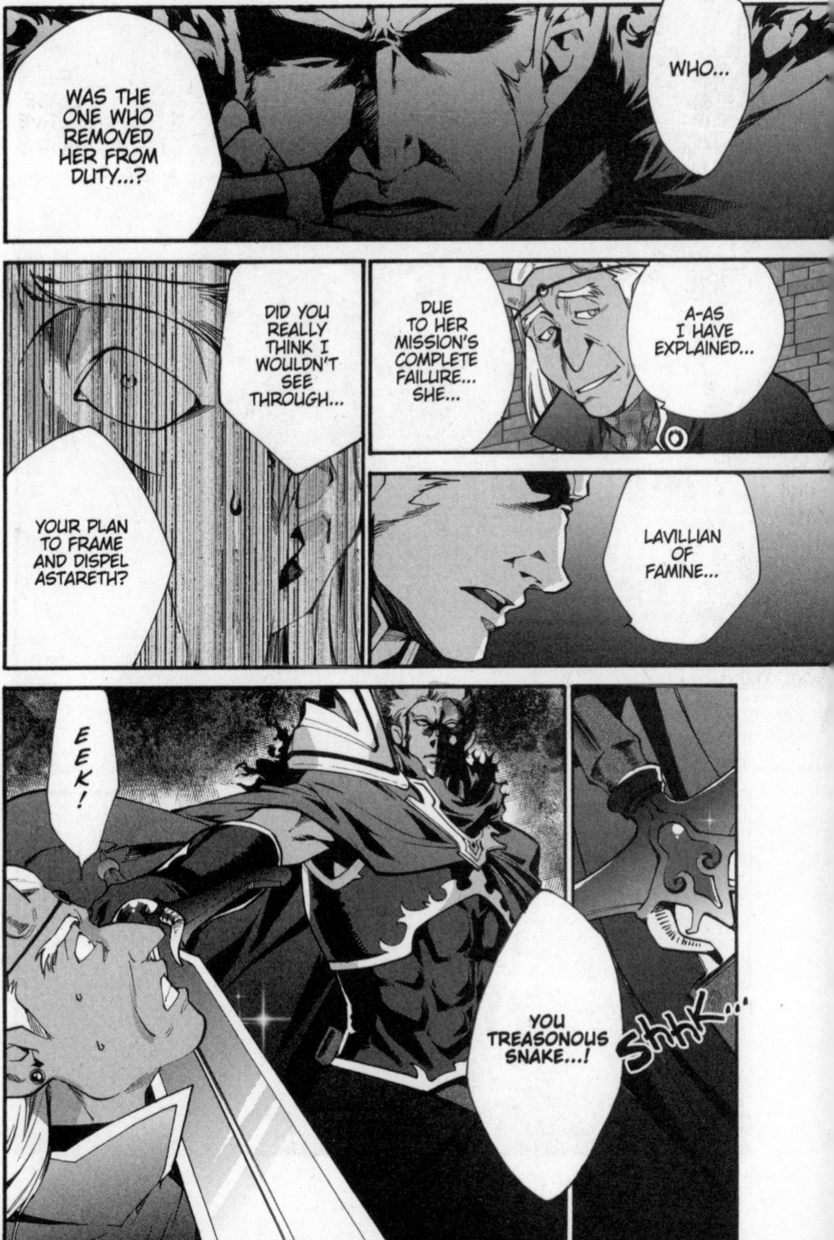
WHO...
WAS THE ONE WHO REMOVED HER FROM DUTY...?
A-AS I HAVE EXPLAINED...
DUE TO HER MISSION'S COMPLETE FAILURE... SHE...
LAVILLIAN OF FAMINE...
DID YOU REALLY THINK I WOULDN'T SEE THROUGH...
YOUR PLAN TO FRAME AND DISPEL ASTARETH?
SHHK...
YOU TREASONOUS SNAKE...!
EEK!

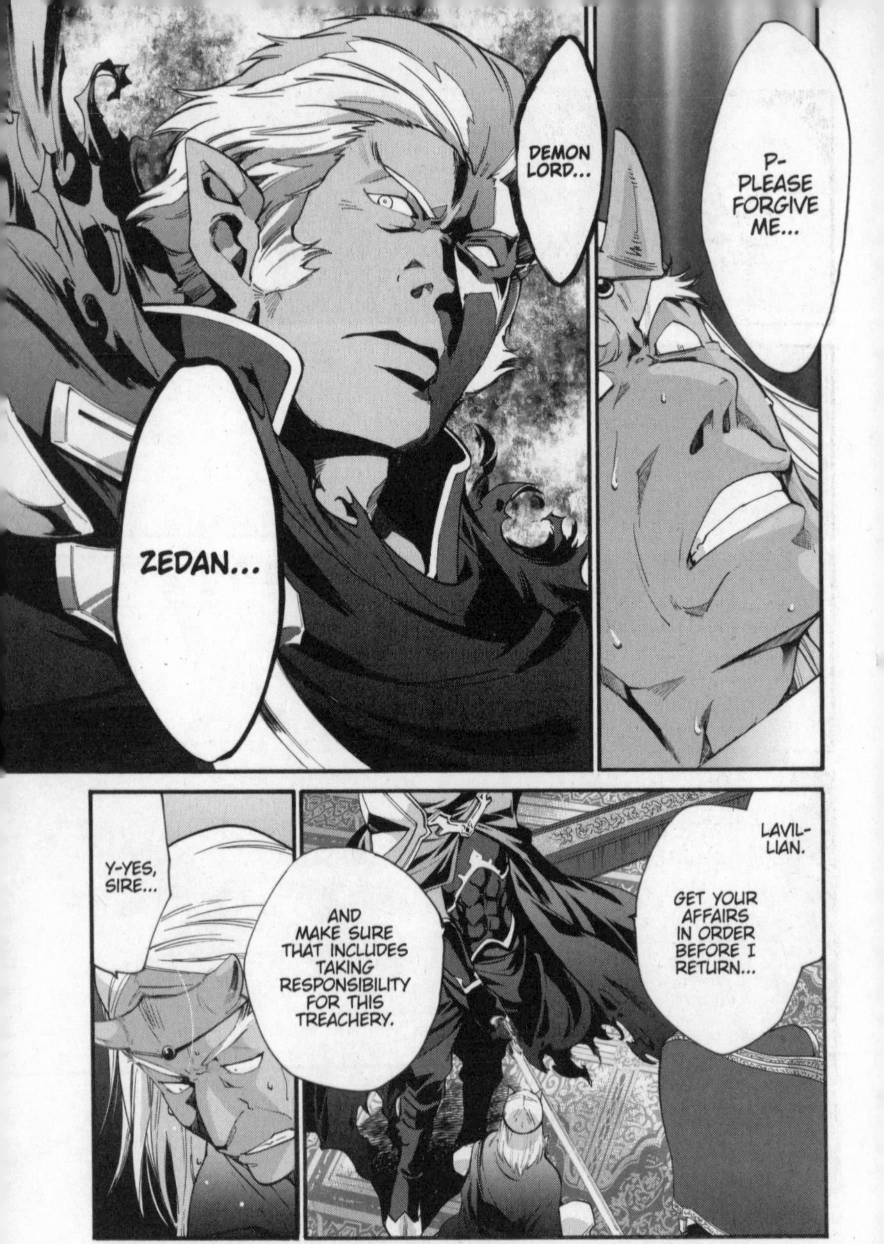
P- PLEASE FORGIVE ME...
DEMON LORD...
ZEDAN...
LAVIL- LIAN.
GET YOUR AFFAIRS IN ORDER BEFORE I RETURN...
AND MAKE SURE THAT INCLUDES TAKING RESPONSIBILITY FOR THIS TREACHERY.
Y-YES, SIRE...

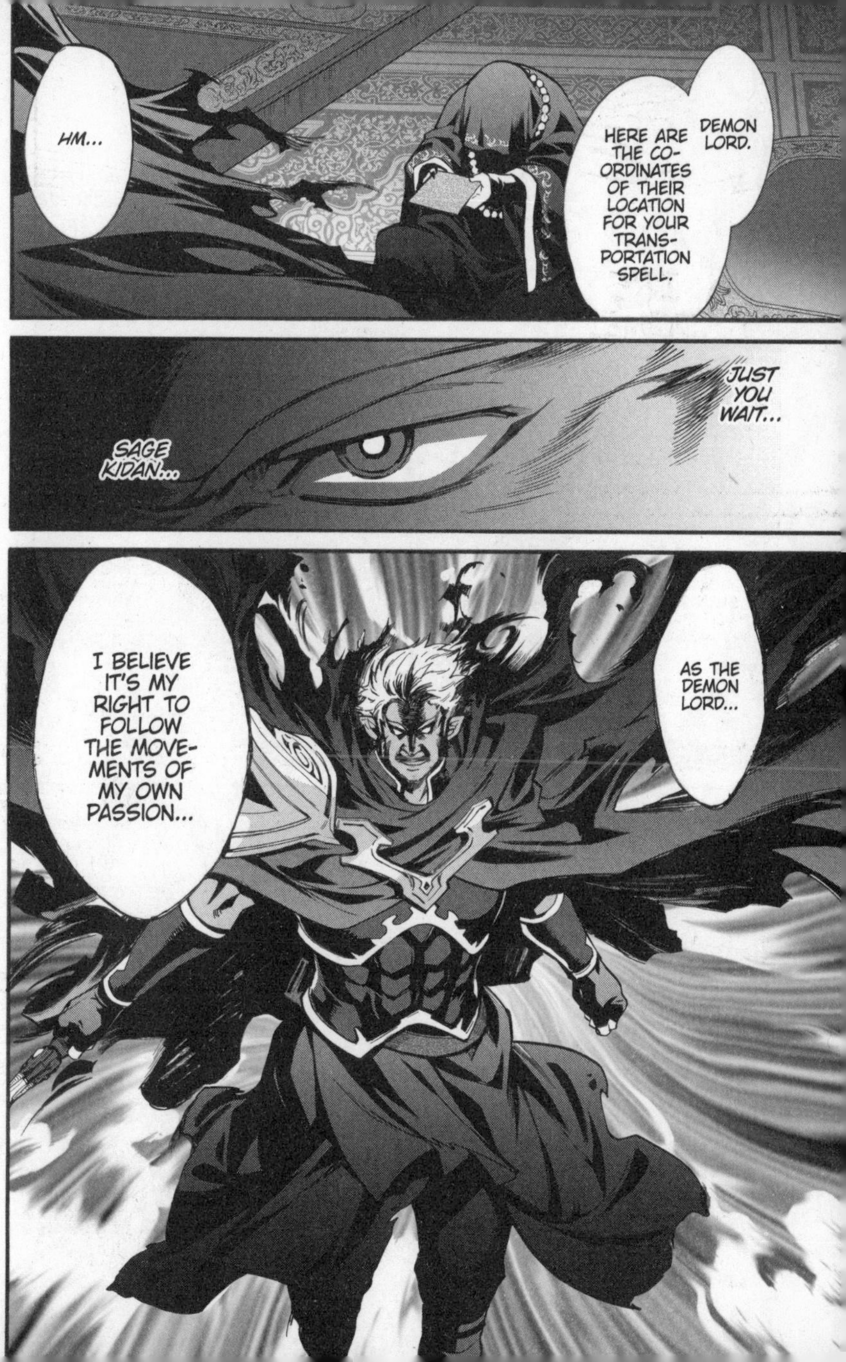
DEMON LORD.
HERE ARE THE CO-ORDINATES OF THEIR LOCATION FOR YOUR TRANS-PORTATION SPELL.
HM...
JUST YOU WAIT...
SAGE KIDAN...
AS THE DEMON LORD...
I BELIEVE IT'S MY RIGHT TO FOLLOW THE MOVE-MENTS OF MY OWN PASSION...

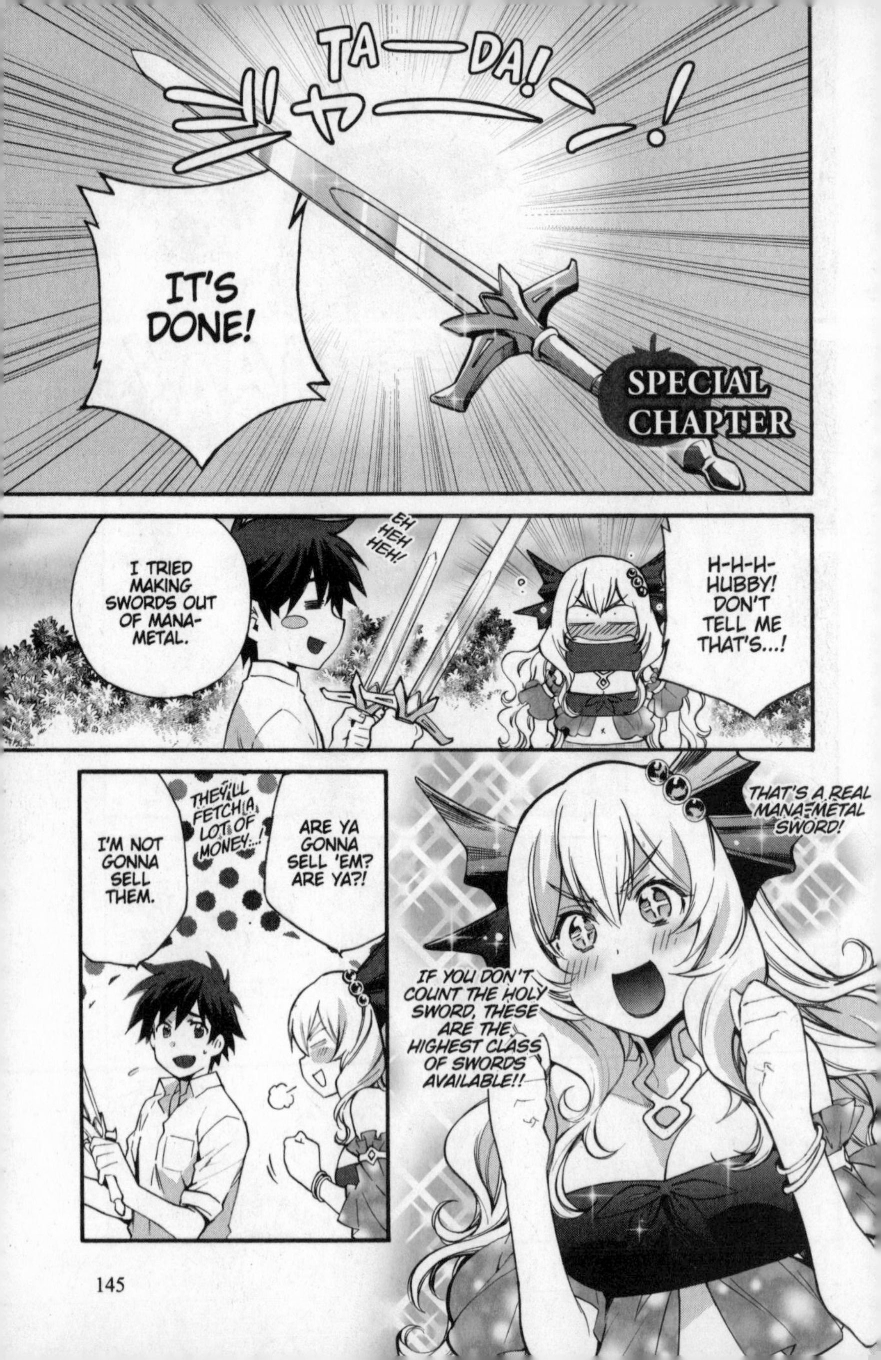
TA—DA!
IT'S DONE!
SPECIAL CHAPTER
H-H-H-HUBBY! DON'T TELL ME THAT'S...!
EH HEH HEH!
I TRIED MAKING SWORDS OUT OF MANA-METAL.
THAT'S A REAL MANA-METAL SWORD!
IF YOU DON'T COUNT THE HOLY SWORD, THESE ARE THE HIGHEST CLASS OF SWORDS AVAILABLE!!
ARE YA GONNA SELL 'EM? ARE YA?!
THEY'LL FETCH A LOT OF MONEY...!
I'M NOT GONNA SELL THEM.

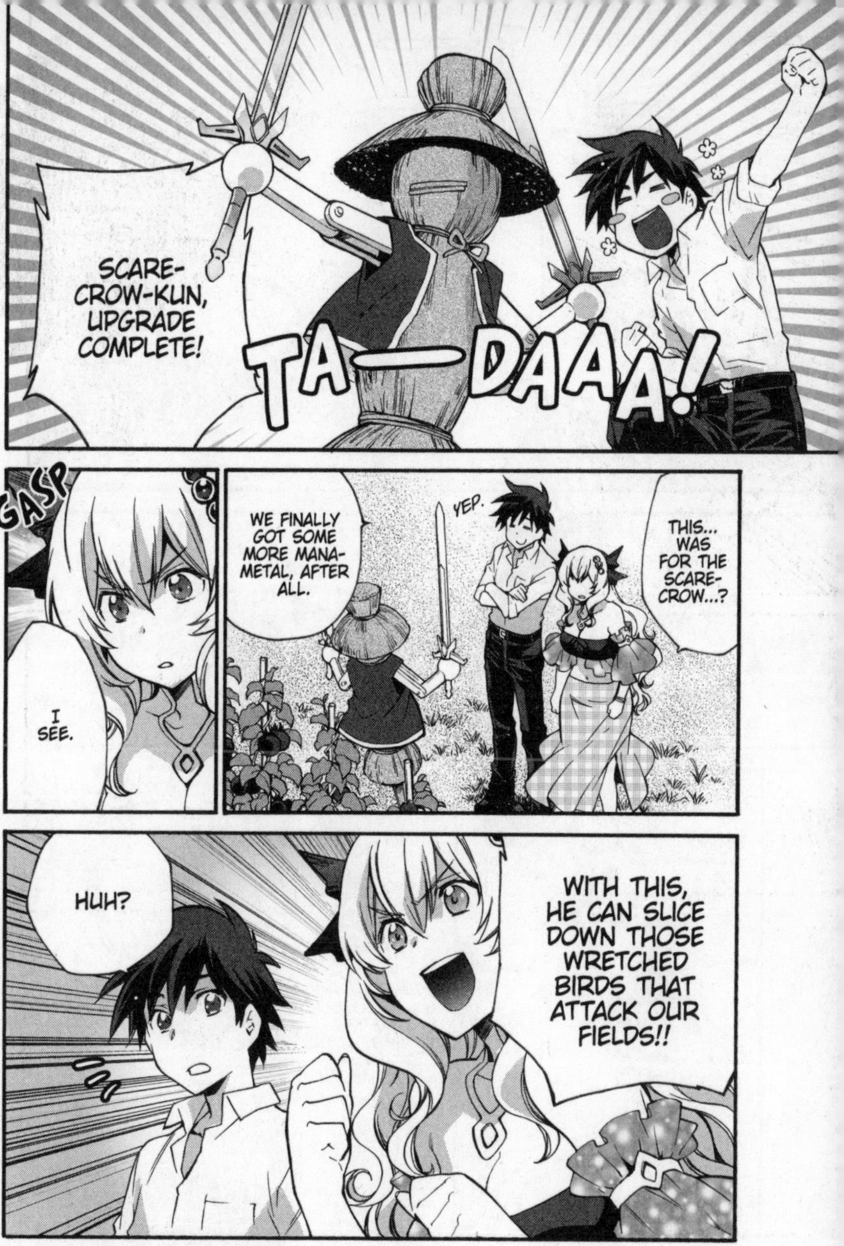
TA—DAAAA!
SCARE-CROW-KUN, UPGRADE COMPLETE!
THIS... WAS FOR THE SCARE-CROW...?
YEP.
WE FINALLY GOT SOME MORE MANA-METAL, AFTER ALL.
GASP
I SEE.
WITH THIS, HE CAN SLICE DOWN THOSE WRETCHED BIRDS THAT ATTACK OUR FIELDS!!
HUH?

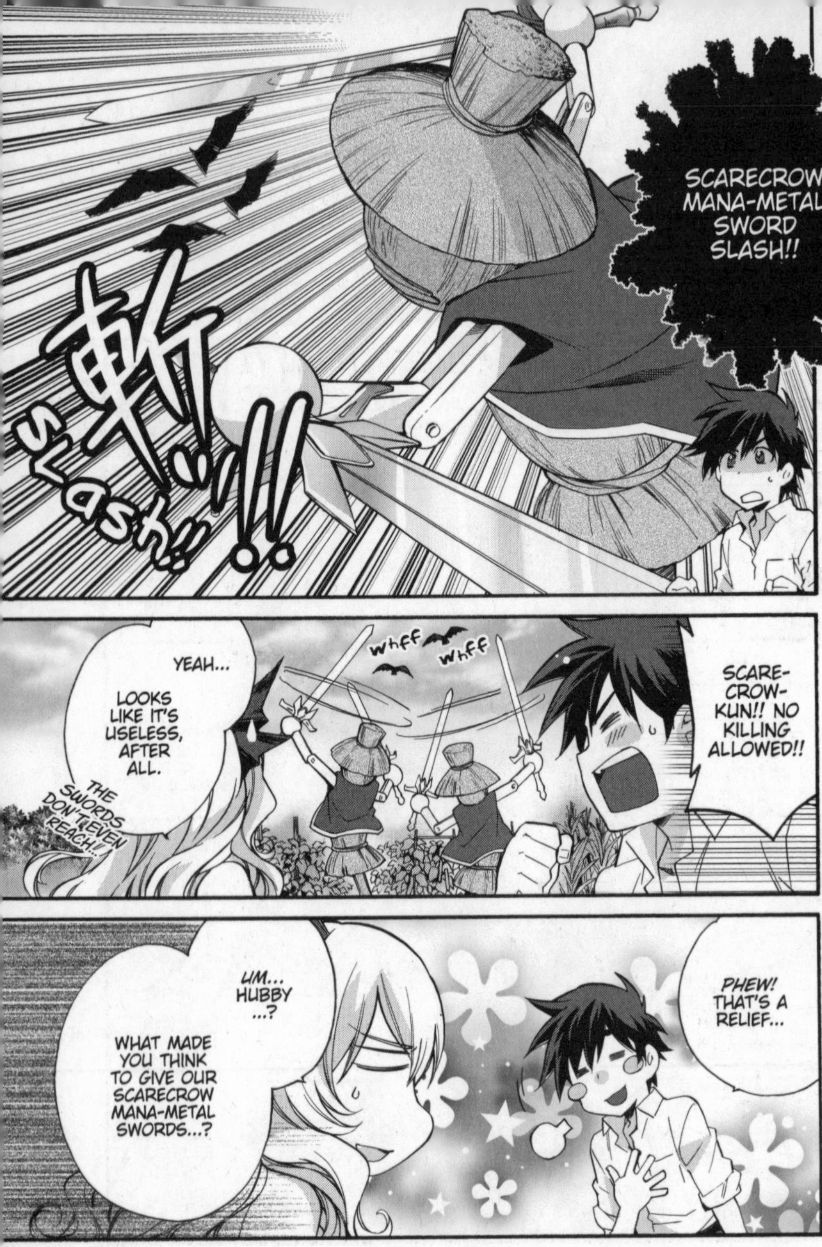
SCARECROW MANA-METAL SWORD SLASH!!
斬!!
SLASH!!
SCARE-CROW-KUN!! NO KILLING ALLOWED!!
WHFF
WHFF
YEAH...
LOOKS LIKE IT'S USELESS, AFTER ALL.
THE SWORDS DON'T EVEN REACH...
PHEW! THAT'S A RELIEF...
UM... HUBBY ...?
WHAT MADE YOU THINK TO GIVE OUR SCARECROW MANA-METAL SWORDS...?

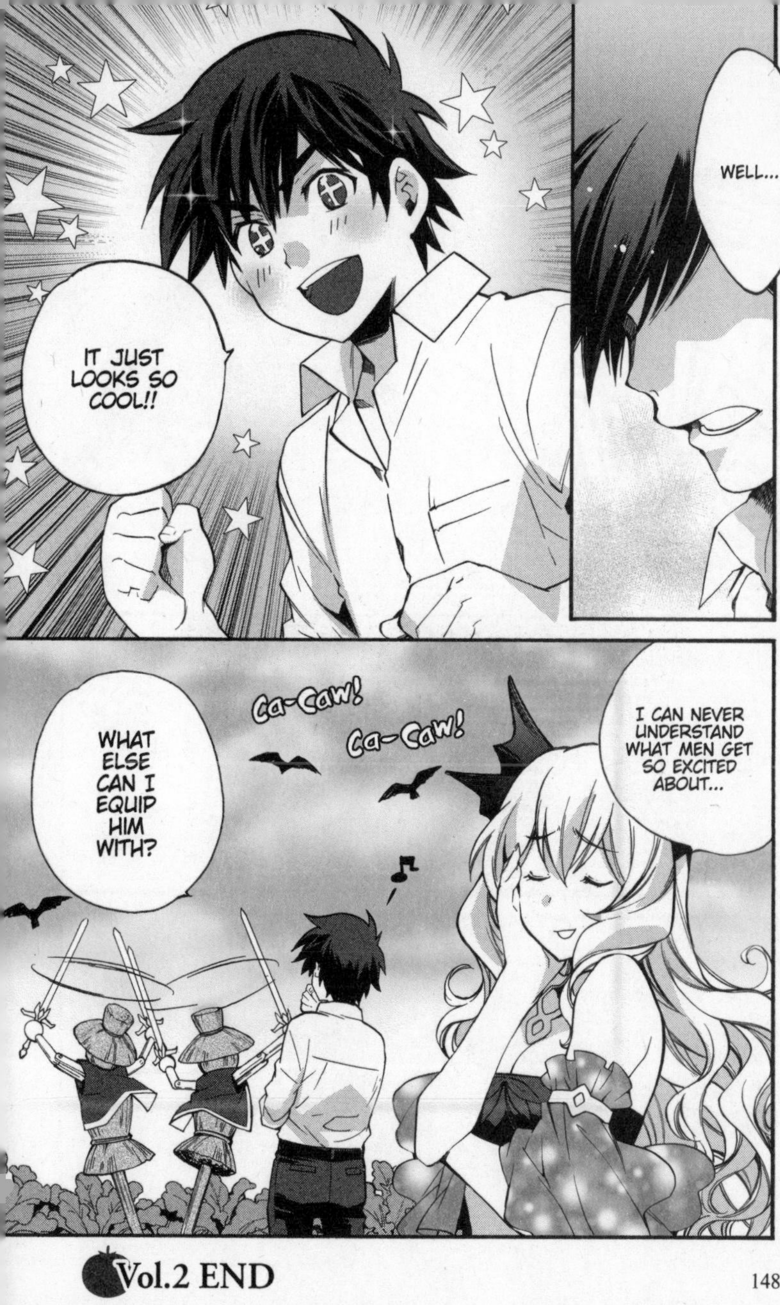
WELL...
IT JUST LOOKS SO COOL!!
I CAN NEVER UNDERSTAND WHAT MEN GET SO EXCITED ABOUT...
Ca-Caw!
Ca-Caw!
WHAT ELSE CAN I EQUIP HIM WITH?

Vol.2 END

to be continued

LET'S BUY THE LAND and CULTIVATE IT IN A DIFFERENT WORLD

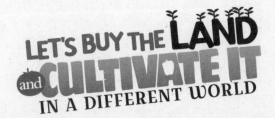

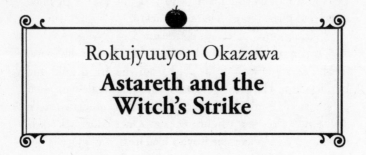

Rokujyuuyon Okazawa
**Astareth and the
Witch's Strike**

ASTARETH OF CHAOS had horrible back pain. Recently, she had been laboring over many tasks like weeding grass and spreading seeds with her back constantly in a stooped position. Because of the burden that was placed on her back doing all of these things…

"Aaaugh …! My *back*…!!" yelped Astareth, bent almost in two.

After that, she left the fields and lay face down on the bed, suffering from horrible pains in her lower back. Bati and Belena, two of her most trusted friends since her days in the Demon Lord's army, stood by her side, tending to her injury.

"Are we supposed to cool down the area where it's painful?" pondered Bati as she slapped a wet towel on to Astareth's back. Plep.

"Eep!! Cold!!" screeched Astareth.

"Don't you think we should warm it up?" suggested Belena, the other attendant, who brought over a steamed towel and placed it on Astareth's back.

"Hoooooot!!" Astareth complained.

Apparently, Belena had heated the towel a little too much. Astareth writhed in pain from the frigid cold and burning heat. Her two attendants were not gentle with their patient at all. But honestly, back pain that accumulated from daily stress was a sort of chronic pain. Once your back starts hurting, there's no simple way to heal it. If the injury is not treated correctly, the pain may become a lifelong companion.

I couldn't stand the idea of Astareth having this pain for the rest of her life, so I felt I had to take responsibility as the overseer of my farm.

"I'm so ashamed…! As a former member of the Four Heavenly Kings, I cannot allow myself to appear so ungraceful…!" cried Astereth, levering herself to her feet.

"Astareth, no!" I yelled out. *Is it all right for her to stand up already? Shouldn't she take more time to lay down and rest…?*

"Even if I was standing in a way that I was not used to, the pain is only proof that I lack the right training. A stronger body wouldn't feel pain like this! Oh, I know!"

What's this now? I wondered.

"If I had more muscle, I wouldn't have to be troubled by this back pain!" exclaimed Astareth, trying to push herself for the first time since she'd come here. Her determination only made me feel *more* anxious about the situation.

"I might have been fired, but I'm still one of the Four Heavenly Kings of the Demon Lord! I swear on my honor,

I will conquer this back pain! To do that, I must build back muscle strength through training!!" proclaimed Astareth. For some reason, she went out and pulled a large boulder aloft from the ground.

"Whoooa! A boulder!"

"It's so large, I have to crane my neck to see the whole thing!"

Where did she find something like that on my farm? I wondered.

Astareth lifted this boulder that was far larger than her with her two bare hands. Lifting the boulder past her shoulders—no, her head—with the form of someone hefting a barbell.

"*What*?! Is she *really* using that big boulder as a barbell weight?!" I asked, shocked. *Does she plan to do reps lifting that thing up and down to build back muscle?*

"Then, to really train my back muscles...I need to bend forward, while holding onto this boulder!!" Astareth shouted through gritted teeth.

Astareth bent forward as if she were bowing while propping up the boulder on her shoulders, and then raised her body back up to a standing position.

"If I keep repeating this motion, I should be able to build considerable muscle! And then it's farewell to my back pain!!" This was definitely weightlifting.

Imagine Astareth's body as a sideways "V" where at the top she held a massive boulder. That's kind of what her form was like. It was something a weightlifter would call a "Good Morning." The exercise put a considerable burden on her back, though doing it often enough would definitely

build muscle on the lower back. But if Astaroth's already-injured body wasn't up to the strain…

Crick.

Hm…? I thought I heard an unpleasant noise.

"Gwaaaah!! My back! *My baaaaaaack*!!" shrieked Astareth.

Lo and behold, Astareth's back could no longer take the weighty burden, and the sound of her destroyed back giving out echoed through the air.

"Whaaa?! I can't hold up the rock anymore? Gwah!!" Astareth complained loudly as she stumbled, rock slipping from her grip.

"Kyaaah! Lady Astareth is gonna turn into a pancake!" screamed one of the girls.

If you don't train your muscles at the right pace, then you might damage your health instead. Please take care of your bodies, everyone.

✻✻✻

After further diagnosis, we found that she strained her back. If you keep carrying heavy things and put a burden on your back, of course you'd throw it out! Astareth's back had already been hurt from the beginning, but this time it was seriously injured and she was no longer able to leave the bed.

"Urrrgh…!! I can't move and I can't stand!" Astareth grumbled from her position face down on the bed. She wouldn't be able to do any fieldwork for the time being, either.

"I tried to work on myself so I could still move well, but now I can't even move at all! Now even the sage is going to abandon me...!!" Astareth bawled out, hopelessly.

"Lady Astareth!" Bati shouted.

"Lady Astareth! Don't tremble like that! You'll only add more stress to your back!" Belena also seemed very worried.

"How weak do I look now?! No wonder I was fired from my position as one of the Four Heavenly Kings. I'm just some oblivious fool who doesn't even know her own worthlessness!" Astareth fussed.

She's really making a big deal out of her strained back, I thought. Nobody has ever died from a strained back, but in this case, it seemed the patient's mental situation was far more serious than her physical symptoms. *Is it my turn to say something soon?*

"Crying on and on and on about your back... How pitiful." Just as I was about to say something, Plattie interjected first.

Plattie chuckled. "Ha ha ha! I guess it's my time to shine with my magical potions! Potions are helpful when people are not in good health. With the most advanced techniques from my home, the merfolk Kingdom, my potions can make you even healthier than you were before!"

Honestly, I'm much more worried about the side effects...

"*Take this!* My super-powerful, all-curing potion!!" exclaimed Plattie.

"Aaaaaughhh!" screamed Astareth.

Plattie aimed and struck her hand down swiftly and firmly on Astareth's back, as if she was a karate master chopping through bricks. *How could she do this to the most*

delicate part of her patient?!

But after she moved her hand away, there was a square piece of fabric on Astareth's back. *What is that…?* "A compress patch?" I asked.

"After listening to what you said before, I decided to try to make my own. I thought it was a good idea to apply a sticky potion on a piece of cloth and then stick the whole thing on. This way, the potion won't wash away and can stay applied to the affected area for a long time," replied Plattie.

When it comes to treating back pain, I think about the compress patches that we had back home. *Wait, did Plattie just make a completely original medical compress out of the information I casually brought out during one of our chats?! What a genius!*

"Liquid potions usually melt away in the ocean water, so this kind of idea could only be thought of by a land-dweller, you know?" Plattie said, smirking at me.

"But usually, you would lay down a compress patch in a gentler way…" I said, averting my eyes. *Why did she have to get down low to forcefully apply the patch?*

"This potion is still under development. If I don't slap it down with full force, then it won't stick," Plattie responded.

Really…? I wasn't so sure about that.

"Lady Plattie…?! I once tried to capture you away with brute force! And yet, you do this favor for me…?!" Astareth said, eyes shining.

"That's all water under the bridge. As long as you're living here with us, it's my job as Hubby's wife to help you out when you're in trouble!" Plattie said, looking more gracious than ever.

Plattie's deep compassion moved Astareth to tears.

"Then, allow me…" I was feeling myself fading into the background, so I rushed to show my contribution. "I made this for you!" I presented her with a supporter that wrapped tightly around the waist. If she worked while wearing this, her back would be secured and her pain alleviated!

"I still can't make any cloth yet, but after weaving some tree bark and grasses together, I made this makeshift belt. It should help with your back pain. Try wearing it around your waist whenever you're working!"

"I used the scraps of fabric that you had for my compress, Hubby!" confessed Plattie.

Pushing your body past its limits is a terrible thing to do to yourself. Physical work is best taken at your own pace and should not be rushed.

"You two are incredibly kind…I think I've finally come to understand it! The reason your sagely power is so great is because of your kindness…?!" asked Astareth.

No, it's nothing that profound. I'm only doing what is common sense to me as a human being, I thought to myself. Then I turned to Astareth's companions. "Oh yeah! Bati, Belena, are you two all right? I mean, your backs. You two are probably not used to doing all that farm work, either…"

"No need to worry! As I mentioned before, I am of common birth and used to farm work! I have a method to not get so exhausted from bending over!" answered Bati. She went on to explain, "It's all in your knees, feet, and hips. The trick is to distribute your power evenly between these three areas so you don't strain your body! I already taught this to Belena, so we weren't as sore!"

"Why didn't you teach that to Astareth?" I asked.

"Okay, like…I was a little tired of being ordered around all the time, so I was all, if she's not gonna ask, let her hurt her back!"

Well, there you have it. At least Bati told the truth. Astareth, however, was hearing this for the first time.

"You insolent *wenchhhh*!!" Astareth said, reaching up from the bed like a corpse rising from the dead and grabbing Bati.

"*Gyaaaah!!* Owowowowow! Lady Astareth, have *mercyyyy*!!" The infuriated Astareth put all her energy into locking Bati into an Argentine Backbreaker. In the end, Bati would probably join her mistress in bed with a bad back.

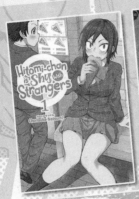
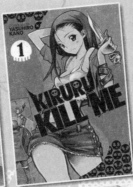
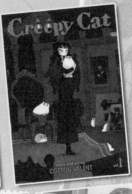
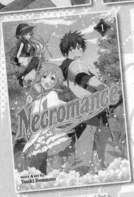
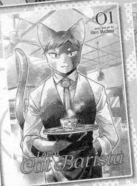
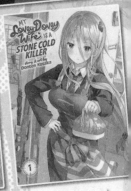
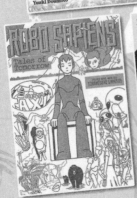
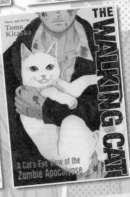
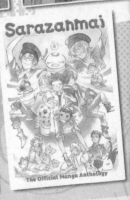

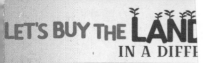

SEVEN SEAS ENTERTAINMENT PRESENTS

LET'S BUY THE LAND
IN A DIFFE[RENT]

story by ROKUJUUYON OKAZAWA   art by JUN SASAMEYUKI   character designs by YUICHI MURAKAMI

MW00526226

TRANSLATION
Jess Leif

LETTERING
Mx. Struble

LOGO DESIGN
George Panella

COVER DESIGN
Nicky Lim

PROOFREADER
Leighanna DeRouen

COPY EDITOR
B. Lillian Martin

EDITOR
Abby Lehrke

PRODUCTION DESIGNER
Christa Miesner

PRODUCTION MANAGER
Lissa Pattillo

PREPRESS TECHNICIAN
Melanie Ujimori
Jules Valera

EDITOR-IN-CHIEF
Julie Davis

ASSOCIATE PUBLISHER
Adam Arnold

PUBLISHER
Jason DeAngelis

Isekai de Tochi wo katte Noujou wo tsukurou volume 2
© OKAZAWA ROKUJUUYON, SASAMEYUKI JUN/OVERLAP,
GENTOSHA COMICS 2020
Originally published in Japan in 2020 by GENTOSHA COMICS INC., Tokyo.
English translation rights arranged with GENTOSHA COMICS INC., Tokyo.
through TOHAN CORPORATION, Tokyo.

Seven Seas press and purchase enquiries can be sent to Marketing Manager Lianne
Sentar at press@gomanga.com. Information regarding the distribution and purchase of
digital editions is available from Digital Manager CK Russell at digital@gomanga.com.

Seven Seas and the Seven Seas logo are trademarks of
Seven Seas Entertainment. All rights reserved.

ISBN: 978-1-68579-342-5
Printed in Canada
First Printing: January 2023
10 9 8 7 6 5 4 3 2 1

////// READING DIRECTIONS //////

This book reads from *right to left*,
Japanese style. If this is your first time
reading manga, you start reading from
the top right panel on each page and
take it from there. If you get lost, just
follow the numbered diagram here.
It may seem backwards at first,
but you'll get the hang of it! Have fun!!

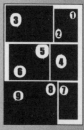

Follow us online: www.SevenSeasEntertainment.com